FROZEN IN TIME

FROZEN
THE FATE OF THE
IN TIME
FRANKLIN EXPEDITION

OWEN BEATTIE & JOHN GEIGER

Introduction by **MARGARET ATWOOD**
Foreword by **WADE DAVIS**

GREYSTONE BOOKS
Vancouver/Berkeley/London

This book was published originally by Bloomsbury Publishing Ltd.
in the United Kingdom, E.P. Dutton in the United States, and, in Canada,
by Western Producer Prairie Books.

23 24 25 26 27 9 8 7 6 5

Greystone Books Ltd.
greystonebooks.com

Cataloguing data available from Library and Archives Canada

ISBN 978-1-77164-173-9 (pbk.)
ISBN 978-1-77164-174-6 (epub)

Editing by Anne Rose
Cover design by Naomi MacDougall
Text design by Jessica Sullivan and Nayeli Jimenez
Cover art by J Franklin Wright
Printed and bound in Canada on FSC® certified paper at Friesens.
The FSC® label means that materials used for the product have been responsibly sourced.

Greystone Books thanks the Canada Council for the Arts, the British Columbia
Arts Council, the Province of British Columbia through the Book Publishing Tax Credit,
and the Government of Canada for supporting our publishing activities.

Greystone Books gratefully acknowledges the xʷməθkʷəy̓əm (Musqueam),
Sḵwx̱wú7mesh (Squamish), and səl̓ílwəta?ɬ (Tsleil-Waututh) peoples on
whose land our Vancouver head office is located.

For Shirley F. Keen.—J.G.
For my first grandchild, Akasha (a.k.a. Pumpy)—O.B.

Sir John Franklin

CONTENTS

Foreword xi
Introduction 1

PART ONE: THE SKELETONS
1 King William Island, 29 June 1981 11
2 A Subject of Wonder 18
3 Into the Frozen Seas 36
4 Puny Efforts 47
5 Isthmus of the Graves 58
6 Region of Terror 67
7 Terror Camp Clear 73
8 Scattered Bones 105
9 The Boat Place 118
10 A Doorway Opens 140

PART TWO: THE ICEMEN
11 Across the Precipice 151
12 The Face of Death 178
13 The Evidence Mounts 191
14 Hartnell Redux 201
15 The Royal Marine 222
16 Understanding a Disaster 235

Epilogue 244
Afterword 256
Acknowledgements 263
Appendix One: List of the officers and crews
of HMS *Erebus* and HMS *Terror* 266
Appendix Two: Major expeditions involved in the
search for HMS *Erebus* and HMS *Terror* 269
Bibliography 271
Index 278

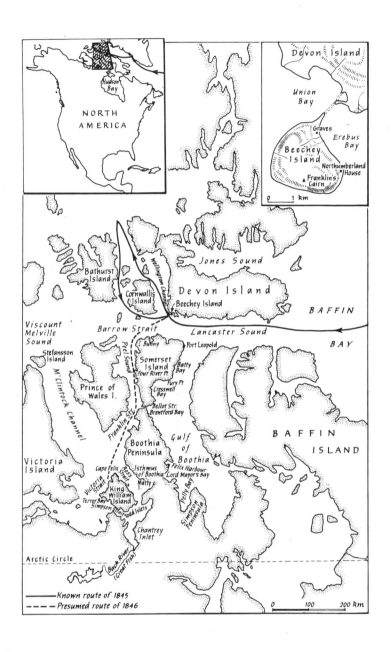

Inset (top left):
NORTH
AMERICA

Hudson
Bay

Inset (top right):
Devon Island

Union
Bay

Graves
Erebus
Bay

Beechey
Island

Northumberland
House

Franklin's
Cairn

0   1 km

Main map:
Jones Sound

Bathurst
Island

Wellington Channel

Cornwallis
Island

Devon Island

Beechey Island

BAFFIN

Viscount
Melville
Sound

Barrow Strait

Lancaster Sound

BAY

Stefansson
Island

Peel Sound

C. Bunny

Port Leopold

Somerset
Island

Batty
Bay

McClintock Channel

Prince of
Wales I.

Four River Pt.

Fury Pt.

Cresswell
Bay

Bellot Str.
Brentford Bay

Franklin Str.

Gulf
of
Boothia

BAFFIN

Boothia
Peninsula

ISLAND

Victoria
Island

Cape Felix

Ross Strait

Isthmus
of Boothia

Felix Harbour
Lord Mayor's Bay

Victoria
Strait

King
William
Island

Matty
I.

Pelly Bay

Terror Bay

Simpson Strait

Todd Islets

Simpson
Peninsula

Chantrey
Inlet

Arctic Circle

Back River
(Great Fish)

——— Known route of 1845
– – – Presumed route of 1846

0   100   200 km

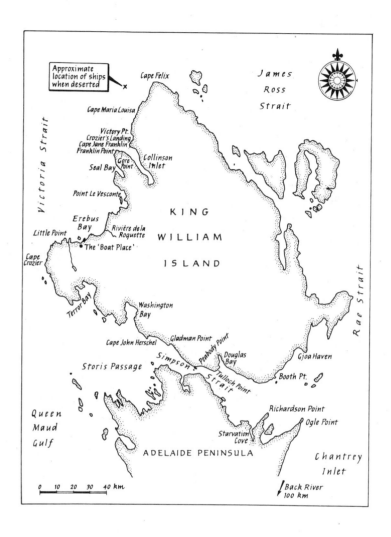

Approximate
location of ships
when deserted   ×

James
Ross
Strait

Cape Felix

Cape Maria Louisa

Victory Pt.
Crozier's Landing
Cape Jane Franklin
Franklin Point
                        Collinson
Seal Bay   Gore   Inlet
             Point

Victoria Strait

Point Le Vesconte

KING

Erebus
Bay
Little Point   Rivière de la   WILLIAM
                 Roquette
      The 'Boat Place'
Cape   ISLAND
Crozier

                                                      Rae Strait

Washington
Bay
                                         Cape John Herschel   Gladman Point
Terror Bay

                        Cape John Herschel   Gladman Point
                                         Peabody Point
                        Simpson   Douglas   Gjoa Haven
Storis Passage   Bay   Bay
                                        Strait
                                         Tulloch Point   Booth Pt.

Queen   Richardson Point
Maud   Ogle Point
Gulf
                                  Starvation
                                  Cove   Chantrey
            ADELAIDE PENINSULA   Inlet

0   10 20 30 40 km   Back River
                                          100 km

Foreword

THE EARLY HISTORY of European exploration in the Arctic was dominated by a single theme. Those who mimicked the ways of the native people—fur traders such as Alexander Mackenzie and Samuel Hearne—achieved great feats of discovery. Those who failed to do so—naval officers, for example, who viewed the quest for the Northwest Passage as but dangerous sport pitting British pluck against the elements—more often than not suffered terrible deaths.

Sir John Franklin, whose initial travels through the barren lands of Keewatin taught him a great deal about the ways of the Inuit, evidently failed to transfer such knowledge to his ill-fated Arctic command of 1845. Long after his own death on board the HMS *Erebus* in June of 1847, remains of his crewmembers were found far to the south, where they perished during a desperate quest for survival. Their shriveled remains were found in leather traces. They died dragging behind them an oak and iron sledge built in Manchester and weighing several hundred pounds. On it was a dory with all the personal effects of British naval officers, including silver dinner plates and even a copy of the novel *The*

Vicar of Wakefield. Somehow they expected to haul this unwieldy load across the frozen wastes several hundred miles to possible rescue.

Not one of the 129 men who sailed with Franklin in 1845 survived. It was the greatest disaster in the history of Arctic exploration, and it gave rise to a mystery that would haunt the British for generations until finally the truth emerged in the wake of the events so powerfully chronicled in this elegant book. *Frozen in Time* is a story of mystery and adventure, an account of maritime sleuthing and discovery worthy of the pen of the great Victorian master of intrigue, Sir Arthur Conan Doyle. Like many great tragedies it begins in a sea of pride and blinding ambition.

The search for a polar route to Asia, which started during the reign of Elizabeth I with the voyages of Martin Frobisher, William Baffin, John Davis and Henry Hudson, had by the 19th century grown into an epic quest, a mission of redemption and destiny for a seafaring nation that, against all odds, had emerged triumphant from the Napoleonic Wars. For young officers in a peacetime navy—men such as Franklin, John Ross and William Edward Parry—the only route to advancement and promotion lay in exploration.

In 1818 the Admiralty dispatched two expeditions to the Arctic. Franklin went north, second in command of two ships with impossible orders to traverse the North Pole and descend upon the Beaufort Sea. John Ross and William Edward Parry went west into Baffin Bay and Lancaster Sound, the actual mouth of the passage. They sailed on until Ross discerned a range of mountains blocking the horizon, a ridge that no one but he could see. Returning to England, ridiculed for his folly, Ross yielded command of the second voyage to Parry, who in 1819 managed to sail all the way to Melville Sound, crossing the meridian of 110 degrees west, allowing him to lay claim to a prize of £5,000, a small fortune at the time. In a season of limited ice, the likes of which would not be known in the Arctic for decades, he came tantalizingly close to victory. Only the permanent pack ice of McClure Strait kept him from reaching the open waters of the Beaufort Sea. Parry's experience led many to underestimate the enormity of the challenge. In the end his very success would lure scores of seamen to their deaths.

Even as Parry in 1819 made plans for a winter in the ice, Franklin set out overland from Hudson Bay to map the Arctic coast. Before he could explore he needed to learn to walk in snowy conditions unlike anything he had known. It took him three years just to reach the mouth of the Coppermine River. Soon after, with most of his men dead or dying and unable to move on, one started to grow healthier by the day. It turned out the man had killed two of his companions and cached their frozen corpses in the snow. Each day he hacked off chunks of meat, allowing him to grow plump as the others, including John Franklin, withered in the cold. When this was discovered, the culprit was summarily executed.

By the end of Franklin's second expedition in the North in 1827, he had travelled thousands of miles on foot or by water, and the entire northern shore of the continent had been mapped, an astonishing achievement for which he would be knighted upon his return to London. Amid the fanfare he met and married Lady Jane, a proud and indefatigable woman who would make his destiny her own.

After nearly a decade as governor of Tasmania, Franklin came back to England at age fifty-nine, just as the British government was about to sanction the first expedition in seven years to search for a way through the polar ice. Despite his age, he managed to talk his way into the command of what promised to be the crowning achievement of his life. The two ships, *Erebus* and *Terror*, were completely refitted and equipped with the first screw steamers ever to be used in the Arctic. To man them, Franklin had the pick of the British Navy. It took three years before they were ready to sail, with every stage of the process, every technical innovation and each hour of training only increasing expectations and the certainty of success.

Sailing down the Thames on May 19, 1845, along riverbanks lined with thousands of well-wishers, Franklin readied his crews for a run across the sea, wind at their stern. His orders were to go where Parry had gone, and succeed where Parry had failed. They made for Lancaster Sound. Finding Barrow Strait blocked with ice, they went north, exploring Wellington Channel before returning south along Cornwallis Island to a winter anchorage at Beechey Island.

Come spring, with the way west still blocked by pack ice, they sailed south following an uncharted waterway along the west coast of North Somerset Island. Approaching King William Island, surrounded on both sides by open water, Franklin made a fateful decision, ordering his ships down the western side of the island, where they became beset in ice not twelve miles offshore. It was September. Through a long and harsh winter they drifted west of the mainland with the pack ice, even as men succumbed to tuberculosis, scurvy and madness brought on by lead poisoning. Half of the tinned rations had gone bad. Weakened by lack of food, poisoned by what little they had, men began to die.

In the spring, sledging parties went out, only to discover that had Franklin chosen the eastern side of the island they would have avoided the ice that trapped their ships, and quite possibly have reached the open waters of the Beaufort Sea, the very passage of their dreams. Demoralized, they returned to their ships, only to find their commander on his deathbed. Sir John Franklin, who died on June 11, 1847, mercifully did not live to witness the unbearable agonies of his men and their final descent into depravity.

Even as a third dark winter came upon them, the survivors found themselves still beset, their vessels some fifteen miles from shore. With the ice tightening as a vice, threatening to crush the hulls at any moment, they had no choice but to abandon the ships at the first sign of the return of the sun. Their only hope was to head south down King William Island, across Simpson Strait to the mainland of the continent, where if they could find their way to the mouth of Back River they might fight their way a hundred miles upriver to the nearest outpost of civilization.

They set out April 22, 1848, 105 survivors, all suffering from scurvy and starvation, each man responsible for a two hundred pound load, which he was expected to drag 250 miles (400 km). As the bedraggled caravan trudged south, it left in its wake a trail of detritus, castaway medicine chests and canvas tents, picks, shovels, blankets and bodies. A few survived the trek and managed to row to the mainland. Of these, one or two may have managed to drag themselves inland. But in the end all would perish.

The uncertain fate of the Franklin expedition dismayed the Admiralty and British government, even as it aroused the passions of a nation bound together by a mystic sense of patriotism. Lady Franklin, influential at court, shameless in her dealings with the newspapers, did all that was humanly possible to inflame public sentiments. In doing so, she effectively shifted the narrative from grotesque failure to epic saga of survival and hope. She alone ensured that her husband's greatest achievement would be his disappearance, for it was the search for Franklin that heralded the greatest period of exploration in the history of the Arctic.

In the decade after his death, no fewer than forty major expeditions set out from Britain, some sponsored by the government, at least four by Lady Franklin herself. Six went overland to search the northern shores of the continent. Most went by sea, either through the Bering Strait on the chance that Franklin had reached the Beaufort Sea, or through Lancaster Sound, following his last known trajectory. Each extended its range by sending out sledging parties, some of which travelled as much as 300 miles (480 km) from their mother ships. With every journey, more and more of the Arctic became known, its waterways charted, the blank spots on the map filled.

As the months and years went by, and any hope of rescuing the men faded, the search shifted into an obsession with discovering their fate, and salvaging their remains for proper burial at home.

Beginning in 1850, ships brought back bits and pieces of evidence, tin cans and compasses, a chronometer, scraps of cloth, several bibles. Formally exhibited as "Franklin Relics," they took on almost religious significance.

Then, even as the search narrowed, unsettling news stunned the British public. In 1853 John Rae, exploring overland from the south, met Inuit who claimed to have encountered in the winter of 1849 forty white men heading south, dragging a sledge. They had been starving, and the Inuit traded a small seal for bits of metal. Later that season, the Inuit had come upon some thirty corpses on the mainland, another five on a nearby island, not far from the mouth of a large river. With this account in hand, Rae returned to England and claimed the £10,000 prize that Parliament had put up for the first to solve the Franklin mystery. He also brought back enticing evidence of a darker story. From the descriptions of the mutilated state of the bodies, and the reported contents of their kettles, there could be little doubt that Franklin's men in their desperation had resorted to cannibalism.

The expedition had consumed a decade, only to yield a result that challenged all Victorian notions of moral certainty and superiority. As to the fate of Franklin himself and his ships, nothing whatsoever had been unveiled. If this was not enough to dampen enthusiasm for the search, the outbreak of war in Crimea most assuredly was. With thousands of British boys dying before the walls of Sebastopol, it became increasingly difficult to arouse sympathy for 129 officers and crew, gone for a decade and marred by their final acts in life, deeds that provoked only repulsion in the hearts and minds of their countrymen. In March 1854, the Admiralty officially declared that all of Franklin's men were dead, and formally removed their names from the Navy List. There was only one dissenting voice, that of Lady Jane Franklin.

In July 1857, she sent out a final expedition, captained by Francis Leopold M'Clintock. Like so many others it became beset in sea ice, and after two years returned, with nothing but more disturbing news. Accounts of human bones scattered along the shores, two corpses found inside a dory along with forty pounds of chocolate, new stories from the Inuit of cannibalism and madness. Evidence not of imperial glory, but of complete cultural failure and betrayal by men who insisted on importing their environment with them, rather than adapting to a new one in which they found themselves struggling to survive.

For nearly two centuries the fate of Franklin's ships remained unknown. Such was the allure of the mystery that their location, though never established, was registered as a Canadian national historic site. For years it was the only such maritime site that visitors could not visit, for it was nothing more than an abstract point on a map, delimited by a 200 yards (180 m) radius, an approximate place just west of King William Island where it was believed the ships went down. Like the Northwest Passage itself, the location lay only in the realm of dreams and the imagination.

Then came the astonishing discovery of *Erebus*, and later *Terror*, shadowy silhouettes lying in shallow waters, anchored if you will in geopolitical reality. Ottawa may call for the landmarks and all the surrounding waters to be designated UNESCO World Heritage Sites, if only to boost the nation's claim that the Northwest Passage is an internal Canadian waterway, and not as the Americans and others claim, an international strait. At stake is the sovereignty of the Arctic, control of maritime traffic across the polar north, and with it ownership of the vast mineral and oil and gas resources waiting to be discovered. Thus the discoveries so elegantly described in this book have political implications that go far beyond this moment in time. In a manner he could never have envisioned, fully 170 years after his death Sir John Franklin remains very much a force to be reckoned with in the Arctic. Lady Franklin would be pleased.

Wade Davis

Introduction

FROZEN IN TIME is one of those books that, having once entered our imaginations, refuse to go away. As I've been writing this introduction, I've described the project to several people. *"Frozen in Time,"* I say. They look blank. "The one with the picture of the Frozen Franklin on the front," I say. "Oh yes. *That* one," they say. "I read that!" And off we go on a discussion of forensic anthropology under extreme conditions. For *Frozen in Time* made a large impact, devoted as it was to the astonishing revelations made by Dr. Owen Beattie—including the high probability that lead poisoning had contributed to the annihilation of the 1845 Franklin expedition.

I read *Frozen in Time* when it first came out. I looked at the pictures in it. They gave me nightmares. I incorporated story and pictures as a subtext and extended metaphor in a short story called "The Age of Lead," published in a 1991 collection called *Wilderness Tips.* Then, some nine years later, during a boat trip in the Arctic, I met John Geiger, one of the authors of *Frozen in Time.*

Not only had I read his book, he had read mine, and it had caused him to give further thought to lead as a factor in northern exploration and in unlucky nineteenth-century sea voyages in general.

Franklin, said Geiger, was the canary in the mine, though unrecognized as such at first: until the last years of the nineteenth century, crews on long voyages continued to be fatally sickened by the lead in tinned food. Geiger has included the results of his additional research in this expanded version of *Frozen in Time*. The nineteenth century, he said, was truly an "age of lead." Thus do life and art intertwine.

BACK TO THE FOREGROUND. In the fall of 1984, a mesmerizing photograph grabbed attention in newspapers around the world. It showed a young man who looked neither fully dead nor entirely alive. He was dressed in archaic clothing and was surrounded by a casing of ice. The whites of his half-open eyes were tea-coloured. His forehead was dark blue. Despite the soothing and respectful adjectives applied to him by the authors of *Frozen in Time,* you would never have confused this man with a lad just drifting off to sleep. Instead he looked like a blend of *Star Trek* extraterrestrial and B-movie victim-of-a-curse: not someone you'd want as your next-door neighbour, especially if the moon was full.

Every time we find the well-preserved body of someone who died long ago—an Egyptian mummy, a freeze-dried Incan sacrifice, a leathery Scandinavian bog-person, the famous iceman of the European Alps—there's a similar fascination. Here is someone who has defied the general ashes-to-ashes, dust-to-dust rule, and who has remained recognizable as an individual human being long after most have turned to bone and earth. In the Middle Ages, unnatural results argued unnatural causes, and such a body would either have been revered as saintly or staked through the heart. In our age, try for rationality as we may, something of the horror classic lingers: the mummy walks, the vampire awakes. It's so difficult to believe that one who appears to be so nearly alive is not conscious of us. Surely—we feel—a being like this is a messenger. He has travelled through time, all the way from his age to our own, in order to tell us something we long to know.

THE MAN IN the sensational photograph was John Torrington, one of the first three to die during the doomed Franklin expedition of 1845. The stated goal of the expedition was to discover the Northwest Passage to the Orient and claim it for Britain, the actual result was the obliteration of all participants. Torrington had been buried in a carefully dug grave, deep in the permafrost on the shore of Beechey Island, Franklin's base during the expedition's first winter. Two others—John Hartnell and William Braine—were given adjacent graves. All three were painstakingly exhumed by anthropologist Owen Beattie and his team in an attempt to solve a long-standing mystery: Why had the Franklin expedition ended so disastrously?

Beattie's search for evidence of the rest of the Franklin expedition, his excavation of the three known graves, and his subsequent discoveries, gave rise to a television documentary and then—three years after the photograph first appeared—to the book you are holding in your hands. That the story should generate such widespread interest 140 years after Franklin filled his fresh-water barrels at Stromness in the Orkney Islands before sailing off to his mysterious fate is a tribute to the extraordinary staying powers of the Franklin legend.

For many years the mysteriousness of that fate was the chief drawing card. At first, Franklin's two ships, the ominously named *Terror* and *Erebus*, appeared to have vanished into nothingness. No trace could be found of them, even after the graves of Torrington, Hartnell and Braine had been found. There is something unnerving about people who can't be located, dead or alive. They upset our sense of space—surely the missing ones have to be somewhere, but where? Among the ancient Greeks, the dead who had not been retrieved and given proper funeral ceremonies could not reach the Underworld; they lingered in the world of the living as restless ghosts. And so it is, still, with the disappeared: they haunt us. The Victorian age was especially prone to such hauntings, as witness Tennyson's *In Memoriam*, its most exemplary tribute to a man lost at sea.

Adding to the attraction of the Franklin story was the Arctic landscape that had subsumed leader, ships and men. In the nineteenth century very few Europeans—apart from whalers—had ever been to the far north. It was one of those perilous regions attractive to a public still sensitive to the spirit of literary Romanticism—a place where a hero might defy the odds, suffer outrageously, and pit his larger-than-usual soul against overwhelming forces. This Arctic was dreary and lonesome and empty, like the windswept heaths and forbidding mountains favoured by aficionados of the Sublime. But the Arctic was also a potent Otherworld, imagined as a beautiful and alluring but potentially malign fairyland, a Snow Queen's realm complete with otherworldly light effects, glittering ice-palaces, fabulous beasts—narwhals, polar bears, walruses—and gnome-like inhabitants dressed in exotic fur outfits. There are numerous drawings of the period that attest to this fascination with the locale. The Victorians were keen on fairies of all sorts; they painted them, wrote stories about them, and sometimes went so far as to believe in them. They knew the rules: going to an otherworld was a great risk. You might be captured by non-human beings. You might be trapped. You might never get out.

EVER SINCE Franklin's disappearance, each age has created a Franklin suitable to its needs. Prior to the expedition's departure there was someone we might call the "real" Franklin, or even the Ur-Franklin—a man viewed by his peers as perhaps not the crunchiest biscuit in the packet, but solid and experienced, even if some of that experience had been won by bad judgment (as witness the ill-fated Coppermine River voyage of 1819). This Franklin knew his own active career was drawing to an end, and saw in the chance to discover the Northwest Passage the last possibility for enduring fame. Aging and plump, he was not exactly a dream vision of the Romantic hero.

Then there was Interim Franklin, the one who came into being once the first Franklin failed to return and people in England realized that something must have gone terribly wrong. This Franklin was neither dead nor alive, and the possibility that he might be either caused him to loom large in the minds of the British public. During this period he acquired the adjective "gallant," as if he'd been engaged in a military exploit. Rewards were offered, search parties were sent out. Some of these men, too, did not return.

The next Franklin, one we might call Franklin Aloft, emerged after it became clear that Franklin and all of his men had died. Not only had they died, they had perished, and they had not just perished, they had perished miserably. But many Europeans had survived in the Arctic under equally dire conditions. Why had this particular group gone under, especially since the *Terror* and the *Erebus* had been the best-equipped ships of their age, offering the latest in technological advances?

A defeat of such magnitude called for denial of equal magnitude. Reports to the effect that several of Franklin's men had eaten several others were vigorously squelched. Those bringing the reports—such as the intrepid John Rae, whose story was told in Ken McGoogan's 2002 book, *Fatal Passage*—were lambasted in the press; and the Inuit who had seen the gruesome evidence were maligned as wicked savages. The effort to clear Franklin and all who sailed with him of any such charges was led by Jane, Lady Franklin, whose social status hung in the balance: the widow of a hero is one thing, the widow of a cannibal quite another. Due to Lady Jane's lobbying efforts, Franklin, in absentia, swelled to blimp-like size. He was credited—dubiously—with the discovery of the Northwest Passage and given a plaque in Westminster Abbey and an epitaph by Tennyson.

After such inflation, reaction was sure to follow. For a time in the second half of the twentieth century we were given Halfwit Franklin, a cluck so dumb he could barely tie his own shoelaces. Franklin was a victim of bad weather (the ice that usually melted in summer had failed to do so, not in just one year, but in three), but in the Halfwit Franklin reading, this counted for little. The expedition was framed as a pure example of European hubris in the face of Nature: Sir John was yet another of those Nanoodles of the North who came to grief because they wouldn't live by Native rules and follow Native advice—"Don't go there" being, on such occasions, Advice #1.

But the law of reputations is like a bungee cord: you plunge down, you bounce up, though to diminishing depths and heights each time. In 1983, Sten Nadolny published *The Discovery of Slowness,* a novel that gave us a thoughtful Franklin, not exactly a hero but an unusual talent, and certainly no villain. Rehabilitation was on the way.

Then came Owen Beattie's discoveries and the description of them in *Frozen in Time.* It was now clear that Franklin was no arrogant idiot. Instead he became a quintessentially twentieth-century victim: a victim of bad packaging. The tins of food aboard his ships had poisoned his men, weakening them and clouding their judgment. Tins were quite new in 1845, and these tins were sloppily sealed with lead, and the lead had leached into the food. But the symptoms of lead poisoning were not recognized at the time, being easily confused with those of scurvy. Franklin can hardly be blamed for negligence, and Beattie's revelations constituted exoneration of a kind for Franklin.

There was exoneration of two other kinds, as well. By going where Franklin's men had gone, Beattie's team was able to experience the physical conditions faced by the surviving members of

Franklin's crews. Even in summer, King William Island is one of the most difficult and desolate places on earth. No one could have done what these men were attempting—an overland expedition to safety. Weakened and addled as they were, they didn't have a hope. They can't be blamed for not making it.

The third exoneration was perhaps—from the point of view of historical justice—the most important. After a painstaking, finger-numbing search, Beattie's team found human bones with knife marks and skulls with no faces. John Rae and his Inuit witnesses, so unjustly attacked for having said that the last members of the Franklin crew had been practising cannibalism, had been right after all. A large part of the Franklin mystery had now been solved.

ANOTHER MYSTERY has since arisen: Why has Franklin become such a Canadian icon? As Geiger and Beattie report, Canadians weren't much interested at first: Franklin was British and the North was far away, and Canadian audiences preferred oddities such as the well-known midget Tom Thumb. But over the decades, Franklin has been adopted by Canadians as one of their own. For example, there were the folksongs, such as the traditional and often-sung "Ballad of Sir John Franklin"—a song not much remembered in England—and Stan Rogers' well-known "North-west Passage." Then there were the contributions of writers. Gwendolyn MacEwen's radio drama *Terror and Erebus* was first broadcast in the early 1960s; the poet Al Purdy was fascinated by Franklin; the novelist and satirist Mordecai Richler considered him an icon ripe for iconoclasm, and, in his novel *Solomon Gursky Was Here*, added a stash of cross-dresser women's clothing to the contents of Franklin's ships. What accounts for such appropriation? Is it that we identify with well-meaning non-geniuses who get tragically messed up by bad weather and evil food suppliers? Perhaps. Or perhaps it's because—as they say in china shops—if you break it, you own it. Canada's North broke Franklin, a fact that appears to have conferred an ownership title of sorts.

It's a pleasure to welcome *Frozen in Time* back to the bookshelves in this revised and enlarged edition. I hesitate to call it a groundbreaking book, as a pun might be suspected, but groundbreaking it has been. It has contributed greatly to our knowledge of a signal event in the history of northern journeying. It also stands as a tribute to the enduring pull of the story—a story that has passed through all the forms a story may take. The Franklin saga has been mystery, surmise, rumour, legend, heroic adventure and national iconography; and here, in *Frozen in Time*, it becomes a detective story, all the more gripping for being true.

Margaret Atwood

PART ONE

The
SKELETONS

Ah, Franklin!
To follow you, one does not need geography.
At least not totally, but more of that
Instrumental knowledge the bones have,
Their limits, their measurings.
The eye creates the horizon,
The ear invents the wind,
The hand reaching out from a parka sleeve
By touch demands
that the touched thing be.

GWENDOLYN MACEWEN, *Terror and Erebus*

Ah, for just one time,
I would take the Northwest Passage
To find the hand of Franklin
reaching for the Beaufort Sea
Tracing one warm line through a land
so wide and savage
And make a Northwest Passage to the sea.

STAN ROGERS, "Northwest Passage"

KING WILLIAM

Island, 29 June 1981

KING WILLIAM ISLAND is one of the most desolate places in the world, a virtually featureless polar semidesert of limestone and mud interspersed with ice-water lakes. Located in the Canadian Arctic archipelago, separated from the north coast of the North American continent by Simpson Strait, the island is large—5,244.5 square miles (13,111 sq km)—but indistinct, rising to a maximum elevation of only 450 feet (137 metres). Yet the indifference of the landscape stands in stark contrast to the island's dramatic history.

For it was here, in 1848, that the finely outfitted and trained British Arctic expedition commanded by Sir John Franklin ended in extraordinary tragedy. Not one of the 129 men came out of the Arctic to tell of their accomplishments or suffering, and both of the expedition's ships, HMS *Erebus* and HMS *Terror*, were lost, as were whatever written accounts of the journey that had existed. British and American searchers grasping to understand the disappearance were confounded by what little remained of the expedition. Sketchy stories told by the native Inuit, some artefacts, human remains and one tragic note found by nineteenth-century searchers are all that historians have been able to rely on for their reconstruction of events.

Walking along the gravel and sand beaches on a blustery and near freezing June day in 1981, members of an archaeological team from the University of Alberta surveyed a spit of land near Booth Point, on the south coast of King William Island, for human skeletal remains. They hoped their research would uncover clues to the events of the expedition's agonizing final days. They knew that some of the last survivors had crossed from here to a place on the mainland known as Starvation Cove, where the tragedy had reached its inevitable conclusion. The researchers were following the lead of one of the early Franklin searchers, an American explorer named Charles Francis Hall, who in 1869 recorded an Inuit account of a grave belonging to a member of the lost expedition:

> After traveling about half an hour, the party halted on a long low spit, called by the natives Kung-e-ark-le-ar-u, on which the men . . . 'knew that a white man had been buried.' This, however, was chiefly from the accounts which they had had from their people; only one of these had ever seen the grave. The spot was pointed out, but the snow covered all from view. A monument was erected, and its bearings . . . carefully noted.

The first day of survey work in 1981 failed to turn up anything. It was on the second morning, 29 June, that field assistant Karen Digby walked up to forensic anthropologist Owen Beattie and archaeologist James Savelle clutching what looked like a broken china bowl in her right hand. "I think this is something important. Is it human?" Digby asked as she handed the white skull bone to Beattie.

It was the first major discovery of their fieldwork, representing the starting point of Beattie's forensic investigation. Having marked the location of her find, Digby led the rest of the crew to the spot. Still visible in the sandy soil was the depression where the human skull fragment had rested, and, placing the discovery back in the depression, the researchers began the process of meticulously searching the finger of land for other remains.

At first, only a few fragments of bone were found. But after six hours of careful survey work, in which every inch of ground was covered, the researchers had discovered, photographed, mapped and then collected thirty-one pieces of human bone. Most of the remains were found exposed on the surface, others were hidden by occasional pockets of vegetation or had been nearly swallowed by the sand.

The texture of the bone illustrated the severity of the northern climate. Exposed portions were bleached white, and powdery flakes of the outer bone surface cracked and fell off if handled too roughly. Sharing the exposed surfaces were small and brightly coloured colonies of mosses and lichens, anchored firmly on the sterile white of the bone as if braced for another harsh winter. By contrast, the ivory-brown undersides of the bones, never exposed to the sun or elements, were found to be in extremely good condition, with all anatomical detail preserved. The researchers also discovered several artefacts at the site, including a shell button common in the early and mid-nineteenth century and a clay pipe stem like those carried on the Franklin expedition. The skeletal remains and artefacts were found over a 33- by 50-foot (10- by 15-metre) area, at the centre of which lay the remnants of what had been a stone tent circle.

One of the first and most important questions that forensic anthropologists ask when examining human remains is, "How many individuals are represented?" Carefully studying the remains, Beattie was able to determine that there were no duplications of bones or anatomical features and that the size and characteristics of the bones supported the theory that they belonged to a single individual.

The shape of the skull's frontal bone and characteristics of the eye socket revealed the remains to be likely of European ancestry.

Heavy brow ridges and well-developed muscle markings on the skull and limb bones identified the skeleton as male. The skull sutures (the joints between the various bones of the skull that slowly disappear as an individual grows older) were still clearly visible, indicating that the individual was only twenty to twenty-five years of age at the time of his death.

To many, skeletal remains of a Franklin sailor would serve only as an intimation of a distant Arctic disaster. But to Beattie, the discovery of the Booth Point skeleton was as if one of the last of Franklin's crewmen to die had come forward through time to answer his questions. For there was evidence of metabolic stress, suggestive of serious dietary problems, in porous lesions on the orbital roofs of the skeleton. (Such lesions are associated with various anaemias, but most particularly with iron deficiency anaemia.) There was also the first physical evidence ever discovered that supported the long-held belief among historians that expedition members suffered from the debilitating effects of scurvy during their final months. Areas of shallow pitting and scaling on the outer surfaces of the bones were like those seen in documented cases of vitamin C deficiency, the cause of scurvy. Bone changes due to inflammation (called periostitis) of the thin, parchment-like skin adhering tightly to the surface of living bone, were also easily identified. Other bone changes showed the effects of haemorrhaging between this thin skin and the long bone surfaces. With scurvy, these subperiosteal haemorrhages and resulting bone remodelling can occur even during the physical stresses and strains of everyday activities.

The tremendous impact of scurvy was felt throughout much of the period of European expansion and maritime exploration, which started in the sixteenth century. The diet of the mariners of the age, who endured long voyages without fresh fruit and vegetables, made them particularly susceptible to the ravages of the disease. More Royal Navy charges succumbed to this scourge than died in battle in the eighteenth century. When British commodore George Anson led a squadron into the Pacific in the 1740s to raid Spanish shipping routes, for instance, he lost thirteen hundred men out of his entire two thousand complement to scurvy. In his account of that voyage, Anson's expedition chaplain, Richard Walter, provides a grisly inventory of the symptoms, including ulcers, rictus of the limbs, spontaneous haemorrhages in almost all parts of the body—and a bloom of gum tissue that enveloped what teeth had not already fallen out, producing a terrible odour. Walter also noted strange sensory and psychological effects. The smell of lotus blossoms wafting from the shore caused men to writhe in agony; the sound of a musket firing could be fatal to patients with advanced cases. The sailors also found themselves crying inconsolably at the slightest provocation and swept by hopeless longings.

Unknown until 1917 was the root cause: Scurvy is the result of a deficiency of vitamin C (ascorbic acid), which today can be effectively cured within twenty-four hours with the intake of large doses of the vitamin. In 1753, Scottish physician James Lind published his classic *A Treatise on the Scurvy,* in which he advanced the plausibility of such a treatment by providing experimental proof of the benefits of citrus juice as an antiscorbutic. The Royal Navy, which one critic would later damn as "a hierarchy as soul-chilling, as rigorous, as iron-bound, as any Brahmin caste," initially failed to reform dietary regimens, however, with the result that the disease continued to wreak havoc. Only in 1795 did the Royal Navy heed decades of advice and begin enforcing the consumption of lime juice on its ships (giving rise to the term "limey").

While slow to enforce the benefits of lime juice, the Royal Navy nevertheless moved swiftly to embrace a technology that it was convinced also had powerful antiscorbutic properties: tinned food. Prior to the 1810 introduction of tinned meats and vegetables, expeditions were reliant on dry foods that could be stored for long periods of time, such as salt beef and salt pork, biscuits, pemmican and flour. However, spoilage, insects and rodents played havoc with such stores—none of which had antiscorbutic properties.

Therefore, the discovery of the value of preserving food in airtight metal containers offered a liberation of sorts. In theory, expeditions of ever-greater duration might now be planned, knowing that there would be a reliable onboard source of meats, vegetables, fruits and soups that would maintain their nutritive value throughout an expedition. It was this simple invention, tinned meats and vegetables, together with the navy's success with lime juice, that convinced the Admiralty that lengthy Arctic discovery voyages such as Franklin's were possible.

Yet, though tinned foods enjoyed a great reputation for warding off scurvy, their antiscorbutic benefits had not been proven, and, in fact, were grossly overrated. The nature of the canning process of the day, which required that tins be nearly immersed in boiling water or saltwater, destroyed any ascorbic acid they may have contained, so that their tinned meats, vegetables, soups and even fruits were virtually useless as antiscorbutics. Still, received opinion held that scurvy could be staved off on Arctic voyages by liberal diets of tinned meats and vegetables, along with a daily allotment of lime juice.

The skeleton found near Booth Point by the University of Alberta researchers in 1981 proved otherwise. It left little doubt that, during the final year of the Franklin expedition (and probably earlier), scurvy was a factor in the declining health of the crews and an important contributor to the expedition's disastrous outcome.

Other findings also preyed upon the minds of the researchers, however: the unusual distribution of the bones near the entrance of the tent circle, the fact that certain bones were present yet others were missing and the discovery of cut marks on the skeleton's right femur. Also noted by Beattie were the angularity of the cranial fragments and the identifiable convergence of fracture lines, indicating that the skull was forcibly broken. He paused over the evidence before him and briefly considered the possibility that this young sailor had suffered an end far more terrible than that described in the historic Inuit accounts—that Franklin's crew "fell down and died as they walked along." Was this the first physical evidence found to support another Inuit claim: that in their final days, the sailors had been reduced to cannibalism?

The discovery of the bones at Booth Point would prompt, over the next five years, three further scientific expeditions into the Canadian Arctic. With each of these investigations, new leads would be pursued and unravelled, culminating in the exhumation of the preserved corpses of three of Franklin's sailors on Beechey Island in 1984 and 1986, allowing Beattie and his colleagues an unprecedented look into a world very different from our own. By opening this window into the past, they became the first to piece together accurately the events that led to the destruction of the greatest enterprise in the annals of polar exploration.

A Subject of
WONDER

"THE DISCOVERY OF a north-west passage to India and China has always been considered as an object peculiarly British." With these words, John Barrow, Second Secretary to the Admiralty, announced that, at the end of the Napoleonic Wars, Britain was to embark on a great age of polar discovery. For in the nineteenth century, the greatest epoch of geographic exploration ever known, a primary British aim was to establish the existence of a Northwest Passage (the successful navigation from the Atlantic to the Pacific around America's northern extremity); another was to reach the North Pole. In a little over five decades, from 1818 to 1876, dozens of Royal Navy ships would reach the polar sea. In the process, the Arctic archipelago, that vast labyrinth of land and ice that lies to the north of America, was made almost entirely known.

In most respects, this age of marine exploration was a triumph of geographic and scientific advancement. Yet, despite an enormous investment of resources and manpower, the Royal Navy failed to achieve the two goals set for it by Parliament. When the last official British Arctic expedition returned in 1876 to newspaper headlines proclaiming "The Polar Failure," no ship had succeeded in navigating the Northwest Passage and no one had yet reached the North Pole. Those prizes were left for others. It was not until 1905 that Roald Amundsen, a Norwegian, would complete the first successful navigation of the Northwest Passage; in 1909, the North Pole was claimed by Robert Peary, an American.

Is it possible that the forensic investigation of human remains from that era, specifically the Franklin expedition disaster of 1845–48, would provide some insight into this larger failure? Certainly the terrible fate of Sir John Franklin's expedition marked the nadir of Arctic exploration: a disappearance of two ships with all 129 of their men, which preyed strongly upon the British mind. Alongside the Franklin disaster, though, were numerous more routine exploration failures that, whilst lacking the sheer melancholic grandeur of the Franklin disaster, were just as frightful and inexorable. For one word appears time and again in their expedition narratives, a word that represents none of the usual suspects: neither ice traps nor perpetual darkness, marauding polar bears nor the minus 50°F (-46°C) cold—but simply, "debility."

"Debility" plagued Arctic expeditions of the 19th century.

In his 1836–37 voyage of discovery, for instance, Captain George Back complained of the "languor," "incoherency" and "debility" suffered by his crew. In 1848–49, Sir James Clark Ross similarly reported that many of his men were made "useless from lameness and debility." Five years later, in 1854, Captain George Henry Richards also wrote of a "general debility" afflicting his crew; four years after that, in 1859, all members of Captain Leopold M'Clintock's expedition aboard the *Fox* were struck down by "debility."

It is an endless catalogue strung together by one simple word.

AT THE OUTSET, the Admiralty's John Barrow believed that the Northwest Passage was easily navigable and predicted this would be achieved in a matter of months. There was simply no conception of the impediment an ocean of ice would pose to Britain's

The polar regions, as perceived by Victorian England.

exploration ambitions. Those hopes would first be set back in 1818, when Captain John Ross sailed into Lancaster Sound—the true entrance of the passage—only to adjudge it a bay, then compounded his blunder by naming the "bay" in Barrow's honour. Then in 1819, Barrow dispatched twenty-eight-year-old Lieutenant William Edward Parry with two ships, the *Hecla* and *Griper,* and a youthful crew to do that which, in Barrow's words, "Ross, from misapprehension, indifference or incapacity, had failed to do."

Parry entered Lancaster Sound and, with a stiff wind behind him, bore westward. A vast, unexplored channel lay open before the two ships. The masts were crowded with officers and men the entire day. Parry, every bit the Regency gentleman, sought to conceal his own excitement, but did remark upon the "almost breathless anxiety . . . now visible in every countenance." The *Hecla* and *Griper* blew past the precipitous cliffs and stratified buttresses of Devon Island to the north and, to the south, passed a series of channels to which Parry assigned names: Navy Board Inlet, Admiralty Inlet and Prince Regent Inlet. He saved for Barrow a particular distinction: naming the channel that lay due west after him. Thus, Lancaster Sound gave way to Barrow Strait.

Parry had blind luck on his side. His ships pushed rapidly west, cruising through a channel normally closed fast by ice, even in summer. When ice did finally obstruct his progress, he opted to overwinter at Melville Island, a rugged outcrop of 1,200-foot (370-metre) cliffs that he named for Viscount Melville, the First Lord of the Admiralty. Parry fully expected the ice to clear from the remainder of the passage the following summer. In fact, he had unknowingly breached the dominion of ice, a possibility that dawned on him during the depths of the polar winter, when the temperature outside plunged to minus 55°F (-48°C). He realized that he had taken an incalculable risk and secretly began to craft an escape, titled "Plan of a Journey from the North coast of America towards Fort Chipewyan, should such a measure be found necessary as a last resource." He doubtless realized it would have been an exercise in futility. The nearest white men, Hudson's Bay Company fur traders, were more than 700 miles (1,130 km) away across some of the bleakest, coldest terrain on earth.

Parry, however, did just about everything right in the circumstances. It was 1 October, and he "immediately and imperiously" set about securing the ships and stores for the onset of the polar winter, a responsibility that had, he wrote accurately if immodestly, "for the first time devolved on any officer in his majesty's navy, and might, indeed, be considered of rare occurrence in the whole history of navigation." Most particularly, Parry determinedly set about defending against scurvy. He sent out hunting parties and enforced a ruling that "every animal killed was to be considered as public property; and, as such, to be regularly issued like any other kind of provision, without the slightest distinction between the messes of the officers and those of the ships' companies." In addition, Parry diligently seized upon two dietary reforms that had only recently been introduced by the Royal Navy: The lime juice—prepared from fresh fruit—he carried onboard was dispensed daily in the presence of an officer to ensure that the bitter concoction was consumed by reluctant sea-hands; also distributed were the stores of "embalmed provisions"—tinned meats, vegetables and soup. So new was the technology that no one had yet invented the can opener; the cans had to be cleaved open with an axe. (The Royal Navy had begun conducting trials with tinned foods in 1813.)

Parry had yet another plan: to keep his men so thoroughly occupied that they had no time to consider their predicament. Their days were filled with activities, but Parry's most useful tool for staving off monotony was a barrel organ for singalongs and bimonthly polar melodramas put on by officers in petticoats. His second officer even produced a newspaper called the *North Georgia Gazette and Winter Chronicle*, filled with bad puns and abominable poesy, but which had the "happy effect of . . . diverting the mind from the gloomy prospect which would sometimes obtrude itself on the stoutest heart."

Despite Parry's best efforts, however, the living conditions the men were forced to endure were appalling. On 3 November, the sun disappeared below the horizon and did not return until 84 days later, just before noon on 3 February 1820, when a crewman spotted it from the *Hecla*'s maintop. By then, the temperature inside the ships was so cold that the theatrical performances could not be enjoyed by anyone, but most particularly by the cast of female impersonators. Large patches of skin were left behind any time the men touched a metal surface. Wrote Parry: "We found it necessary, therefore, to use great caution handling our sextants and other instruments, particularly the eye-pieces of telescopes." The lime juice froze and shattered its glass containers. Even the mercury froze in the thermometers.

Rations, at least, were better than the more experienced hands were used to, as "a pound of Donkin's preserved [tinned] meat, together with one pint of vegetable or concentrated soup, per man" replaced salt beef weekly. Yet despite this measure and the daily allotment of lime juice, the first case of scurvy was reported on 1 January 1820. Parry tried to conceal it from the crew, and set about curing the victim by starting a tiny garden of mustard and cress on the warm galley pipes of the *Hecla*. The measure worked. Nine days later, the man boasted that he was fit enough to "run a race."

Soon, however, illness gained a firmer hold: a quarter of the ninety-four-strong crew fell ill, half of them from scurvy—though even as the symptoms appeared, the worst of the crew's hardships were behind them. By May, ptarmigan were seen, and soon a brace or two were bagged daily for the sick. It was, wrote Parry, "of the utmost importance, under our present circumstances, that every ounce of game which we might thus procure should be served in lieu of other meat." During the expedition's twelve months on Melville Island, the men would consume 3 musk oxen, 24 caribou, 68 hares, 53 geese, 59 ducks, 144 ptarmigans—totalling 3,766 pounds (1,710 kg) of fresh meat. To cap it off, when the snow melted, Parry noticed that sorrel grew in abundance around the harbour, and the men were sent out every afternoon to collect it: "Of the good effects produced upon our health by the unlimited use of fresh vegetable substances, thus bountifully supplied by the hand of Nature, even where least to be expected, little doubt can be entertained, as it is well known to be a never-failing specific for scorbutic affections." In the end, Parry lost just one man to scurvy during his seventeen-month voyage. Relative to what might have been expected in such circumstances, the achievement was, wrote Parry, "a subject of wonder."

Parry's expedition had become the first to overwinter in the Arctic archipelago. He also came closer to completing the Northwest Passage than any other person would come for the next three decades. He was tempted to push on to the Pacific. But, facing an impermeable barrier of multiyear ice, with depleted stores and the very real risk of being forced to spend a second winter in the region, he relented.

The expedition had encountered no Inuit during its long winter at Melville Island, but on its homeward journey, the crew finally met some natives on Baffin Island; one of those meetings would be laden with irony. One of the Inuit elders was, Parry noted, "extremely inquisitive" and observed gravely as a tin of preserved meat was opened for dinner: "The old man was sitting on the rock, attentively watching the operation, which was performed with an axe struck by a mallet." When the tin had been opened, the man "begged very hard for the mallet which had performed so useful an office, without expressing the least wish to partake of the meat, even when he saw us eating it with good appetites." Parry, however, insisted the man try some: "[He] did not seem at all to relish it, but ate a small quantity, from an evident desire not to offend us."

Unfortunately, the elder's distaste for tinned foods was not shared by British authorities. After Parry's return, expedition surgeon John Edwards praised such supplies as "acquisitions of the highest value." C.I. Beverley, the assistant surgeon on Parry's expedition, also produced a glowing endorsement of the expedition's tinned provisions, ascribing to them both the preservation of the general health of the officers and crew and the eventual recovery of one man who had been "attacked by the scurvy." This assessment ended with a statement that encouraged ever-greater reliance on tinned goods: "I have every reason to believe that the anti-scorbutic quality of the vegetable is not injured in its preparation." Yet this notion—that tinned foods retained powerful antiscorbutic properties—was entirely anecdotal. The comparative immunity enjoyed by Parry's men might, with hindsight, have been more accurately attributed to other factors, not the least of which was the amount of game shot and wild sorrel collected. Unfortunately, no mention of these measures was made. The British were enamoured of technology, and, after Parry's successful overwintering in the Arctic, the antiscorbutic benefits of tinned foods became accepted wisdom in the Royal Navy, a premise that would go untested and unchallenged for much of the next century. Indeed, starting with William Edward Parry's voyage of 1819–20, British Arctic expeditions used tinned foods first as a supplement, then, by the time of George Back's 1836–37 voyage, as a critical component of their food stores.

STILL, NOT EVERY SHIP captain shared the navy's enthusiasm for tinned provisions. In fact, the privately financed 1829–33 expedition of Captain John Ross was a feat of physical endurance and survival precisely because Ross sought to avoid reliance on preserved foods.

Following his 1818 maritime blunder, when Barrow rained such derision upon him that he never again received a Royal Navy command, Ross had been forced into semi-retirement at half-pay. He watched from the sidelines as his rival, Parry, undertook two further polar expeditions (in 1821–23 and 1824–25), at the end of which, Barrow conceded that knowledge about the Northwest Passage was "precisely where it was at the conclusion of his [Parry's] first voyage." Parry had even managed to lose one of His Majesty's ships, the *Fury*, which was nipped by an iceberg in Prince Regent Inlet. Ross seized on the opening. He raised a private expedition and found a wealthy gin merchant, Felix Booth, to underwrite a voyage to complete the Northwest Passage aboard the *Victory*, a second-hand steamer that Ross refitted with state-of-the-art technology and manned with 23 officers and men.

It appeared at first that Ross would succeed. In Greenland, he received reports that it was an unusually warm summer. On 6 August 1829, the expedition entered Lancaster Sound, the site of his 1818 humiliation. Believing Prince Regent Inlet would eventually reveal an opening to the west, Ross tacked south, calculating correctly that the land mass, which had been named Somerset by Parry, was an island. He pressed further into these waters than any European before him, but missed Bellot Strait, the only opening to the west, and with time concluded that the western shore of Prince Regent Inlet was not an island but a peninsula, which he named Boothia, for his sponsor. By then it was too late to continue. With conditions deteriorating, the expedition established winter quarters at a place Ross called Felix Harbour. From here, the expedition embarked on the first of four winters in the Arctic, a harrowing saga that is remarkable—in equal measure—for the courage and endurance needed to survive it.

The following summer, the ice freed the *Victory*, allowing 3 miles (5 km) of hope before it closed in again and held the ship fast, trapping it for a second winter. In 1830, Ross's young nephew, Commander James Clark Ross, led a sledge journey far to the west. He named the farthest place he reached Victory Point, and the adjoining territory was claimed in the name of King William IV. Unaware that he had crossed an ice-covered strait on his journey, Ross named the territory King William Land. In fact, it was King William Island. James Ross also noted an accumulation of pack-ice off the northwest coast, the "heaviest masses that I had ever seen in such a situation." His sledge journey was a remarkable achievement in itself. The *pièce de résistance*, however, was his subsequent discovery of the North Magnetic Pole, which "Nature," he wrote, "had chosen as the centre of one of her great and dark powers." With that, the expedition became a triumph. "Nothing now remained for us but to return home and be happy for the rest of our days," the younger Ross wrote. But by the summer of 1831, the *Victory* had been allowed only another 4 miles (6.5 km) of passage before the impenetrable ice barrier returned.

"To us," John Ross declared, "the sight of ice was a plague, a vexation, a torment, an evil, a matter of despair." The depth of this despondency is further revealed in his journal, where he confided: "I confess that the chances are now much against our being ever heard of." He was faced with a critical decision: risk sitting out the following spring in the hope that by summer the ice would finally give way and the *Victory* would be freed, which seemed unlikely, or abandon the *Victory* and undertake a 300-mile (480-km) overland trek north while snow remained on the ground, allowing for sledge travel. Ross elected for the latter. His destination would be Fury Beach on Somerset Island, where there was a store of provisions left by Parry on an earlier expedition and the greater likelihood of open water. From there, Ross believed he could use the ship's small boats to make a dash for Baffin Bay, to rendezvous with the summer whaling fleet.

Sledges were fashioned to haul the small boats loaded with provisions, and the captain ordered advance parties to establish a string of caches en route. Then, on 29 May 1832, the expedition abandoned the *Victory* and, in sub-zero temperatures and on two-thirds rations, headed north. But off Fury Beach, where open water had been expected, the ice had also failed to clear and the men were forced to endure a fourth winter in the Arctic. They barricaded themselves in a house of wood and snow they hurriedly constructed. It was little better than an igloo, yet Ross gave it a pompous name—Somerset House—and enforced rigid delineations of rank. It was a snow house divided. On one side, ordinary seamen were crammed together in their rank furs, muttering obscenities; the structure's other half was segregated quarters for the officers, where John Ross continued to be waited upon hand and foot like the country squire he aspired to be. Ross grimly speculated whether "it should be the fortune of any one to survive after another such year as the three last." But he maintained a stiff upper lip, and not only because of the cold.

To make matters worse, the men's provisions were inadequate. Ross ordered half-rations, but by now, these consisted mainly of preserved meat and tinned turnip and carrot soup from the stores left by Parry. The crew's only fresh meat came from the few Arctic foxes, and fewer hares, they could snare, with roast fox served on Sundays. The expedition surgeon made note of the deteriorating conditions: "we had scarcely any animal food . . . The development of severe scurvy at once served to heighten our misery, and to show how poor a defence a [tinned] vegetable regimen is . . . " It was, he wrote, "during our stay at the *Fury*'s stores that the worst form of the disease appeared." The ship's carpenter died of the illness in February 1833. John Ross was also suffering the effects of the dread disease: ancient wounds long-healed began to open as scar tissue dissolved. The captain wondered whether, "I might not be ultimately able to surmount all the present circumstances."

Yet survive he did, and, in late summer, a lane of open water appeared into which, on 15 August 1833, the men launched their boats with a fine westerly breeze. Having "almost forgotten what it was to float at freedom on the seas," they made 72 miles (116 km) on 17 August alone. Propelled by the wind when it blew, they rowed on amongst the icebergs when it dropped—once for a stretch of twenty hours without rest. After nine days heading east, they finally spotted a sail in the distance. The men desperately rowed towards the vessel, but after several hours a wind came up and the ship moved off to the southeast. Soon another sail was sighted, but that ship too sailed on. Wrote John Ross: "it was the most anxious moment that we had yet experienced, to find that we were near to no less than two ships, either of which would have put an end to all our fears and all our toils, and that we should probably reach neither." But an hour later the wind dropped, and they again began to close on one of the ships. Finally, they saw it lower a boat that rowed over to meet them. Stunned, the mate in command assured Ross that he couldn't be who he said he was, as Ross was known to have died two years earlier. That conclusion, Ross replied, had been "premature." They were unshaven, filthy, "dressed in the rags of wild beasts," gaunt and starved to the bone. But they were definitely alive.

That John Ross is not celebrated today as one of the epic heroes of polar exploration is remarkable. Perhaps his all-too human failings militated against such a reputation, for John Ross was the antithesis of what one might expect in a hero: corpulent, irritable and overly solicitous of class. In contrast to Parry, who did his best to provide for the comfort of his men, Ross held in contempt the entire notion of the importance of creature comforts in maintaining morale. While still aboard the *Victory,* for instance, Ross had reduced the heat each winter to lessen the effects of condensation. He then responded to complaints from the freezing crew by bragging loudly about his unusual capacity for generating body heat. No one ever got close enough to him to notice. There was something improbable, even absurd, about John Ross. And he paid a terrible price for his haughtiness when a disgruntled underling later helped publish an unofficial account of the expedition: a remarkable rant called *The Last Voyage of Capt. John Ross*—vilifying Ross's character and mocking his physical attributes. More damaging still was the book's inventory of his alleged shortcomings as a leader, culminating in a declaration that while "the men were conscious that they owed him obedience; they were not equally convinced that they owed him their respect and esteem."

Such criticisms aside, the expedition's return was a triumph of human ingenuity and survival. Its success was due to one simple measure: Ross's emulation of the Inuit, the Earth's hardiest survivors, who eke out a living on the margins of the habitable world and yet who do so without any trace of scurvy. The Inuit treat the contents of a caribou's stomach and the testicles of the musk-ox as delicacies, for example, food sources that have since been proven to be powerful antiscorbutics. And whilst unwilling to consume these igloo specialities, John Ross had his men eat a diet of fresh meat and salmon, concluding that "the large use of oils and fats is the true secret of life in these frozen countries." Where possible, therefore, he replaced supplies such as salt beef and tinned foods with fresh meat, resulting in a "very salutary change of diet to our crew." By doing so, Ross also solved the mystery of Arctic survival. Through contact with the locals, he correctly surmised that their diet of fresh meat had antiscorbutic properties, observing that "the natives cannot subsist without it, becoming diseased and dying under a more meager diet." As he wrote in his log, "The first salmon of the summer were a medicine which all the drugs in the ship could not replace." The Inuit had saved John Ross's hide and those of his crew, and he knew it, though his praise was tempered by characteristic pomposity. They were, he said, "among the most worthy of all the rude tribes yet known to our voyagers, in whatever part of the world." It was only in his fourth winter, after he had lost contact with the Inuit and moved north to Somerset Island, where game was scarce and the expedition became dependent upon tinned foods, that scurvy had made a run at the expedition.

UNFORTUNATELY, Captain George Back, on his 1836–37 Arctic expedition, failed to learn from Ross's example. A veteran of three expeditions across the barren lands of northern Canada, two of them under the command of John Franklin, R.N., George Back was by turns ambitious, conceited and utterly charming. An inveterate womanizer, dandy and accomplished watercolourist, Back was a knowingly Byronic figure who dabbled in poetry and possessed a certain élan, having spent five years as a prisoner of war in Revolutionary France.

Back sailed for the Arctic on 14 June 1836, with orders to travel to Repulse Bay, beyond the northwestern reaches of Hudson Bay, then to send sledge parties across the isthmus of the Melville Peninsula (an arm of the American continent) to explore its western coast. The expedition was an appalling failure. Back's ship, the *Terror*, like the *Victory*, was caught in the Arctic's thrall of relentless ice. At one point it was hurled 40 feet (12 metres) up a cliff face, only to be mauled by an iceberg. Wrote Back: "To guard against the worst I ordered the provisions and preserved meats, together with various other necessaries, to be got up from below and stowed on deck, so as to be ready at a moment to be thrown on the large floe alongside." Men slept in their clothes, ready to abandon ship at a moment's notice. On some nights, the ice could be heard gently caressing the hull, on others it wailed and pounded against the ship's sides. At one point the ice reached up alongside to form a cradle, then, after holding the ship tight in the air, the floe let go its grasp and the vessel plunged into the sea. Back was astonished to glimpse in those moments a mould of the ship "stamped as perfectly as in a die in the walls of ice on either side." Next, a huge square mass of ice of many tons collapsed, throwing up a wave 30 feet (9 metres) high that rolled over the stricken *Terror*. George Back:

> It was indeed an awful crisis rendered more frightful from the mistiness of the night and the dimness of the moon. The poor ship cracked and trembled violently and no one could say that the next minute would not be her last, and, indeed, his own too, for with her our means of safety would probably perish.

Compounding the desperate situation, there had been a sudden, serious and—to the expedition's captain and medical officer— inexplicable onset of illness aboard the *Terror* within a fortnight of the last live domestic animal being slaughtered on board. Six months into the expedition, Back complained in his journal on

26 December that the crew had been inflicted by "perverseness," "sluggishness" and "listlessness."

As his men began complaining of debility, Back concluded they were suffering from scurvy. Yet he made no serious attempt to secure fresh meat. Instead, he increased the provision of tinned meat, soup and vegetables, as well as lime juice and other alleged anti-scorbutics. But on 13 January 1837, one of the men died. As well, ten of the ship's crew of sixty—both officers and men—were now sick, complaining of "languor" and "shooting pains or twitches betokening weakness" in the ankles and knees. One, named Donaldson, "evinced a disposition to incoherency." Another was suddenly "seized with syncope," or dizziness. The provision of canned meat and "anti-scorbutics of every kind" failed to help. While Back had suffered through horrific privations before—scurvy and starvation amongst them—during previous overland expeditions, he was unnerved by the disease eating away at the *Terror*'s crew: "Who could help feeling that his hour also might shortly come?" He felt utterly helpless, that the situation was "beyond our comprehension or control." At one point, he wondered if the cause might not in fact have been an illness carried aboard by one of the crew, at another he mused about the influence of the dank, hothouse atmosphere inside the ship and the freezing dry cold without.

Donaldson, the man who had shown signs of incoherency and who remained in a "drowsy stupor," died on 5 February. On 26 April, he was followed by a Royal Marine named Alexander Young who, before dying, had requested that he be autopsied. The ship's surgeon found Young's liver enlarged, water in the region of the heart and the quality of his blood "poor." When Back demanded in an official letter to the surgeon, Dr. Donovan, "his opinion of the probable consequences if the ship were detained another winter in these regions," Donovan's answer was that "it would be fatal to many of the officers and men." And so, when the *Terror* was finally released by the ice after ten months, Back ordered the ship, badly leaking, to make for home. With a hull bound round with chain cables to seal the cracks caused by the ice and "in a sinking condition," the *Terror* somehow limped across the Atlantic. Even then, in July, Back watched in impotent fury as the disease continued to spread: "The whole affair, indeed, was inexplicable to the medical officers as we had the advantage of the best provisions." As the *Terror* made towards Ireland, the "apprehension of sickness had induced most of the men to go without food." Back himself remained an invalid for six months after the dreadful voyage.

The Back expedition was an enormous setback for the Admiralty. Still, there was no attempt by British authorities to examine the causes of the illness amongst Back's crew. Even if there had been, the probable cause—the expedition's heavy reliance on tinned foods and the absence of fresh meat—would almost certainly have eluded suspicion. Indeed, four years after Back's return there was a push within the Royal Navy to replace all livestock on expeditions with tinned food. Wrote Captain Basil Hall:

> Meat thus preserved eats nothing, nor drinks—it is not apt to die—does not tumble overboard or get its legs broken or its flesh worked off its bones by tumbling about the ship in bad weather— it takes no care in the keeping—it is always ready, may be eaten hot or cold, and this enables you to toss into a boat as many days' cooked provisions as you require.

In 1844, Second Secretary to the Admiralty John Barrow argued for one final attempt to complete the Northwest Passage. Barrow wanted to finish what he had started a quarter-century before, fearing that England, having "opened the East and West doors, would be laughed at by all the world for having hesitated to cross the threshold." Glossing over Back's setback, Barrow, in his bid for funding, opted to focus instead on a gloriously successful trio of Antarctic cruises undertaken by John Ross's nephew, James Clark Ross, from 1839–43:

There can be no objection with regard to any apprehension of the loss of ships or men. The two ships that recently were employed among the ice of the Antarctic sea after three voyages returned to England in such good order as to be ready to be made available for employment on the proposed North-West expedition; and with regard to the crews, it is remarkable that neither sickness nor death occurred in most of the voyages made into the Arctic regions, North or South.

As far as Barrow was concerned, he had the right ships, the *Erebus* and *Terror*, and he had the right commander in Ross.

James Clark Ross's Antarctic expedition had charted some 500 miles (805 km) of the southern continent's coastline, discovered the Antarctic ice shelf and sighted a smoking volcano, which Ross named Mount Erebus after his ship (a nearby crater was named Mount Terror after the smaller of the two vessels). When he returned to England in the autumn of 1843, Ross had earned himself the title of the world's leading polar discoverer. The expert in ornithology and the science of terrestrial magnetism was knighted and presented with the Founder's Medal of the Royal Geographical Society. He cut quite a dash in Victorian society, and was once said to be "the handsomest man in the Royal Navy," no small compliment given the preening to which the officer class was prone.

The *Erebus* and *Terror* were not nearly so handsome. Royal Navy bomb vessels designed for shore bombardment, they were sturdily built to withstand the recoil of their 3-ton (3.1-tonne) mortars. But the *Terror*, in particular, had an interesting history. Built in 1813, a ship of that name was engaged the following year in the Battle of Baltimore, which saw British ships of war firing bombs, rockets and cannons at Fort McHenry. The 25-hour barrage failed to dislodge the Americans and gave rise to the U.S. National Anthem, the *Star-Spangled Banner*, with its reference to "the rockets' red glare." The *Terror* later saw service in the Mediterranean before it was sailed into Hudson Bay under the command of George Back. After its narrow escape from the Arctic, the *Terror*, together with the *Erebus*, was reinforced for protection against the ice for Ross's Antarctic voyages.

Further reinforcements were made for the planned Northwest Passage expedition, set to embark in May 1845, including covering the ships' bows with sheet iron. Other changes were made to assist the expedition as it made its way through Arctic waters. The ships were fitted with a tubular boiler and steam-forming apparatus, which conveyed hot water in pipes under the decks to warm the men's berths and all other parts of the vessels. Desalinators were built into the galley stoves. In a revolutionary step, entire steam locomotives with specially adapted screw propellers were also installed, for emergency use. A 25-horsepower locomotive from the London and Greenwich Railway was bought for the *Erebus*, stripped of its front wheels and installed in the ship's hold. The engine of the *Terror*, at 20 horsepower, was placed in the after-hold.

On 12 May 1845, the *Times* reported:

> The Lords Commissioners of the Admiralty have, in every respect, provided most liberally for the comforts of the officers and men of an expedition which may, with the facilities of the screw-propeller, and other advantages of modern science, be attended with great results.

It was, in short, the most technologically advanced and best-equipped exploration team ever. However, it was not to be commanded by James Clark Ross, who declined due to a promise he had made his wife—to never again undertake a polar expedition—and a rumoured problem with the drink. Instead, the honour fell to an aging navy veteran, Sir John Franklin.

— 3 —

Into the Frozen
SEAS

T FIFTY-NINE, Sir John Franklin was widely considered too
old for the command. Lord Haddington, First Lord of the
Admiralty, shared the doubts of many about Franklin's
fitness but agreed to interview him. During that meeting, the
First Lord told Franklin of his concerns. "You are sixty," he said.
Franklin was nonplussed: "No, my lord, I am only fifty-nine." Still,
the Admiralty was nothing if not an old boys' club, and William
Edward Parry lobbied on Franklin's behalf, telling Haddington:
"If you don't let him go, the man will die of disappointment." On
7 February 1845, Franklin was given the job.

Born in Spilsby, Lincolnshire, on 16 April 1786, Franklin entered the Royal Navy when he was fourteen and served in a number of famous battles during the Napoleonic Wars, including the
Battle of Trafalgar. In 1814, he would be injured in a disastrous attempt to capture New Orleans. When the Duke of Wellington
finally defeated Bonaparte in the Battle of Waterloo in 1815, the
Royal Navy was forced to look for new assignments for its best

Daguerreotype of Sir John Franklin.

young officers. Arctic exploration was one way for such officers to distinguish themselves in peacetime. And so it was that, in May 1818, Franklin began his polar service as second-in-command of Captain David Buchan's failed voyage into the Spitsbergen ice.

In 1819 Franklin again headed north, this time in command of an overland expedition ordered by the British Admiralty to travel from Hudson Bay to the polar sea, where he was to map North

America's unexplored Arctic coast. George Simpson of the Hudson's Bay Company was highly skeptical of Franklin's qualifications for such a journey:

> Lieut. Franklin, the Officer who commands the party has not the physical powers required for the labor of moderate Voyaging in this country; he must have three meals p diem, Tea is indispensible, and with the utmost exertion he cannot walk above Eight miles in one day, so that it does not follow if those Gentlemen are unsuccessful that the difficulties are insurmountable.

Franklin succeeded in surveying 211 miles (340 km) of the icy shoreline east of the Coppermine River before a tragic return journey over the Canadian tundra, or "Barren Grounds," during which expedition members were reduced by starvation to eating an old leather shoe and caribou excrement. Ten men died from the cold and hunger, exacerbated in part by Franklin's unfamiliarity with northern conditions. Franklin himself nearly succumbed to starvation before relief arrived. Yet when he returned to London, Franklin's account of heroic achievement marred by murder, cannibalism and his own suffering caught the public's imagination, and he became known as the man who ate his boots. Promoted to the rank of captain, he then returned in 1825–27 to the Arctic for a well-organized second overland expedition, resulting in the mapping of another 397 miles (640 km) of Arctic shoreline, for which he was knighted. Finally, after a six-year stint as colonial governor of Van Diemen's Land (today, the Australian state of Tasmania), Franklin was placed in command of the greatest single expedition of discovery Britain had ever mounted.

Royal Navy officers Captain Francis Crozier and Commander James Fitzjames were also appointed to the expedition. The veteran Crozier had served in a number of earlier attempts at finding both a Northwest Passage and reaching the North Pole and had been second-in-command of James Clark Ross's Antarctic expedi-

Captain Francis Crozier.

tions as commander of the *Terror*. As for Fitzjames, he had served as mate aboard the first steamer to successfully navigate the Euphrates, and had served on ships operating in the Middle East and China, where he first became interested in the romantic lure of the Northwest Passage.

The days before the *Erebus* and *Terror* set sail were filled with social engagements and a general sense of excitement. The confidence of the expedition team was palpable. In a letter to his brother dated 11 April 1845, Harry D.S. Goodsir, the assistant surgeon on the

Commander James Fitzjames.

Erebus, wrote: "All the Officers are in great hopes of making the passage and expect to be in the Pacific end of next summer." Franklin and his officers were entertained at the Admiralty on 8 May. The crews were paid in advance of the sailing, and it can be assumed that at least some of the money was spent at the pubs dotting the docklands along the Thames. On 9 May, the final official inspection of the ships took place, attended by leading civil and naval figures and other specially invited guests. The *Illustrated London*

News reported that "the arrangements made for the comfort of the officers and crews are excellent. The quantity of stores taken on board is considerable." According to a *Times* reporter, those stores included "numerous chests of tea, although the crews are not expected to become teetotalers, an ample supply of rum having been provided for their use in the frozen regions."

Among the food supplies were nearly 8,000 tins of preserved meats (including boiled and roast beef, boiled and roast mutton, veal, seasoned beef and ox-cheek), vegetables (potatoes, parsnips, carrots and mixed vegetables) and soup (of 1-, 2-, 4-, 6- and 8-pound/.5-, 1-, 2-, 3-, 4-kg capacity). They also carried 1,203 pounds (546 kg) of tinned pemmican. Other supplies included 7,088 pounds (3,218 kg) of tobacco, 200 gallons (909 litres) of "wine for the sick" and 9,450 pounds (4,290 kg) of chocolate. Some 9,300 pounds (4,222 kg) of lemon juice were also taken, to be rationed to all during the expedition.

With such vast quantities of provisions and fuel, enough to last three years, the accommodations were congested. Of the living quarters, only Franklin's cabin on the *Erebus* was of any significant size. Commander Fitzjames had a cabin less than 6½ feet (2 metres) wide, with the crew of the *Erebus* berthed in what little space remained (many slung their hammocks alongside one another on the mess deck). Yet despite the cramped quarters, the *Erebus* had a library of 1,700 volumes, the *Terror* carried 1,200, including everything from narratives of earlier Arctic expeditions and geographical journals to Charles Dickens's *Nicholas Nickleby* and bound copies of *Punch* magazine. Each ship also had a hand organ that could play fifty tunes, including ten hymns. There were mahogany writing desks for officers and school supplies for teaching illiterate sailors to read and write. Instruments for research in geology, botany and zoology and for magnetic observation were also taken. The Franklin expedition was also one of the first voyages of discovery to carry that relatively new invention: a camera.

Commander Fitzjames's cabin on the HMS Erebus.

No Arctic expedition had ever been so lavishly outfitted. The same could be said even for the men, who were issued gear for extreme weather, suggesting a greater willingness on the part of British officialdom to adapt and learn from the Inuit than is generally credited. Indeed, Goodsir reported being issued sealskin gloves, a sealskin cap and greatcoat and a pair of "Deer-skin" trousers.

On 5 May, Franklin received his official instructions: essentially to sail to Baffin Bay and Lancaster Sound through to the Bering Strait and, in so doing, complete a Northwest Passage—all the while collecting valuable scientific and geographical information. There were no plans for Admiralty assistance or relief should the expedition encounter difficulty or fail to complete its voyage within the three years it had been supplied for. As a cursory precaution, the Hudson's Bay Company, with its fur-trading outposts at Fort Good Hope and Fort Resolution in what is now Canada's Northwest Territories, was asked to aid the expedition should word of trouble be received. The company was also instructed to alert native traders to watch for Franklin's crews.

In the last few days before he sailed, Franklin may have experienced a premonition of his fate. Suffering from the flu, he was resting at home with his wife, Jane, who had just finished sewing a silk Union Jack for him to take. Concerned about his illness, she draped the flag over his legs for warmth. He sprang to his feet: "There's a flag thrown over me! Don't you know that they lay the Union Jack over a corpse?" But on Sunday 18 May, the eve of his departure, with his wife and daughter present, the profoundly religious Franklin read Divine Service for the first time to his crews. And when the expedition sailed from the Thames the next morning, carrying 134 officers and men, most felt the Franklin expedition could not fail. Franklin's only child, Eleanor, wrote to an aunt:

> Just as they were setting sail, a dove settled on one of the masts, and remained there for some time. Every one was pleased with the good omen, and if it be an omen of peace and harmony, I think there is every reason of its being true.

The expedition was already out of view when the *Times* trumpeted:

> There appears to be but one wish amongst the whole of the inhabitants of this country, from the humblest individual to the highest in the realm, that the enterprise in which the officers and crew are about to be engaged may be attended with success, and that the brave seamen employed in the undertaking, may return with honour and health to their native land.

One week later, the president of the Royal Geographical Society, Sir Roderick Murchison, summed up the public mood in a speech: "The name of Franklin alone is, indeed, a national guarantee." Besides, the geographical obstacles were by now judged to be not all that great: The cumulative discoveries of preceding Arctic expeditions—Parry, John Ross, George Back, and Franklin's among them—had resulted in the mapping of much of the southern Arctic archipelago. By 1845, stretches of less than 62 miles (100 km) remained to be explored, and it was to close those gaps that Franklin sailed.

After calling briefly at Stromness Harbour on the island of Orkney, the expedition left Britain for the last time. A transport vessel, the *Barretto Junior,* laden with stores such as ten live oxen, accompanied the ships to the Whalefish Islands in Disco Bay on the west coast of Greenland, where the oxen were slaughtered for fresh meat and supplies transferred to the *Erebus* and *Terror.* Harry Goodsir wrote to his uncle from Greenland that, "we have got 10,000 cases of preserved ready cooked meats on board the Erebus alone so you see there is no chance of starving." It was also while at the Whalefish Islands that the first tins of preserved meat, carrots and potatoes were opened, and the contents served to the expedition's officers.

Franklin also wrote a letter in which he said his final goodbye to Lady Franklin. It was a message full of optimism:

> Let me now assure you, my dearest Jane, that I am amply provided with every requisite for my passage, and that I am entering on my voyage comforted with every hope of God's merciful guidance and protection, and that He will bless, comfort and protect you, my dearest . . . and all my other relatives. Oh, how much I wish I could write to each of them to assure them of the happiness I feel in my officers, my crew, and my ship!

Fitzjames sent home a journal in which he described the journey from Stromness to Disco—as well as many of his companions—

and outlined his feelings for Franklin: "We are very happy, and very fond of Sir John Franklin, who improves very much as we come to know more of him. He is anything but nervous or fidgety: in fact I should say remarkable for energetic decision in sudden emergencies."

The respect felt for Franklin was widely shared. A formal but affable character, Franklin was well-liked by his men. Lieutenant James Walter Fairholme, a 24-year-old officer aboard the *Erebus,* wrote to his family explaining, "he has such experience and judgement that we all look on his decisions with the greatest respect. I never felt that the Captain was so much my companion with any-one I have sailed with before."

After saying farewell, Lieutenant Edward Griffiths, command-ing the *Barretto Junior,* sailed back to Britain. He took with him members of the expedition, making a total of five who had already become ill enough to be sent home: three petty officers, one Royal Marine and an able seaman. Griffiths later described the spirits of the expedition as high and observed that the supplies, including the quality of the tinned foods, seemed quite satisfactory for the planned voyage.

A dog named Neptune and a pet monkey named Jacko accom-panied the 129 sailors when, on 12 July, they pushed westward. Their last contact with the outside world came at the end of July, in Baffin Bay, where they met two whaling ships, one named *Prince of Wales,* the other, *Enterprise.* Franklin was waiting for conditions to allow for a crossing of Baffin Bay to Lancaster Sound. Captain Dannett of the *Prince of Wales* reported inviting Franklin and sev-eral of his officers aboard. "Both ships' crews are all well, and in re-markable spirits, expecting to finish the operation in good time. They are made fast to a large iceberg, with a temporary observa-tory fixed upon it," Dannett recorded in his log.

Captain Robert Martin of the *Enterprise* noted that Franklin said he had provisions for five years, and if it were necessary he could "make them spin out seven years." Martin added that

Franklin told him he would "lose no opportunity of killing birds and whatever else was useful that came in the way, to keep up their stock, and that he had plenty of powder and shot for the purpose."

Martin was invited to dine aboard the *Erebus,* but shifting winds sent the ships apart, and so it was that in early August 1845, Franklin and his crews lost contact with their world. The *Erebus* and *Terror* were last seen making for Lancaster Sound, the eastern entrance to the Northwest Passage, where they would enter the desert of silence beyond.

4

Puny

EFFORTS

HERE WAS NO anxiety at first. Unease about the status of the Franklin expedition only crept into the minds of the Admiralty's London officials at the end of 1847. In March 1848, the need for a relief expedition was first raised in the House of Commons, where a confidant of Jane, Lady Franklin asked what, if any, steps the government might take regarding a search. The response confirmed that there was cause for concern, because the expedition had enough food only for three years, meaning its supplies would shortly be exhausted. None could have guessed that their worst nightmares were already about to play themselves out on the desolation of King William Island.

In 1848, the Admiralty dispatched three expeditions to relieve Sir John Franklin. Captain Henry Kellet was instructed to sail to the Bering Strait, where Franklin was to break free of the Arctic ice; a second expedition, under the command of Sir James Clark Ross, was sent into Lancaster Sound, following Franklin's original route, and an overland party led by Dr. John Rae and Sir John

Richardson was sent down the Mackenzie River. It was the failure of all three of these relief expeditions to find a trace of Franklin that finally sparked the fear that something might have gone terribly wrong. Ross's experiences especially contributed to the growing sense of foreboding.

With Franklin's disappearance, Ross's wife's entreaties—now coloured by the knowledge that it might have been her husband for whom they sought—were overridden by the Admiralty's orders for Ross to command one of the relief expeditions. Rather than relieve Franklin, however, Ross very nearly replicated the disaster.

Ross, with his wealth of Arctic experience, well understood the need to defend against scurvy. When the *Enterprise* and *Investigator,* two barque-rigged sailing vessels, departed the Thames in tow of two steam tugs on 12 May 1848, the ships had been provisioned for three years, with an additional year's stores for Franklin's crews. The ships carried plenty of preserved meats as well as canned potatoes, carrots and mixed vegetables such as beets and cabbage; while the expedition still carried salt beef and salt pork, tinned foods constituted the bulk of the provisions. In consequence, Ross remarked that his Franklin relief voyage was exceptionally outfitted by the navy. "Long experience and liberal means gave us many comforts that no other expedition had enjoyed," Ross would later write, "yet it is remarkable that the health of the crew suffered more during this winter than on any former occasion."

As winter quarters for the *Enterprise* and *Investigator* (the latter commanded by Captain Edward Henry Bird), Ross chose Port Leopold, on the northeast coast of Somerset Island. Here, on the eastern shore of the harbour, a narrow beach stretches out in a series of ridges below a bluff. The western side is steep and very high; its headland named Cape Seppings. On arrival, the two ships sent rockets up every evening and morning in the event that Franklin's men were in the vicinity. But the ships, moored some 200 yards (183 metres) apart, were soon frozen fast, and the crew immediately set to work in preparation for winter. A wall of snow

Men of the search expedition commanded by
James Clark Ross construct their winter quarters.

7 feet (2.1 metres) high was built linking one ship to the other, to aid with crossings during blizzards. In mid-October, winter awnings of "stout wool" were erected over the decks of each ship to afford protection from the wind and snow.

A concise account of the expedition was kept by James D. Gilpin, clerk-in-charge on the *Investigator*, and he recorded the news of the first death on 27 October 1848. "William Coombes, of the carpenter's crew, died: he had been long wasting away and expired at noon this day. The disease I understood was in the brain, and contracted previous to his servitude in the *Investigator*." Coombes was buried three days later, during the gloom of a heavy snowfall. Wrote Gilpin:

All hands attended the funeral, a mournful duty at all times, but particularly so here where the wild prospect around us contributed so much to the melancholy of the occasion. A more affecting spectacle cannot be than to behold a number of men in mournful procession, walking through deep snow, and drawing after them a sledge bearing a coffin shrouded with the bright colours of Old England.

The scene was a harbinger of the difficult winter ahead. For the expedition's outbreak of illness was every bit as rapacious as that experienced by George Back in 1836–37, and also attributed to scurvy—a debilitating toll aggravated by the urgency of Ross's quest.

Several days after Coombes's funeral, on 9 November, the sun disappeared. It would not return until 9 February 1849. The dreary winter routine aboard-ship was interrupted only by the trapping of Arctic foxes. The animals were fitted with copper collars around the neck, upon which were punched the name of the ship, their position and date "in the hopes that Sir John Franklin, or some of his people, might in the ingenious manner be apprised of assistance."

In March, Gilpin wrote that "two men are now lying seriously ill in their cots, one of them afflicted with scurvy, the first case of that malignant disease, so much dreaded in these voyages." A short time later, Gilpin recorded the death of a seaman on the *Enterprise*, noting that "for some time previous to his illness, he had been very melancholy, and from the time he was placed on the sick list never once rallied." The seaman, a Jamaican named James Gray, had been one of the most cheerful men on the ship for the first months of the expedition, but by December 1848 he had become "gloomy, distant and solitary." On 27 December he sought medical attention and was diagnosed as "suffering from Nostalgia." John Robertson, surgeon on the *Enterprise*, described the curious affliction:

The symptoms which appeared most prominent in this unusual malady amongst British seamen was depression of spirits, a fearful foreboding of the future, an extraordinary anxiety for the welfare of his friends in England and an eternal craving to return home . . . [He] could not sleep for thinking of home and what a fool he was to come to a dark world like this, at Port Leopold.

Gray was placed on a diet of tinned meat and tinned vegetables, yet he continued to deteriorate, developing symptoms such as pains in the chest, exhaustion and incoherency. Bronchitis then intervened "on the pre-existing constitutional debility," and he died on 16 April 1849. Robertson was impressed by Gray's inconsolable longing to return to Jamaica: "This being the only mulatto we had on board, it would seem that children of the torrid zone have a greater love of home than 'the children of the night' of whom we had many."

A second death followed on the *Enterprise*, on 30 April. The man, an able-bodied seaman named David Jenkins, had slipped while securing the ship to an iceberg nine months earlier. While no symptoms of the blow were visible for a lengthy period of time after the incident, his demise was attributed to a tumour that later developed. He suffered a "most lingering and painful illness." Because of the unusual symptoms, an autopsy was conducted.

Then on 12 May, William Cundy, captain of the hold of the *Investigator*, died. Wrote Gilpin: "He was a weak, ill-made man, and his recovery despaired of soon after he was taken into the sick bay, his first illness was scurvy, but many unseen causes hastened his death."

On 15 May, Sir James Clark Ross led the first of the sledging parties out in the search for Franklin. Ross marched west along the north coast of Somerset Island, then turned south, charting the island's west coast and travelling in the general direction of the North Magnetic Pole and King William Land, which he had first visited nearly two decades earlier. Just over two weeks out, however, Ross was confronted with the near-total breakdown in the health of one of his party. Lieutenant Francis Leopold M'Clintock, who was also accompanying Ross, described the man's condition:

"James Bonnett now complained of spasmodic pains, loss of strength, giddiness, & c. He continued ailing, and unable to labour, for the remainder of the journey." Three days later, M'Clintock recorded that the problem had spread to others: "Bonnett continues full of pains and devoid of strength, and all the other men are greatly reduced in strength; although our sledge gets lighter, they seem to be less able to drag it."

The work was onerous, at times desperate, as the crew struggled southward over the hummocks and heavy crushed ice that served to fringe the "impregnable and forbidding" western coastline of Somerset Island. They travelled 250 miles (400 km) before Ross finally called an end to the search. At this point, a large cairn was constructed on a headland and a note deposited in a copper cylinder:

> The cylinder which contains this paper was left here by a party detached from Her Majesty's ships Enterprise and Investigator under the command of Captain Sir James C. Ross, Royal Navy in search of the expedition of Sir John Franklin; and to inform any of his party that might find it that these ships, having wintered at Port Leopold in long. 90°w, lat 73° 52′N have formed there a depot with provisions for the use of Sir John Franklin's party sufficient for six months; also two very small depots about fifteen miles south of Cape Clarence and twelve miles south of Cape Seppings. The party are now about to return to the ships, which, as early as possible in the spring, will push forward to Melville Strait, and search the north coast of Barrow Strait; and, failing to meet the party they are seeking, will touch at Port Leopold on their way back, and then return to England before the winter shall set in.

> *7th June 1849. James C. Ross. Captain.*

Ross's party then began the return journey. He had sought to relieve Franklin, but concern for the health of his own men seriously hindered the efficacy of his search. Despite carrying with them lime juice as an antiscorbutic and the provision of a preferred diet of preserved beef and pea soup, several of his party were now "useless from lameness and debility," so ill in fact that they had to be hauled on the sledges by the remaining men. M'Clintock recorded that five of the twelve men had "quite broken down." Upon reaching Port Leopold thirty-nine days after setting out, Ross described his party as "so completely worn out by fatigue that every man was, from some cause or other, in the doctor's hands for two or three weeks, and I am sorry to say that two of them are not yet recovered." Gilpin remarked upon the "haggard looks and the attenuated forms of all of them."

Unknowingly, at the furthest point of this sledge trek, Ross's party came within 200 miles (320 km) of where Franklin's ships had been deserted the previous summer. Ross had travelled south along Peel Sound, the very route that Franklin had taken in 1846. Later, M'Clintock lamented this failure, "because we were marching in the right direction, as [subsequent] discoveries ... have proved."

Other sledging parties were also dispatched from the two ships, though as Ross later discovered, "The labours of these parties were of comparatively short durations; still they, like ourselves, all suffered from snow blindness, sprained ankles, and debility." One of the search parties travelled down the west shore of Prince Regent Inlet to Fury Beach, but the rigours of the journey also resulted in breakdowns in the health of some in the party. They did locate Somerset House, the structure occupied by the men under old Sir John Ross in 1832–33, and found it still standing. A tent was erected inside, fires were lit for warmth and two men—who were "too much fatigued to go any further"—were left as temporary occupants. The remainder of the party travelled only 25 miles (40 km) farther before erecting a cairn and returning to collect the invalids. The stores of the *Fury* were then examined and the contents tested. The tinned soup was declared "as good as when manufactured ... most delicious, and in flavour and consistency, superior to any of our preserves of the same kind."

Sailors' dinner at Cape Seppings, Somerset Island, during James Clark Ross's voyage of 1848–49 in search of Franklin. By Lieutenant William Browne

While the physical demands of these sledge searches doubtless contributed to the outbreak of illness, those left aboard also fell sick. On 15 June 1849, Henry Mathias, assistant surgeon on the *Enterprise,* died. The death was blamed on consumption, which, "im-

perceptibly gaining on his strength, brought him to the grave."
John Robertson wrote that Mathias was "greatly beloved and re-
spected by all in the expedition," but that there was no hope of
"getting him alive out of Port Leopold the grave of so many." Ross
observed: "Several others of the crews of both ships were in a declining state, and the general report of health was by no means
cheering." Even the *Enterprise*'s surgeon fell seriously ill. Robertson wrote that he suffered from scurvy and only "narrowly escaped destruction," though he would continue to suffer active
symptoms of "this abominable scourge" seven months later, even
after his return to England.

There was another death on 8 July.

Before the ships departed from Port Leopold, Ross ordered that
a depot be established. In it, he left behind a steam launch (with
fuel), a shelter with carpenter's tools, blankets, sleeping bags,
stoves, provisions and other essential supplies, and an account of
the expedition and its future plans. Gilpin: "Here then should any
of Sir John Franklin's people reach, they would find the means of
subsistence and escape."

After departing Port Leopold, Ross attempted to travel west,
but the ships were beset on 1 September and carried by ice towards
Baffin Bay. After three weeks they were freed, but with the intensi-
fying malevolence of the disease amongst his men, Ross was forced
to cut his losses, abandon his search and make a run for home. The
Investigator's cook died on 16 September during the homeward
passage; the last case appeared less than a week before the ships
limped into the English port of Scarborough in November 1849.
Some of the sailors remained ill enough to require hospitalization,
and one died shortly afterwards.

On 17 November, the *Illustrated London News* announced the
expedition's disappointing results, reporting the "great difficulty"
encountered by the sledge parties and noting the deaths: "The assistant-surgeon, a very intelligent young man, and three able seamen of the *Enterprise*, with three of the crew of the *Investigator*,

have died since the vessel left Woolwich in the spring of 1848." The *Athenaeum* declared the search for Franklin "very incomplete":

> ... the public mind can arrive at no conclusion for its anxiety from what has been done. But the issue of such examination as Sir James Ross *has* been enabled to institute makes a painful addition to the melancholy suggestions arising out of the long and death-like silence which has fallen over the former Expedition.

Ross's own health was broken. While many critics felt he should have braved a second winter, lamenting his "puny efforts," John Robertson, the surgeon on the *Enterprise*, thought most of the men would not have survived another year:

> There were few men in the ship who were not more or less afflicted by scurvy, and I cannot help fearing that had we remained out another winter, few if any would have ever returned—this the more certain since our antiscorbutics proved such perfect failures.

One officer on the expedition wrote: "We have certainly had to grapple with difficulties of no ordinary nature." Years later, M'Clintock reflected that "we underwent as much privation and fatigue as in any equal period of my subsequent travel." Yet the truth was that Ross's expedition was the only one with at least a theoretical chance of saving some of Franklin's men. When his ships reached Port Leopold, some of the men may still have been alive; with Ross's defeat, any chance of their being saved was lost.

Struggling to understand the severity of the sickness suffered aboard Ross's ships, some historians have theorized that the problem might have been compounded by the crews being accepted for the expedition without medical examinations. Ross's own officers complained that the ships' canned provisions were not only under-weight but of inferior quality, in Robertson's words, "a disgrace to the contractor." The same contractor—Stephan Goldner—had supplied Franklin's expedition. Doubts about the antiscorbutic value of the lime juice carried on-ship were also raised, with subsequent chemical analysis concluding that there was no guarantee of "the initial soundness of the fruit." This grave conclusion unfastened an exhaustive inquiry by Sir William Burnett, the navy's medical director-general. All juice then in the victualling stores was analyzed, with the conclusion that it was all below the proper standard of acidity. It was, of course, a mistake to suppose that acidity was the vital element.

In the end, the Admiralty attributed the health problems that beset the expedition, and the unusual number of deaths, to scurvy. Ross, who had seen scurvy's effects on some of his earlier expeditions, was unconvinced. He pointedly did not use the word "scurvy" in his official report of the expedition nor, indeed, did his men when later examined, saying that there had been "debility but no scurvy." The ferocity of the illness was unequalled in nineteenth-century Arctic exploration. Not even Franklin's expedition during its first year came close to experiencing the crippling losses encountered by James Clark Ross's during its lone Arctic winter; at one point, twenty-six men were on the sick list. The mortality on Ross's expedition was more than twice that of Franklin's 1845–46 winter losses.

— 5 —

Isthmus of the
GRAVES

O N 4 APRIL 1850, the *Toronto Globe* published an advertise-
ment announcing a £20,000 reward to be given by "Her
Majesty's Government to any party or parties, of any country,
who shall render efficient assistance to the crews of the discovery
ships under the command of Sir John Franklin." A further £10,000
was offered to anyone able to relieve any of the crews or bring information leading to their relief. Finally, another £10,000 was offered
to anyone succeeding in ascertaining the fate of the expedition.

By the autumn of 1850, a fleet of ships was combing the Arctic's
waterways for a sign of the missing explorers. The British Admiralty alone sent three expeditions consisting of a total of eight ships
into the Arctic. One of the search expeditions, made up of the HMS
Enterprise and HMS *Investigator* under the command of Captain
Richard Collinson and Commander Robert McClure, was sent
through the Bering Strait; Captain Horatio Thomas Austin, with
second-in-command Captain Erasmus Ommanney, was ordered to
take four ships into Lancaster Sound, while the third expedition,

led by Arctic whaling master Captain William Penny, was sent north into Jones Sound.

As early as February 1849, Jane, Lady Franklin travelled to Hull, a port from which whalers sailed to Baffin Bay, "with a view to plead her anxieties and distresses and to animate the commanders to her cause." She was among those active in the race to save her husband and his men, and with the help of supporters sent a ship to join in the search. As well, the United States Navy Department assisted New York merchant Henry Grinnell, who outfitted two ships under Lieutenant Edwin J. De Haven, while aging explorer Sir John Ross led an expedition funded by the Hudson's Bay Company and public subscription.

The Hudson's Bay Company also sent John Rae, an expert in Arctic survival, to assist with what would be his second search. Rae, who travelled overland and by boat to Victoria Island, would discover two pieces of wood on the southern shore of the island, wood that could only have come from a ship. Yet there was no proof that the debris was from either the *Erebus* or *Terror*, and his survey ended on the southeastern corner of the island, where the ice that clogged Victoria Strait prevented him from crossing to nearby King William Island.

View of the spot on Cape Riley, Devon Island, where in 1850 Captain Ommanney of the HMS Assistance *found evidence of a Franklin expedition encampment.*

Finally, on 12 October 1850, the *Illustrated London News* was able to report: "some faint gleams of hopeful light have at last been thrown upon the gloom of uncertainty which hangs over the fate of Sir John Franklin and his companions." For on 23 August 1850, Captain Erasmus Ommanney and some of the officers of the search ship HMS *Assistance* found signs of Franklin's expedition at Cape Riley, on the southwest shore of Devon Island. After two years of disappointments, the Royal Navy at last had leads in the search for the missing men. Ommanney recalled:

> I had the satisfaction of meeting with the first traces of Sir John Franklin's expedition, consisting of fragments of naval stores, ragged portions of clothing, preserved meat tins, &c . . . and the spot bore the appearance of an encampment.

But those relics told only of a brief stop, perhaps for magnetic observation early in the expedition, and gave away nothing in regard to Franklin's whereabouts.

Ommanney pushed on, combing the shoreline for clues, until a large cairn was spotted high up on the headland of a nearby islet named Beechey Island. Lieutenant Sherard Osborn, commander of the steamship HMS *Pioneer*, which was also part of the Royal Navy search expedition under the overall command of Captain Horatio Thomas Austin, painted a dramatic picture of the men rushing towards the "dark and frowning cliffs . . . too steep for even [a] snow-flake to hang upon":

> A boatful of officers and men proceeded on shore. On landing, some relics of European visitors were found; and we can picture the anxiety with which the steep slope was scaled and the cairn torn down, every stone turned over, the ground underneath dug up a little, and yet, alas! no document or record found.

Osborn was undeterred; he still held great hope that more discoveries would follow: "[The cairn] seemed to say to the beating heart, 'follow them that erected me!' "

A flotilla of search ships converged on the area, among them the *Lady Franklin* under Captain William Penny. The gritty Scot swore to scour the area "like a blood-hound" until answers to the mystery were found. More traces of Franklin's crew were discovered on Devon Island, this time at nearby Cape Spencer. Penny found the remains of a hut built of stones, artefacts that included scraps of newspaper dated September 1844, a fragment of paper with the words "until called," more food tins, torn gloves—and that was all. Then, on 27 August, a breathless sailor brought Penny startling news: "Graves, Captain Penny! Graves! Franklin's winter quarters!"

Dr. Elisha Kent Kane, ship's surgeon under American searcher Edwin De Haven, was present when the news arrived and described what happened next:

> Captain De Haven, Captain Penny, Commander Phillips, and myself . . . hurried on over the ice, and, scrambling along the loose and rugged slope that extends from Beechey to the shore, came, after a weary walk, to the crest of the isthmus. Here, amid the sterile uniformity of snow and slate, were the head-boards of three graves, made after the old orthodox fashion of gravestones at home.

The tombs lay side by side in a line with the headboards facing Cape Riley. Two of the grave mounds were "neatly paved round" with limestone slabs. Their inscriptions, chiselled into the headboards, read:

Sacred

to the

memory of

William Braine, R.M.,

H.M.S. Erebus

Died April 3d, 1846

aged 32 years

'Choose ye this day whom ye will serve'

Joshua, ch. xxiv., 15.

The second was:

> Sacred to the memory of
> John Hartnell, A.B. of H.M.S.
> Erebus,
> died January 4th, 1846
> aged 25 years.
> 'Thus saith the Lord of Hosts, consider your ways.'
> Haggai, i., 7.

The third grave, representing the earliest death, was not as carefully finished as the others, but Kane felt "its general appearance was more grave-like." The headboard was inscribed:

> Sacred
> to
> the memory of
> John Torrington
> who departed
> this
> life January 1st,
> A.D. 1846,
> on board of
> H.M. ship Terror
> aged 20 years

Osborn noted that some seashells from the bay had been collected and "prettily arranged . . . by some old messmates." The orderly arrangement of what Kane called the "isthmus of the graves" reminded Osborn of a parish cemetery.

> . . . it breathes of the quiet churchyard in some of England's many nooks . . . and the ornaments that nature decks herself with, even in the desolation of the frozen zone, were carefully culled to mark the seaman's last home.

The searchers hoped the discovery of the expedition's winter campsite and the graves of its first three victims would somehow

The three Franklin expedition graves on Beechey Island.
Drawn from a sketch by Dr. E.K. Kane

point to Franklin's whereabouts. The dates inscribed on the head-boards showed that the doomed expedition had passed the winter of 1845–46 nestled in a small bay on the east side of Beechey Island, and there was more.

Searchers sweeping the windblown island during the shorten-ing days of late summer found other signs, including the remains of tenting sites, an armourer's forge, a large storehouse, a carpen-ter's house and a few other, smaller structures. Deep ruts left by sledges were found on the gravel terraces of Devon Island, leaving Osborn to observe "how little Franklin's people were impressed with the importance of rendering their travelling equipment light and portable." A polar bear killed by one of the searchers revealed an earlier bullet wound. The bullet was retrieved from the beast's flesh and identified as having been fired from a weapon like those supplied to Franklin. Kane found "inexpressibly touching" the dis-covery of a little garden scraped into the gravel, with anemones still growing. Wrote Kane: "A garden implies a purpose either to remain or to return: he who makes it is looking to the future." This discovery on Beechey Island, especially moving to a nation of gardeners, inspired a verse by Charles Dickens:

O then
Pause on the footprints of heroic men,
Making a garden of the desert wide
Where PARRY conquer'd and FRANKLIN died.

Another large cairn was discovered, this one made of more than 600 discarded food tins filled with gravel, but nowhere was there a message telling where Franklin and his crews had sailed. Why these empty cans had been stacked 7 feet (2.1 metres) high in such a manner was unclear. It was usual for Arctic expeditions to leave messages under cairns describing their current status and plans—but here there was no note. Such was the scale of popular interest in each development during the Franklin searches that even this peculiar discovery—a cairn of tins built without apparent purpose—found its way into another literary work, *Walden,* where Henry David Thoreau asked, "Is Franklin the only man who is lost, that his wife should be so earnest to find him?"

Wrote Thoreau: "Explore your own higher latitudes with shiploads of preserved meats to support you, if they be necessary; and pile the empty cans sky-high for a sign." But a sign of what in this case? What did it mean? With each discovery the Franklin mystery only seemed to deepen. As well, the trail that began at Cape Riley on Devon Island seemed to end on Beechey Island, just 1¼ miles (2 km) away. Osborn expressed the mood of the searchers this way: "Everyone felt that there was something so inexplicable in the non-discovery of any record, some written evidence of the intentions of Franklin and Crozier on leaving this spot . . . "

Although death was expected on expeditions of discovery through accident or illness, three deaths during the first winter was still considered unusual. The suggestion that the graves at Beechey Island could represent problems with the expedition's food supply was discussed by the searchers and publicly stated by Ommanney in evidence given to the British government in 1852: "We know that 3 of their men (young men) died the first year, from which we may infer they were not enjoying perfect health. It is supposed that their preserved meats were of an inferior quality."

Ommanney was referring to the possibility that some of the canned food was spoiled, or in his words, represented a "putrid abomination." Sherard Osborn also noted angrily that "their preserved meats were those of the miscreant, Goldner." Tinned-food supplier Stephan Goldner had had quality control problems with provisions supplied to later expeditions. In January 1852, it was reported that an examination at Portsmouth of a consignment of Goldner's preserved meat (delivered fourteen months earlier), revealed that most of the meat had putrefied. According to the *Times:* "If Franklin and his party had been supplied with such food as that condemned, and relied on it as their mainstay in time of need, the very means of saving their lives may have bred a pestilence or famine among them, and have been their destruction." Even before the Franklin expedition had sailed, Commander Fitzjames expressed concern that the Admiralty would buy meat from an unknown supplier simply because he had quoted a lower price. Indignation over the spoiled meat led to an inquiry, however it concluded that Goldner's meat had been satisfactory on previous contracts. Wrote one Admiralty official: "From that period (1845) Goldner's preserved meats have been in constant use in the navy, and it is only, I believe, latterly that they have been found to consist of such disgusting material."

Dr. Peter Sutherland, surgeon on Penny's expedition, believing some important clues to the health and the fate of Franklin's expedition might be harboured within the graves, proposed their exhumation:

> It was suggested to have the graves opened, but as there seemed to
> be a feeling against this really very proper and most important
> step, the suggestion was not reiterated. It would have been very

interesting to have examined into the cause of death; it is very probable there would be no difficulty in doing this, for the bodies would be found frozen as hard as possible, and in a high state of preservation in their icy casings.

Sutherland went on to speculate on possible causes of death for the three sailors:

> The cause of Braine's death, which happened in April, might have been scurvy supervening upon some other disease. The first two deaths had probably been caused by accidents, such as frost bite or exposure to intense cold in a state of stupor, or to diseases of the chest, where there might have been some latent mischief before leaving England, which the changeable weather in September and October rekindled, and the intense cold of November and December stimulated to a fatal termination.

In August 1852, a squadron of ships returned to Beechey Island, and the searchers resumed their research there, but these further investigations were hampered by the frenzied activity that had taken place at the time of the discovery of Franklin's first winter quarters two years earlier. Sherard Osborn, in a communication to the Royal Geographical Society, wrote of the destruction of the site:

> after a couple of hundred seamen had, in 1850, turned everything topsy-turvy, and carried and dropped things far from where they were originally deposited, those who first visited the place in 1852 can have but little idea of what the place was like when we found it as it had been left by the 'Erebus' and 'Terror'.

Together, the rescue vessels had traced the first season of Franklin's voyage from its disappearance into silence down Lancaster Sound in August 1845 until as late as September 1846. At most, searchers had found at Beechey Island only a partial record of the expedition's first year beyond the reach of civilization. No one knew where to look next.

— 6 —

Region of

TERROR

RONICALLY, Franklin's failure launched the golden era of Arctic exploration. More than thirty ship-based and overland expeditions would search for clues as to Franklin's fate over the course of the following two decades, charting vast areas and mapping the completed route of the Northwest Passage in the process. Whilst many of these search expeditions were funded by the British government in response to public demand that Franklin be saved, others were raised by public subscription following appeals from Lady Franklin. Seamen volunteered for Arctic service in droves. Yet contemporary journals make it clear that many of these searches were also crippled by illness. In this respect, James Clark Ross was not alone.

Indeed, there was a more sinister enemy on board these Arctic voyages than the usual complaints of frostbite and stifling boredom. Where one captain, George Henry Richards, reported the "general debility" afflicting his crew, another, Sir Edward Belcher, abandoned four of his five ships in order to escape the far north after two years, fearing that a third Arctic year would lead to large-scale loss of life. The crew of another ship, the *Prince Albert*, a privately funded expedition, suffered severely from scurvy during their lone winter, 1851–52. And on the *Enterprise,* Captain Richard Collinson waged a bitter internecine war with his crew; by the end of his command he had placed, amongst others, his first, second and third officers under arrest. When he was subsequently criticized for his conduct, Collinson blamed "some form of that insidious Arctic enemy, the scurvy, which is known to effect the mind as well as the body of its victims."

When another ship, the *Investigator,* commanded by Captain Robert McClure, became trapped at Mercy Bay on Banks Island, several of the men aboard went mad and had to be restrained, their howls piercing the long nights. The crew carried lime juice, specially prepared by the Navy's Victualling Department, and hunted and gathered scurvy grass in the brief Arctic summers. By these methods, McClure was able to forestall the appearance of scurvy, but by the third winter, illness was widespread: "only 4 out of a total of 64 on board were not more or less affected by scurvy." Alexander Armstrong, expedition surgeon, described treating sufferers with "preserved fresh meat," as tinned foods were still considered to have antiscorbutic properties. Even after such interventions, three of the men died. McClure abandoned ship, and his crew were spared only by a fortuitous encounter with yet other search ships. Thomas Morgan, who was seriously ill at the time of this rescue, "sick and covered with scurvy sores," died on 19 May 1854. He was buried on Beechey Island, alongside the men from the *Erebus* and *Terror.*

Yet McClure, who was credited with the first successful transit of the Northwest Passage, even without his ship, was glad for the struggle he had been put through. He, like others of the age, saw self-sacrifice in some noble cause as the pinnacle of human achievement. He captured the spirit of the Franklin searchers this way:

> How nobly those gallant seamen toiled . . . sent to travel upon
> snow and ice, each with 200 pounds to drag . . . No man flinched

from his work; some of the gallant fellows really died at the drag rope . . . but not a murmur arose . . . as the weak fell out . . . there were always more than enough volunteers to take their places.

By far the worst afflicted, however, were two Franklin search expeditions funded by Henry Grinnell, a wealthy American benefactor. The first, commanded by Lieutenant Edwin de Haven of the U.S. Navy, aboard the *Advance* and the *Rescue,* went out in May 1850 and by August was already trapped in winter quarters with temperatures plummeting. Elisha Kent Kane, the ship's surgeon and the scion of a wealthy Philadelphia family, described the appalling living conditions endured by the crew:

> . . . within a little area, whose cubic contents are less than father's library, you have the entire abiding-place of thirty-three heavily-clad men. Of these I am one. Three stoves and a cooking galley, three bear-fat lamps burn with the constancy of a vestal shrine. Damp furs, soiled woolens, cast-off boots, sickly men, cookery, tobacco-smoke, and digestion are compounding their effluvia around and within me. Hour by hour, and day after day, without even a bunk to retire to or a blanket-curtain to hide me, this and these make up the reality of my home.

A pervasive melancholy set in, and scurvy made its first appearance in September. By Christmas, there was a general shortness of breath, and the officers noticed a strange phenomenon that the British searchers had also identified, "a sort of craving" for animal fats. Kane described the complexions of the crewmen as having assumed a "peculiar waxy paleness," even "ghostliness." The men reported outlandish, vivid dreams. One described finding "Sir John Franklin in a beautiful cove, lined by orange-trees." Another dreamt he had visited the desolate nearby coast and "returned laden with watermelons." By January, de Haven was also stricken and forced to relinquish command. Among other complaints, he suffered severe pain from a wound in his hand inflicted by a schoolmaster's ruler twenty-five years before. In February, twelve men were laid out by stiff and painful limbs. Largely dependent on salted and preserved foods, the crew's stores of antiscorbutics, raw potatoes and lime juice were running low. In May, the crew succeeded in killing a large number of seals and walrus, and catastrophe was averted.

The second Grinnell expedition, this time commanded by Elisha Kent Kane, sailed in 1853 with instructions to search Smith Sound, ostensibly for Franklin's missing ships. The expedition was, in fact, a thinly veiled run at the North Pole. This was his first command, and Kane was hardly the image of a grizzled Arctic explorer. Of sickly, almost dainty, constitution, he made up for his physical limitations with the spirit of a dauntless adventurer—his account of this journey is infused with romanticism. He relished the Arctic as a "mysterious region of terrors" as he tacked north through Smith Sound into an unexplored basin that now carries his name. Here, the crew established a winter harbour off the coast of Greenland and lived in a state of perpetual misery. Kane was right with respect to one thing: the terrors abounded. The ship was not insulated, and Kane had miscalculated on the amount of fuel required. By February they could no longer spare fuel to melt water to wash in. It was so cold inside the *Advance* that one man's tongue froze to his beard.

Dependent on "ordinary marine stores," notably pemmican and salt pork, there was also a severe outbreak of scurvy among the twenty men. Kane carefully noted the advance of symptoms. In February 1854, he wrote, "scurvy and general debility have made me short o' wind." In April, Kane dispatched his sledging parties north towards the pole. It was a foolhardy gambit that soon degenerated, the party stricken with frostbite and scurvy. The illness that had gnawed at them all winter now threatened to consume them entirely. Kane himself had to be carried back to the *Advance*, "nearly insensible and so swollen with scurvy as to be hardly recognizable." His condition was regarded as hopeless. When the party reached the ship they were in total disarray, suicidal, incoherent, disease-ridden, gesticulating wildly and conversing with themselves. The ship "presented all the appearances of a mad house." There remained only three men well enough to carry out ordinary duties. To top it all, rats had infested the ship.

Fortunately, with summer's thaw, the hardships that had characterized the winter abated. Hunting parties were sent off and, with a large supply of fresh meat, health was soon restored. But the ice failed to clear from the ship's harbour, and the crew faced a second winter.

Under stress Kane proved to be unfit for command. He became irritable and quarrelsome, and when he wasn't picking an argument with one of his officers he was boasting about his family's status or his amorous conquests back in Philadelphia. His lengthy dinnertime monologues were liberally peppered with Latin phrases, all for the benefit of men he considered his social inferiors. Sick and starved to the bone (on a good day eating the entrails of a fox, on a bad day sucking on their mittens), the crew looked on with a mixture of incredulity and contempt as their commander tried to impress them by speaking the ancient language. Soon, secret meetings were organized, and in September, seven of the men announced to Kane their intention to desert ship and attempt a 700-mile (1,126-km) trek south to Upernavik, the northernmost of Greenland's Danish communities. Yet the mutineers got nowhere near it before returning to the brig nearly frozen to throw themselves at Kane's mercy, which proved a shallow well indeed.

As the second winter set upon them they were nearly out of coal, and Kane ordered the men to use wood from the *Advance* for fuel. They tore off the deck sheathing and removed the ship's rails and upper spars. Unable to secure adequate supplies of raw meat in the fall, the disease returned even more virulently. The symptoms were gruesome. One man had the flesh drop from his ankle, exposing bone and tendons. By December, the only antiscorbutics left were the scrapings of raw potatoes, but there were only twelve of the potatoes left and they were three years old. The entire crew was seriously ill, and Kane was surprised to discover their condition improved or worsened in exact relation to their infrequent ability to obtain fresh meat. Wrote Kane: "Our own sickness I attribute to our civilized diet; had we plenty of frozen walrus I would laugh at scurvy." He later wrote admiringly of the Inuit: "Our journeys have taught us the wisdom of the Esquimaux appetite, and there are few among us who do not relish a slice of raw blubber or a chunk of frozen walrus-beef . . . as a powerful and condensed heat-making and antiscorbutic food it has no rival."

Other searchers had come to the same realization, and one, the surgeon Peter Sutherland, suggested in 1852 that had Franklin needed to increase his stock of provisions, "there is no doubt his ingenuity would suggest to him what the Eskimos have practiced for thousands of years—preserving masses of animal substances, such as whales flesh, by means of ice, during the summer months, when it may be easily obtained, for their use during winter."

The realization came too late for Kane. The health of the crew reached its worst in the spring of 1855, and several men died. At one point, Kane referred to his compatriots in his journal as "my crew," then corrected himself, writing: "I have no crew any longer." Instead, he began referring to the men as "the tenants of my bunks." Kane was, at this point, effectively alone. Of the men on the expedition, only he had remained in comparatively good health throughout the second winter. The reason was simple: Kane had taken to eating the rats infesting the ship. Despite their privations, he could not convince any of the other men to join him.

In the spring, after acquiring fresh walrus meat with the help of some of the natives of Greenland who visited the ship, the bedraggled party abandoned the *Advance* and made its way down the coast, first over the ice and then in small boats. After eighty-four days they flagged down a Danish shallop and were saved. They had done nothing to advance the search for Franklin. In fact, they were some 1,000 miles (1,609 km) away from where the last remnants of the expedition were finally located.

7

Terror Camp

CLEAR

B Y 1854 NINE YEARS had elapsed since Franklin set sail on his voyage of discovery. He had provisions for three years, though it was thought the supplies could have been rationed to last some months longer, perhaps until 1849. What became obvious to the Admiralty was that, regardless of what more could be done to solve the mystery, nothing could be done to save Franklin and his men. On 20 January 1854, a notice in the *London Gazette* stated that unless news to the contrary arrived by 31 March, the officers and crews of the *Erebus* and *Terror* would be considered to have died in Her Majesty's service, and their wages would be paid to relatives up to that date. The expedition's muster books show the sailors buried on Beechey Island, however, were "discharged dead" according to the dates on their headboards: William Braine on 3 April 1846, John Hartnell on 4 January 1846, John Torrington on 1 January 1846.

Despite the official acknowledgement that no more relief expeditions would be sent, interest in the Franklin search—and in the Arctic in general—remained high in Britain. Three Inuit (or

"Esquimaux" as the Victorians called them) were taken to England by a merchant and given an audience with Queen Victoria at Windsor Castle, then "exhibited" in London. "The painful excitement which has so long pervaded the minds of all classes with respect to the fate of Sir John Franklin's Arctic Expedition lends additional interest to the examination of these natives of the dreary North," the *Illustrated London News* commented. Interest among North Americans did not always match that of the British public's, however. In one instance, the *Toronto Globe* complained that only a handful of people attended a lecture on the Arctic and the possible fate of Sir John Franklin, while the same hall had been "filled to overflowing" with those curious to view the famous midget Tom Thumb.

Finally, on Monday, 23 October 1854, under the headline "Startling News: Sir John Franklin starved to death," the *Toronto Globe* reported "melancholy intelligence" that had arrived in Montreal two days earlier. After his failed earlier investigations, the Hudson's Bay Company's John Rae had made the first major discovery of the Franklin searches while surveying the Boothia Peninsula. The *Globe* excitedly outlined the news:

> From the Esquimaux [Rae] had obtained certain information of the fate of Sir John Franklin's party who had been starved to death after the loss of their ships which were crushed in the ice, and while making their way south to the great Fish [Back] river, near the outlet of which a party of whites died, leaving accounts of their sufferings in the mutilated corpses of some who had evidently furnished food for their unfortunate companions.

Two days later, the *Globe* argued that Rae had succeeded "in revealing to the world the mysterious fate of the gallant Franklin and his unfortunate companions, and in proving the folly of man's attempting to storm 'winter's citadel' or light up 'the depths of Polar night.'" By 28 October 1854, word had reached Britain that the veil that obscured the fate of Sir John Franklin had been lifted. In a letter to the Secretary of the Admiralty, Rae outlined his discoveries:

... during my journey over the ice and snow this spring, with the
view of completing the survey of the west shore of Boothia, I met
with Esquimaux in Pelly Bay, from one of whom I learned that a
party of 'whitemen' (Kablounans) had perished from want of
food some distance to the westward ... Subsequently, further
particulars were received, and a number of articles purchased,
which place the fate of a portion, if not all, of the then survivors of
Sir John Franklin's long-lost party beyond a doubt—a fate terrible as the imagination can conceive.

Rae went on to report descriptions of a party of white men dragging sledges down the coast of King William Island, of the discovery a year later of bodies on the North American mainland and
evidence of cannibalism. Contrary to the *Toronto Globe* headline,
there was no proof that Franklin himself had starved to death, but
disaster had clearly befallen his crews. Evocatively, the Inuit also
told Rae that "they had found eight or ten books where the dead
bodies were; that those books had 'markings' upon them, but they
would not tell whether they were in print or manuscript." When
Rae asked what they had done with the books, possibly expedition
logs, he was told that they had given them to their children, "who
had torn them up as playthings." In support of the Inuit accounts,
Rae carried with him items he had been able to purchase from the
natives, including monogrammed silver forks and spoons, one of
them bearing Crozier's initials, and Sir John Franklin's Hanoverian
Order of Merit.

Because Rae's information about the cause of the expedition's
destruction came second-hand, it was judged inconclusive by
many, though the relics were evidence enough that "Sir John
Franklin and his party are no more." The British government, en-
meshed in the Crimean War, asked the Hudson's Bay Company to
follow up on the new information. Its chief factor, James Anderson, was able to add only slightly to Rae's report when he discovered several articles from the Franklin expedition on Montreal

Island and the adjacent coastline, including a piece of wood with the word "Terror" branded on it, part of a backgammon board and preserved meat tins—but no human remains or records. Anderson's search, which lasted only nine days, would be the last official attempt to learn the fate of Franklin. Rae, though attacked by critics for not following up on the Inuit reports and instead hurrying back to London, was given £8,000 in reward money; the men in his party split another £2,000.

The British public and government interest quickly turned to the Crimean War. The very week that news of Rae's discoveries reached Britain, a confusion of orders resulted in a brigade of British cavalry charging some entrenched batteries of Russian artillery. A report in the *Times* captivated Franklin's nephew, the poet Alfred, Lord Tennyson, who immortalized the encounter where so many British horsemen died in his "The Charge of the Light Brigade." Events had finally overtaken the disappearance of Sir John Franklin and his officers and crews, leaving many to believe that the mystery of the expedition's destruction would never be solved. In addition, there were others who questioned the value of research expeditions such as Franklin's, which demanded such a heavy toll. *Blackwood's Edinburgh Magazine* summed up this view better than any other journal in an article published in November 1855:

> No; there are no more sunny continents—no more islands of the blessed—hidden under the far horizon, tempting the dreamer over the undiscovered sea; nothing but those weird and tragic shores, whose cliffs of everlasting ice and mainlands of frozen snow, which have never produced anything to us but a late and sad discovery of depths of human heroism, patience, and bravery, such as imagination could scarcely dream of.

Yet there were still those who had not given up on Arctic expeditions, who still believed that the answers to Franklin's fate lay somewhere on King William Island or on the mainland close to the mouth of the Back River. Foremost among them was Lady Franklin, who made one last impassioned plea to British Prime Minister Lord Palmerston: " . . . the final and exhaustive search is all I seek on behalf of the first and only martyrs to Arctic discovery in modern times, and it is all I ever intend to ask." She failed to convince the British government to send one final search, and launched another expedition of her own. No longer seeking the rescue of Franklin, she now sought his vindication.

Jane, Lady Franklin, neé Griffin, aged twenty-four.

Lady Franklin, born Jane Griffin, personified the romantic heroine with her refusal to give up hope that searchers would one day discover the fate of her husband and his crews. Her determination, coupled with a willingness to spend a large part of her fortune to outfit four such expeditions, haunted the Victorian public as much as it inspired the searchers of her day. "To *know* a loss is a single and definite pain," the *Athenaeum* observed, "to dread it is a complicated anguish which to the pain of the fear adds the pain of the hope . . . The misery is, that if the truth be not known, Lady Franklin will nurse for years her frail hope, almost too sickly to live and yet unable to die."

What makes the devotion of Lady Franklin especially moving is the recognition that she was an independent and free-thinking woman who had not married until her thirties, and who saw more of the world than possibly any other woman of her day. During her long vigil, Lady Franklin not only implored the British for help, but the president of the United States and the emperor of Russia as well. She became an expert in Arctic geography. One famous folk song, "Lord Franklin," captured the passion of her search:

> In Baffin's Bay where the whale-fish blow,
> The fate of Franklin no man may know.
> The fate of Franklin no tongue can tell,
> Lord Franklin along with his sailors do dwell.

> And now my burden it gives me pain,
> For my long lost Franklin I'd cross the main.
> Ten thousand pounds I would freely give,
> To say on earth that my Franklin lives.

With the help of a public appeal for funds and a donation of supplies by the Admiralty, Lady Franklin purchased a steam yacht, the *Fox*, and placed command with the Arctic veteran Captain Francis Leopold M'Clintock, a Royal Navy officer who had been involved in three earlier Franklin search expeditions, beginning with that of James Clark Ross's attempt in 1848–49. M'Clintock chose Lieutenant William Robert Hobson, son of the first governor of New Zealand, as his second-in-command. The *Fox* sailed from Aberdeen, Scotland, on 1 July 1857.

Almost immediately, problems hampered the search and the *Fox* was forced to spend its first winter trapped in ice in Baffin Bay, before being freed in the spring. By August 1858 the *Fox* had reached Beechey Island, where, at the site of Franklin's first winter quarters, M'Clintock erected a monument on behalf of Lady Franklin. The monument, dated 1855, read in part:

> To the memory of Franklin, Crozier, Fitzjames and all their gallant brother officers and faithful companions who have suffered and perished in the cause of science and the service of their country this tablet is erected near the spot where they passed their first Arctic winter, and whence they issued forth, to conquer difficulties or to die. It commemorates the grief of their admiring countrymen and friends, and the anguish, subdued by faith, of her who has lost, in the heroic leader of the expedition, the most devoted and affectionate of husbands.

By the end of September the searchers had travelled to the eastern entrance to Bellot Strait, where they established a second winter base. From there, M'Clintock and Hobson were able to leave their ship in small parties and travel overland to King William Island, early in April 1859. The two groups then split up, with M'Clintock ordering Hobson to scour the west coast of the island for clues while he travelled down the island's east coast to the estuary of the Back River, before returning via the island's west coast.

On 20 April, M'Clintock encountered two Inuit families. He traded for Franklin relics in their possession and, upon questioning them, discovered that two ships had been seen but that one sank in deep water. The other was forced onto shore by the ice. On board they found the body of a very large man with "long teeth." They said that the "white people went away to the 'large river,' taking a boat or boats with them, and that in the following winter their bones were found there." Later, M'Clintock met up with a group of thirty to forty Inuit who inhabited a snow village on King William

The Fox, *trapped in Baffin Bay in 1857–58.*

Island. He purchased silver plate bearing the crests or initials of Franklin, Crozier and two other officers. One woman said "many of the white men dropped by the way as they went to the Great River; that some were buried and some were not."

M'Clintock reached the mainland and continued southward to Montreal Island, where a few relics, including a piece of a preserved meat tin, two pieces of iron hoop and other scraps of metal, were found. The sledge party then turned back to King William Island, where they searched along its southern, then western coasts. Ghastly secrets awaited both M'Clintock and Hobson as they trudged over the snow-covered land.

Shortly after midnight on 24 May 1859, a human skeleton in the uniform of a steward from the lost expedition was found on a gravel ridge near the mouth of Peffer River on the island's southern shore. M'Clintock recorded the tragic scene in his journal:

> This poor man seems to have selected the bare ridge top, as affording the least tiresome walking, and to have fallen upon his face in the position in which we found him. It was a melancholy truth

that the old woman spoke when she said, "they fell down and died as they walked along."

M'Clintock believed the man had fallen asleep in this position and that his "last moments were undisturbed by suffering."

Alongside the bleached skeleton lay a "a small clothes-brush near, and a horn pocket-comb, in which a few light-brown hairs still remained." There was also a notebook, which belonged to Harry Peglar, captain of the foretop on the *Terror*. The notebook contained the handwriting of two individuals, Peglar and an unknown second. In the hand of Peglar was a song lyric, dated 21 April 1847, which begins: "The C the C the open C it grew so fresh the Ever free." A mystery, however, surrounds the other papers, written in the hand of the unknown and referring to the disaster. Most of the words in the messages were spelled backwards and ended with capital letters, as if the end were the beginning. One sheet of paper had a crude drawing of an eye, with the words "lid Bay" underneath. When corrected, another message reads: "Oh Death whare is thy sting, the grave at Comfort Cove for who has any douat how . . . the dyer sad . . . " On the other side of that paper, words were written in a circle, and inside the circle was the passage, "the terror camp clear." This has been interpreted as a place name, a reference to a temporary encampment made by the Franklin expedition—possibly the encampment at Beechey Island. Another paper, written in the same hand, also spelled backwards, includes this passage: "Has we have got some very hard ground to heave . . . we shall want some grog to wet houer . . . issel . . . all my art Tom for I do think . . . time . . . I cloze should lay and . . . the 21st night a gread." The "21st night" could be 21 April 1848, the eve of the desertion of the *Erebus* and *Terror*—a possibility raised because of another discovery. The most important artefact of the Franklin searches had been located three weeks before the skeleton was found, as Hobson surveyed the northwest coast of the island. On 5 May, the only written record of the Franklin expedition—

chronicling some of the events after the desertion of the ships and consisting of two brief notes scrawled on a single piece of naval record paper—was found in a cairn near Victory Point. The first, signed by Lieutenant Graham Gore, outlined the progress of the expedition to May 1847:

> 28 of May 1847. HM Ships Erebus and Terror . . . Wintered in the Ice in Lat. 70° 05′ N. Long. 98° 23′ W. Having wintered in 1846–7 at Beechey Island in Lat. 74° 43′ 28″ N Long. 90° 39′ 15″ W after having ascended Wellington Channel to Lat. 77°—and returned by the west side of Cornwallis Island. Sir John Franklin commanding the Expedition. All well. Party consisting of 2 officers and 6 Men left the Ships on Monday 24th. May 1847. Gm. Gore, Lieut. Chas. F. Des Voeux, mate.

Lieutenant Hobson and his men opening the cairn—
near Victory Point, King William Island—that contained the only
written record of the Franklin expedition's fate.

The document is notable for an inexplicable error in a date—the expedition had wintered at Beechey Island in 1845–46, not 1846–47—and its unequivocal proclamation: "All well." Originally deposited in a metal canister under a stone cairn, the note was retrieved eleven months later and additional text then scribbled around its margins. It was this note that in its simplicity told of the disastrous conclusion to 129 lives:

> (25th April) 1848—HM's Ships Terror and Erebus were deserted on the 22nd April, 5 leagues NNW of this, having been beset since 12th Septr. 1846. The Officers and Crews, consisting of 105 souls, under the command of Captain F.R.M. Crozier landed here—in Lat. 69° 37′ 42″ Long. 98° 41′. This paper was found by Lt. Irving under the cairn supposed to have been built by Sir James Ross in 1831, 4 miles to the Northward, where it had been deposited by the late Commander Gore in June 1847. Sir James Ross' pillar has not however been found, and the paper has been transferred to this position which is that in which Sir J Ross' pillar was erected—Sir John Franklin died on 11th of June 1847 and the total loss by deaths in the Expedition has been to this date 9 Officers and 15 Men.

> James Fitzjames, Captain HMS Erebus.
> F.R.M. Crozier Captain and Senior Offr.
> and start on tomorrow 26th for Backs Fish River.

"So sad a tale was never told in fewer words," M'Clintock commented after examining the note. Indeed, everything had changed in the eleven months between the two messages. Beset by pack-ice since September 1846, Franklin's two ships ought to have been freed during the brief summer of 1847, allowing them to continue their push to the western exit of the passage at Bering Strait. Instead, they remained frozen fast and had been forced to spend a second winter off King William Island. For the Franklin expedition, this was the death warrant. There had already been an astonishing mortality rate, especially among officers. Deserting their ships on 22 April 1848, the 105 surviving officers and men set up camp on the northwest coast of King William Island, preparing for

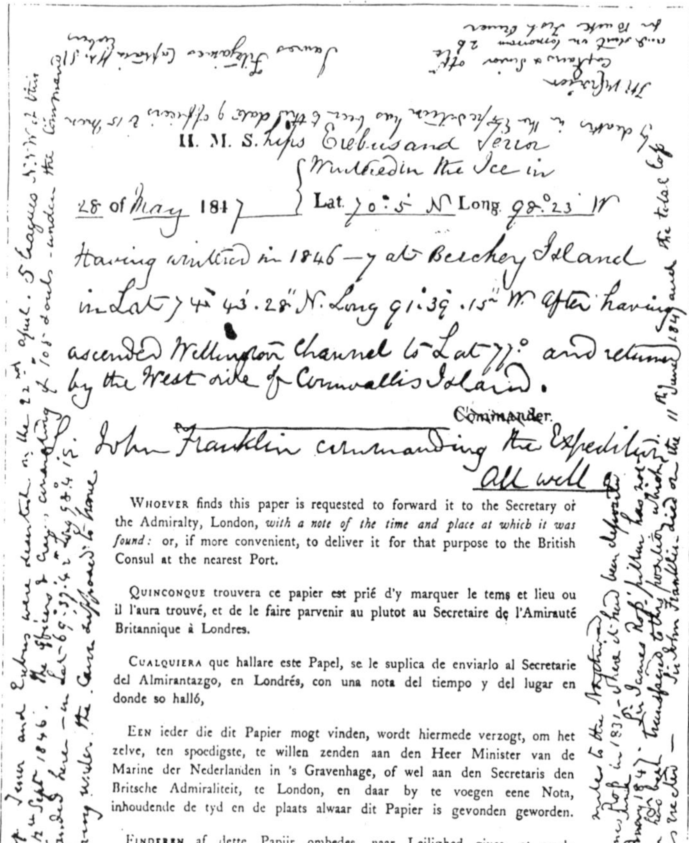

(marginal note, upper right)

H. M. S.hips Erebus and Terror
Wintered in the Ice in
28 of May 1847 } Lat. 70°5' N Long. 98°23' W

Having wintered in 1846—7 at Beechey Island
in Lat 74° 43' 28" N. Long 91°39'.15" W after having
ascended Wellington Channel to Lat 77° and returned
by the West side of Cornwallis Island.

Sir John Franklin commanding the Expedition.
All well

WHOEVER finds this paper is requested to forward it to the Secretary of the Admiralty, London, *with a note of the time and place at which it was found*: or, if more convenient, to deliver it for that purpose to the British Consul at the nearest Port.

QUINCONQUE trouvera ce papier est prié d'y marquer le tems et lieu ou il l'aura trouvé, et de le faire parvenir au plutot au Secretaire de l'Amirauté Britannique à Londres.

CUALQUIERA que hallare este Papel, se le suplica de enviarlo al Secretarie del Almirantazgo, en Londrés, con una nota del tiempo y del lugar en donde se halló.

EEN ieder die dit Papier mogt vinden, wordt hiermede verzogt, om het zelve, ten spoedigste, te willen zenden aan den Heer Minister van de Marine der Nederlanden in 's Gravenhage, of wel aan den Secretaris den Britsche Admiraliteit, te London, en daar by te voegen eene Nota, inhoudende de tyd en de plaats alwaar dit Papier is gevonden geworden.

FINDEREN af dette Papiir ombedes, naar Leilighed gives, at sende samme til Admiralitets Secretairen i London, eller nærmeste Embedsmand i Danmark, Norge, eller Sverrig. Tiden og Stædit hvor dette er fundet ønskes venskabeligt paategnet.

WER diesen Zettel findet, wird hier-durch ersucht denselben an den Secretair des Admiralitets in London einzusenden, mit gefälliger angabe an welchen ort und zu welcher zeit er gefunden worden ist.

(lower handwritten note)
Party consisting of 2 Officers and 6 Men
left the Ships on Monday 24th May 1847
Gm Gore Lieut
Chas F Des Voeux Mate

(caption)
The notes found in the cairn at Victory Point
on 5 May 1859, by Lieutenant Hobson and his men.

a trek south to the mouth of the Back River, then an arduous ascent to a distant Hudson's Bay Company post, Fort Resolution, which lay some 1,250 miles (2,210 km) away. M'Clintock described the scene where the note had been discovered:

> Around the cairn a vast quantity of clothing and stores of all sorts lay strewed about, as if at this spot every article was thrown away which could possibly be dispensed with—such as pickaxes, shovels, boats, cooking stoves, ironwork, rope, blocks, canvas, instruments, oars and medicine-chest.

Why some of these items had been carried even as far as Victory Point is another of the questions that cannot be answered, but M'Clintock was sure of one thing: "our doomed and scurvy-stricken countrymen calmly prepared themselves to struggle manfully for life." The magnitude of the endeavour facing the crews must have been overwhelming, and the knowledge of its futility spiritually crushing. It also ran contrary to the best guesses of other leading Arctic explorers. George Back, who had explored the river named for him in 1834, was certain Franklin's men would not have attempted an escape over the mainland: "I can say from experience that no toilworn and exhausted party could have the least chance of existence by going there." John Rae thought that "Sir John Franklin would have followed the route taken by Sir John Ross in escaping from Regent Inlet."

To this day, the route of the expedition retreat confounds some historians, who, like Rae, believe a much more logical and attainable goal would have been to march north and east to Somerset Island and Fury Beach—the route by which John Ross had made good an escape from an ice-bound ship in 1833. Fury Beach was not much further for the crews of the *Erebus* and the *Terror* than it had been for John Ross's crew of the abandoned *Victory*. It was also the most obvious place for a relief expedition to be sent, and James Clark Ross did indeed reach the area with two ships, five months after the *Erebus* and *Terror* were deserted.

Instead, after quitting their camp on 26 April, the crews moved south along the coastline of King William Island, man-hauling heavily laden lifeboats that had been removed from the ships and mounted on large sledges. Plagued by their rapidly deteriorating health, the crews were then overcome by the physical demands of the task. M'Clintock found what appeared to have been a field hospital established by Franklin's retreating crews only eighty miles into their trek. He suspected scurvy. Speculation also focussed on the tinned food supply. Inuit later told of some of their people eating the contents of the tins "and it had made them very ill: indeed some had actually died." As for Franklin's men, many died along the west and south coasts of King William Island.

Later, Hobson found a vivid indication of the tragedy when he located a lifeboat from the Franklin expedition containing skeletons and relics. Men from Franklin's crews had at last been found, but the help had come a decade too late. When M'Clintock later visited the "boat place," he described his tiny party as being "transfixed with awe" at the sight of the two human skeletons that lay inside the boat. One skeleton, found in the bow, had been partly destroyed by "large and powerful animals, probably wolves," M'Clintock guessed. But the other skeleton remained untouched, "enveloped with cloths and furs," feet tucked into warm boots to protect against the harsh Arctic cold. Nearby were two loaded double-barrelled guns, as if ready to fend off an attack that never came.

M'Clintock named the area, on the western extreme of King William Island, Cape Crozier. The boat, which had been carefully equipped for the ascent of the Back River, was 28 feet (8.5 metres) long; M'Clintock estimated the combined weight of the boat and the oak sledge it was mounted on at 1,400 pounds (635 kg).

Careful lists of the "amazing" quantity of goods also contained in the boat were compiled. Everything from boots and silk handkerchiefs to curtain rods, silverware, scented soap, sponges, slippers, toothbrushes and hair-combs were found. Six books, including a Bible in which most of the verses were underlined,

M'Clintock discovers a lifeboat—containing skeletons—from the Franklin expedition.

A Manual of Private Devotions and *The Vicar of Wakefield,* were
also discovered and scoured for messages, but none were found.
The only provisions in the boat were tea and chocolate. M'Clintock judged the astonishing variety of articles "a mere accumulation of dead weight, of little use, and very likely to break down
the strength of the sledge-crews." Perhaps strangest of all was the

direction in which the boat was pointing, for instead of heading towards the river that was the target of the struggling survivors, the boat was pointed back towards the deserted ships. M'Clintock guessed that the party had broken off from the main body of men under the command of Crozier, and was making a failed attempt to return to the ships for food: "Whether it was the intention of this boat party to await the result of another season in the ships, or to follow the track of the main body to the Great Fish [Back] River, is now a matter of conjecture."

This picture, of dying seamen shambling along, dragging sledges loaded down with the detritus of Victorian England, is the enduring image of the Franklin expedition disaster. Reviewing the evidence in 1881, M'Clintock concluded that surviving members of Franklin's expedition:

> . . . were far gone with scurvy when they landed; and the change from the confined lower decks, and inaction, to extreme exposure in an Arctic temperature, combined with intensely hard sledging labour, would almost immediately mature even incipient scurvy. The hospital tent within 80 miles [130 km] of the spot where their march commenced is, I think, conclusive proof of this. The *Investigator* [McClure's search expedition] is almost the only ship which has ever similarly spent three winters in the ice. Although she had only three deaths in all that time, yet a careful medical examination revealed the fact that only 4 out of a total of 64 on board were not more or less affected by scurvy. Such is the usual results of limitation to salted or preserved provisions, unrelieved by fresh animal or vegetable food. It is evident that disease, not starvation, carried off the earliest and by far the largest number of Franklin's companions, those martyrs to the cause of geographical discovery.

Even among his own sledging parties, M'Clintock observed, "scurvy advanced with rapid strides." Hobson, who had carried tinned pemmican for food, "suffered very severely in health," ulti-

ABOVE *Franklin's men lie dying beside the boat with which they had planned to ascend the Back River, King William Island.* Oil painting by W.T. Smith
BELOW *Burial in mid-winter, from M'Clintock's voyage aboard the* Fox.

mately having to be dragged back on the sledge. Wrote M'Clintock of Hobson's plight: "How strongly this bears upon the last sad march of [Franklin's] lost crews!" Years later, Hobson was asked: "Can you give . . . any opinion as to the cause why scurvy broke out with you?" His answer was, "I can scarcely say that scurvy did break out with us. I said that the men were debilitated, that they lost stamina. There was no cause that I know of, except the fact of not being able to get really fresh meat and fresh vegetables."

The success of their voyage brought both honour and fame to M'Clintock and Hobson, as well as some solace to Lady Franklin. She now knew the exact date of Franklin's death and that he had died aboard-ship long before the final, gruesome events on King William Island, thus preserving his reputation. What is more, he had died close enough to his objective to have justified at least a moral claim to the prize: Discoverer of the Northwest Passage. M'Clintock had produced, it was popularly decided, "melancholy evidence of their success." Sherard Osborn, who had commanded a ship in an earlier search, captured the public mood when he wrote of Franklin:

> Oh, mourn him not! unless you can point to a more honourable end or a nobler grave. Like another Moses, he fell when his work was accomplished, with the long object of his life in view.

The burial of Franklin. Depicted on the monument erected to him at Waterloo Place, London.

In Toronto, the *Globe* echoed:

> Sir John, we now know, sleeps his last sleep by the shores of those
> icy seas whose barriers he in vain essayed to overcome. He died,
> as British seamen love to die, at the post of duty. Surrounded, let
> us hope, by his gallant officers, who, while he lived, would minis-
> ter to his every want, and when dead would bear him to his cold
> and lonely tomb in some rocky bay, with saddened hearts and
> tear-bedewed eyes.

Finally, on 15 October 1859, the *Illustrated London News* attempted
to recapture the emotions felt by Franklin's sailors near Victory
Point in their final desperate struggle to survive:

> Awfully impressing must it have been to Lieutenant Hobson, and
> subsequently Captain M'Clintock, when they thus stood upon the
> intrenched scene where their gallant countrymen had, eleven
> years previously, prepared themselves for that last terrible strug-
> gle for life and home. Who shall tell how they struggled, how
> they hoped against hope, how the fainting few who reached Cape
> Herschel threw themselves on their knees and thanked their God
> that, if it so pleased Him that England and home should never be
> reached! He had granted to them the glory of securing to their
> dear country the honour they had sought for her—the discovery
> of the Northwest Passage.

In their last final march, the crews of the *Erebus* and *Terror* had indeed discovered the Northwest Passage. But by the time they
walked along the shores of Simpson Strait, the triumph must have
been a hollow one, for all around them was despair.

Franklin and his crews entered the Arctic with their primary
goal the completion of the passage. Although geographically there
is no single passage, and on a map it is possible to plot a myriad of
routes around and through the clusters of islands that make up the
Arctic archipelago, in reality, until the advent of ice-breakers, ice

conditions narrowed the possibilities to only a few choices. By 1845, when Franklin sailed, much of the mainland coast of North America had been charted by overland explorers questing for a navigable passage, and when the ship-based explorations up to that point are added to the map of the Arctic, it becomes apparent that only a relatively short distance, in the King William Island region, remained uncharted.

In their first season in the Arctic, Franklin's ships sailed up Wellington Channel to 77°N latitude where they were turned back either by ice or the lateness of the season. The expedition then travelled south to Barrow Strait by a previously unexplored channel between Bathurst and Cornwallis islands. Wrote M'Clintock: "Seldom has such an amount of success been accorded to an Arctic navigator in a single season, and when the *Erebus* and *Terror* were secured at Beechey Island for the coming winter of 1845–46, the results of their first year's labour must have been most cheering." When the sailing season of 1846 began with the break-up of ice in Barrow Strait and in Erebus Bay (their winter harbour off Beechey Island), the two ships sailed roughly south and west, ending beset in the ice off the northwest coast of King William Island in September 1846. What route the ships took to reach this point is still a matter of conjecture, though it is likely the *Erebus* and *Terror* travelled through Peel Sound and what is now Franklin Strait between Somerset and Prince of Wales islands. Franklin believed this route would eventually lead him to parts of the mainland coastline he had explored two decades earlier. His maps told him that, in the King William Island area, he had to complete the stretch along the west side of what was then called King William's Land (a distance M'Clintock estimated at 90 miles/145 km—but, in fact, was actually 62 miles/100 km) to be credited with completing the charting of a Northwest Passage.

The northern extent of this unknown gap was a low point of land on the northwest coast of King William Island, visited by

James Clark Ross from the east in the late spring of 1830. Ross had named the location Victory Point. The southern extent was to be found at Cape John Herschel on the south coast of King William Island. In 1839, Peter Warren Dease and Thomas Simpson explored along the mainland coast; moving eastward along the coast to Boothia Peninsula, they eventually turned back to the south coast of King William Island, exploring the island until they reached Cape John Herschel, where they built a large cairn. From this point they crossed back to the mainland and retraced their route to the west, a route which itself had been extended over time to Bering Strait, the western entrance to the passage.

Curiously, perhaps tragically, both Ross in 1830 and Dease and Simpson in 1839 suggested that the area they had explored was an extension of the mainland—a bulge of land connected directly to the southwestern part of Boothia Peninsula. It is very likely that Franklin, armed with the maps, descriptions and opinions of these earlier explorers as well as his own theories on the geography of the region, believed he had no choice in sailing direction when he eventually encountered Cape Felix, the northern tip of King William Island. Thinking that a route to the east of this point would lead to a dead end, he turned his ships to the southwest, directly into the continuously replenished pack-ice that grinds down the length of McClintock Channel from the northwest. The power and persistence of this ploughing train of ice cannot be overestimated; the northwest coast of King William Island bears the scars as proof. This ice mass does not always clear during the short summers and a lethal trap awaited the two ships, a trap made all the more cruel with the realization that the route along the eastern coast of the island regularly clears during the summer. It was only during their final doomed march that the surviving men from the *Erebus* and *Terror* completed the gap—and the Northwest Passage. In the words of searcher Sir John Richardson, "they forged the last link of the Northwest Passage with their lives."

M'Clintock's discoveries on King William Island thus provided an outline of the expedition's last days. And with this new information, the final clamour for answers to the Franklin mystery died down, even though it was apparent that many questions remained. As the *Illustrated London News* was to explain on 1 January 1881: "[M'Clintock's] search was necessarily a hasty and partial one, as the snow lay thick on the ground, and the parties had to return to their vessel before the disruption of the ice in summer."

In the end, the impetus for continuing to probe the Franklin disaster came not so much from the British but from two colourful Americans, who were without any Arctic experience when they each began their separate searches.

Charles Francis Hall.

Charles Francis Hall, a Cincinnati, Ohio, businessman who became interested in the Arctic following the disappearance of Franklin's expedition, decided in 1859 to conduct a search of his own. Hall argued before potential backers that Franklin survivors might still be alive among the Inuit; besides, the shores of King William Island needed to be searched during the summer for more clues as to the expedition's last days. After a failed first attempt to reach King William Island, Hall returned again in July 1864, finally reaching its southern coast in May 1869. Here, Hall noted Inuit accounts of cannibalism among Franklin's starving crews. He also recorded his anger at learning from the Inuit that, while several native families had provided an officer thought to be Crozier and a group of his men with some seal meat, the Inuit had then left, ignoring pleas for further aid. Forgetting to add that the Inuit themselves only managed to survive at subsistence level, Hall wrote:

> These 4 families could have saved Crozier's life & that of his company had they been so disposed . . . But no, though noble Crozier pleaded with them, they would not stop even a day to try & catch seals—but early in the morning abandoned what they knew to be a large starving company of white men.

Hall itemized Franklin relics found in the possession of the Inuit, including a mahogany writing desk that "had been recently in use as a blubber-tray." He transcribed Inuit testimony of having dug up, and left unburied, a body on King William Island: "This white man was very large and tall, and by state of gums and teeth was terribly sick." The Inuit also recounted having seen a ship in the area of O'Reilly Island, off the Adelaide Peninsula, which Hall took to be evidence that either the *Erebus* or *Terror* had "consummated the Great Northwest Passage." According to their account, the Inuit had at first approached the ship with caution, but when it seemed no one was aboard, a group visited it. In a locked cabin, they told of the discovery of "a dead man, whose body was very large and heavy, his teeth long. It took five men to lift this giant *kob-lu-na*. He was left where they found him." According to Hall's intelligence, the Inuit then began "ransacking" the ship for materials. Among the many items on board, they described seeing meat in cans.

Hall deduced that the Inuit found the ship in the spring of 1849. According to the Inuit account, there was a gangway reaching from the deck to the ice, suggesting that the vessel was still occupied that winter. The ship sank a short time later and debris, masts, boxes and casks drifted to shore. It was after this that an intriguing discovery was made: "fresh tracks were seen of four men and a dog on the land where the ship was. *In-nook-poo-ʒhee-jook,* who had seen Ross and his party on the Victory and Rae in 1854, knew these tracks to be *kob-lu-nas'* . . . " If that is the case, then it is likely that survivors of the Franklin expedition were alive at the time that James Clark Ross made his sledge journey in May 1849.

Searching for remains on King William Island and on nearby islets, Hall in once instance identified a human thigh bone, but his work was constrained because snow remained on the ground. He also found a skeleton, later identified by a gold filling as Lieutenant Henry Le Vesconte of the *Erebus.* Hall conducted a solemn ceremony to honour the dead man, including flying the American flag at half-mast and building a monument of stones. The remains were then collected by Hall and taken to the United States before being returned to England, where they were entombed at a Franklin memorial in Greenwich Hospital.

Much more important American discoveries were to come. On 19 June 1878, Lieutenant Frederick Schwatka, a United States cavalry officer who had served in the Indian wars of the American West at the same time as the famed defeat of Lieutenant Colonel George Custer at Little Big Horn, and who was also a qualified lawyer and medical doctor, led a tiny expedition backed by the American Geographical Society into the Arctic. Schwatka was inspired by Hall's earlier efforts, and by American whalers who, having spoken with the Inuit, reported that documents of the lost expedition might be found.

Travelling by sledge on what was to become a 3,249-mile (5,232-km) return journey, Schwatka was able to reach King William Island and conduct a thorough search in 1878–79 along the route taken during the retreat of the *Erebus* and *Terror* crews. Besides confirming important aspects of M'Clintock's search, Schwatka added immeasurably to the record of relics and human remains scattered along the western and southern coasts of the island.

On 21 July 1879, Schwatka visited the boat place seen by M'Clintock some nineteen years earlier, but instead of an intact boat and contents, he found that the site had "evidently been thoroughly overhauled by the natives." Besides the remnants of the boat, Schwatka found combs, sponges, toothbrushes, bottles and powder cans. He also found the widely distributed bones of four skeletons, including three skulls.

On 24 June that same summer, at what Schwatka called the "very crest" of his long journey, near Victory Point on the island's northwest shores, an opened grave was discovered. A medal with the name of John Irving engraved on it was found at the site, though the grave had been "despoiled by the natives some years before." Schwatka described the scene in his journal:

> In the grave was found the object-glass of a marine telescope, and a few officer's gilt-buttons stamped with an anchor and surrounded by a crown. Under the head was a colored silk handkerchief, still in a fair state of preservation, and many pieces of coarsely stitched canvas, showing that this had been used as a receptacle for the body when interred.

Because of the original care taken in the burial, Schwatka believed that the body had been buried from the ships, where a proper coffin could have been constructed. The gravesite stood in contrast to the final resting places of the other Franklin sailors found on King William Island, where the bones lay scattered on the ground. A human skull and other bones, thought to be Irving's, were found

The grave of Lieutenant John Irving, and relics
from the HMS Terror, found by Lieutenant Schwatka.

scattered over a wide area around the grave. "They were carefully gathered together, with a few pieces of cloth and other articles, to be brought home for interment where they may hereafter rest undisturbed," Schwatka wrote. (Of all the skeletal remains discovered by the American, only those identified as belonging to Irving were removed from the island, to be eventually buried with full naval honours at Dean Cemetery, Edinburgh.)

Schwatka's expedition made other discoveries: a large cairn covering a fragment of paper with a hand drawn on it, the index finger pointing; an Inuit cache with more relics, including several red cans marked "Goldner's Patent." Schwatka also found and interviewed a woman who said that some of the men she had met had "dry and hard and black" mouths, suggesting the presence of scurvy. He also recorded testimony similar to that collected by Hall, from an old man named Ikinnelikpatolok, who told of a large ship frozen in the ice to the west of Adelaide Peninsula, north of O'Reilly Island, and claimed he had seen one white man "dead in a bunk." Among other items, "they found some red cans of fresh meat, with plenty of what looked like tallow mixed with it. A great many had been opened, and four were still unopened."

Before leaving the Arctic, Schwatka met an old Inuk woman and her son who told a grim story of finding relics of the Franklin expedition on the shores of the North American mainland many years before, including one of the lifeboats the retreating crewmen had been dragging. Schwatka recorded the son's account:

> Outside the boat he saw a number of skulls. He forgot how many, but said there were more than four. He also saw bones from legs and arms that appeared to have been sawed off. Inside the boat was a box filled with bones; the box was about the same size as . . . one with the books in it.

The last thirty or forty of Franklin's men had apparently left the tragedy of King William Island behind them near the mouth of the Peffer River and crossed Simpson Strait, only to exhaust their last hopes in the barren reaches of an area Schwatka named Starvation Cove. (It has been argued that the two boxes may have contained the remains of Sir John Franklin and the expedition logs, but they have been lost forever.) A search of the area revealed little, only the partial remains of one sailor. The Inuit explained that the land had reclaimed the rest of the bodies—that the bones had sunk into the sand, mute testimony of the horror that visited the area so long ago.

Schwatka's party returned to the United States in September 1880. The *Illustrated London News* provided detailed coverage of the expedition's journey across King William Island, including an explanation for the absence of proper graves:

> The coast had evidently been frequently visited by natives, who had disinterred those who had been buried for the sake of plunder, and left their remains to the ravages of the wild beasts . . . [Schwatka's party] buried the bones of all those unfortunates remaining above ground and erected monuments to their memory. Their research has established the fact that the records of Franklin's expedition are lost beyond recovery.

The president of the Royal Geographical Society concluded that the Franklin search expeditions had succeeded in surveying much of the Arctic archipelago and "expunged the blot of obscurity which would otherwise have hung over and disfigured the history of this enlightened age." Despite the failure to locate the ships' records, or either of the two vessels, the Franklin searches had also pierced the Arctic long enough to answer the fundamental mysteries of the expedition's disappearance. Its route had been generally established, the reason for the desertion of the *Erebus* and *Terror* was made known and the Inuit accounts and sad discovery of relics on King William Island attested to the crews' final chilling days of life.

With the great search at last over, Tennyson wrote the epitaph for the Westminster Abbey memorial to Franklin:

> Not here: the white North hath thy bones, and thou
> Heroic Sailor Soul
> Art passing on thy happier voyage now
> Toward no earthly pole

Britain transferred sovereignty of the Arctic islands to Canada in 1880. The Northwest Passage was finally sailed by Norway's Roald Amundsen in 1903–06, aboard a wooden sloop named *Gjoa*. It was perhaps fitting that Amundsen should have been the first, for it was the narrative of Franklin's 1819 overland journey that led him to dream of being a polar explorer. "Oddly enough it was the sufferings that Sir John and his men had to go through which attracted me most in his narrative. A strange urge made me wish that I too would go through the same thing," wrote Amundsen, who conquered the passage and later the South Pole, only to die in a plane crash in Arctic waters in 1928. Royal Canadian Mounted Police Sergeant Henry Asbjorn Larsen later sailed the passage from west to east aboard the *St. Roch* in 1940–42, and from east to west in 1944.

Occasionally, bones thought to belong to a Franklin expedition member were discovered. In one case, a partial skeleton was sent to Canada's National Museum in Ottawa, where it remains in storage. And in 1923, the explorer Knud Rasmussen, a native of Greenland, reported interring some remains on the east coast of the Adelaide Peninsula, which, from surviving scraps of clothing and footwear, were "unquestionably the last mortal remains of Franklin's men."

Rasmussen also wrote down Inuit oral history of the discovery of a deserted ship, found when the natives were hunting seals off the northwest coast of King William Island. One old man named Qaqortingneq described what was seen by those who went aboard: "At first they were afraid to go down into the lower part of the ship, but after a while they grew bolder, and ventured also into the houses underneath. Here they found many dead men, lying in the sleeping places there; all dead."

Major L.T. Burwash of Canada's Department of the Interior made several visits to King William Island, interviewing Inuit elders for further clues about the Franklin expedition. In April 1929 he secured a statement from two men named Enukshakak and Nowya who told of finding, forty years earlier, a large cache of wooden cases carrying "tin containers, some of which were painted red." According to the men's account, some of these provisions were tins of preserved meat, purportedly found on a low flat island to the east of King William Island. They expressed their belief that the cache was left by the crew of a ship that had been wrecked off nearby Matty Island. This testimony, coupled with the report, recorded by Schwatka, of a wreck a short distance from O'Reilly Island, prompted Burwash to present the theory that some of Franklin's crews had returned to the *Erebus* and *Terror* and that "the ships were eventually brought to their final resting places while more or less under the control of their crews."

Burwash also included with his account what was purported to be unpublished testimony from a member of Charles Francis Hall's expedition, by then deceased, which strangely never made it into Hall's official account. Attributed to an Inuk hunter, this additional material revealed that Sir John Franklin may have been buried in a cement vault on King William Island: "one man died on the ships and was brought ashore and buried . . . in an opening in the rock, and his body covered over with something that 'after a while was all same stone.' " At the time the remains were interred, "many guns were fired."

In 1930, Burwash and pilot W.E. Gilbert would become the first men to fly to Crozier's Landing. However, there was little more than some rope and broadcloth left for them to see. Gilbert described the scene in an article published in the *Edmonton Journal* on 9 September 1930:

> Bitter winds across the still snow-covered ground made work difficult and the ravages of the tremendous storms encountered here had largely obliterated the remains of the camps in the eighty years which had elapsed.

There was no sustained challenge to Franklin's reputation mounted in Victorian times. It was not until 1939 that Canadian Arctic explorer Vilhjalmur Stefansson wrote his essay, "The Lost Franklin Expedition," and asked how these sea-toughened men, armed with shotguns and muskets, could have "contrived to die to the last man" of hunger so quickly in a land where the Inuit had survived for generations, hunting with Stone Age weapons.

Stefansson concluded that the chief failure of the Franklin expedition, and other nineteenth-century British explorers of the Arctic, was in the refusal to respond to the harsh environment by adopting the ways of the Inuit: "The main cause . . . was cultural." An explorer and ethnographer, and a man who had subsisted on a fresh meat-only diet in the Arctic for seven years, Stefansson repeatedly argued that the Arctic explorers would have thrived had they done the same. As he wrote: "The strongest antiscorbutic qualities reside in certain fresh foods and diminish or disappear with storage by any of the common methods of preservation—

canning, pickling, drying, etc." Yet as late as 1928, Stefansson's theories about the antiscorbutic value of fresh meat continued to be greeted with skepticism. As a result, he submitted to a bizarre experiment in which he ate nothing but raw meat for a year while living in New York City. To the astonishment of medical observers, he remained perfectly healthy.

There is no doubt that an abundance of fresh meat would have offered a means of salvation to Franklin expedition survivors. As Stefansson argued, Franklin and his officers need only have studied the narratives of two then recent expeditions to have had a command of the situation: "When you compare the John Ross expedition of 1829–33 with the George Back expedition of 1836–37, you have the complete answer to how a polar residence should be managed." Stefansson conceded, however, that while John Ross had wisely adopted the Inuit diet, he had not demonstrated that whites could be adequately self-supporting, as most of the food had been obtained from the Inuit through barter. In addition, there is evidence that Franklin expedition survivors did procure limited amounts of fresh meat from the Inuit, but pleas for further aid were then rebuffed.

In truth, the large number of survivors disgorged onto King William Island doomed any hopes of securing adequate quantities of fresh meat. Even among the Inuit, episodes of starvation have been documented in the region of King William Island and the adjacent mainland. Schwatka encountered Inuit who he reported were "in great distress for food" and who had already lost one of their number to starvation. He gave them caribou meat. Knud Rasmussen also wrote that, for the Inuit, life is "an almost uninterrupted struggle for bare existence, and periods of dearth and actual starvation are not infrequent." As late as 1920, Rasmussen documented that eighteen Inuit had died of starvation at Simpson Strait.

More to the point, Stefansson noted the curiously high number of deaths—before the *Erebus* and *Terror* were deserted, "while there were still large quantities of food on the ships." That "scurvy took so heavy a toll" even then, required, he argued, a "special explanation." If scurvy was indeed the cause of those deaths, then that explanation was almost certainly an enduring faith in the antiscorbutic value of tinned foods. As the historian Richard J. Cyriax stated in his 1939 study of the Franklin expedition: "As tinned preserved meat has no antiscorbutic properties, Goldner's meat, if perfectly good, would not have prevented scurvy."

8

Scattered

BONES

O WEN BEATTIE, an assistant professor of anthropology at the
University of Alberta, believed King William Island might
still hold secrets of the Franklin expedition disaster, information that could be exposed by the use of the latest equipment and
methods employed in physical anthropology. He believed at least
one last pilgrimage in the interests of science was warranted. His
initial survey, which would take two Arctic summers to complete,
would again follow that rock-strewn trail down which a straggling
procession of British seamen had made their desperate retreat.

An aura of doom hung over desolate King William Island
during the nineteenth-century visits of M'Clintock, Hall and
Schwatka. And for many years after the Franklin disaster, evidence
of the tragedy remained fresh. Beattie planned his survey of the island's south and west coasts in a manner that would be meticulous,
even though by 1981, 133 years would have passed since the disaster and he wondered what, of the 105 men who died on the island
and in nearby Starvation Cove, endured. He would be the first to

apply the techniques of forensic anthropology to investigations into the Franklin expedition.

Beattie had studied archaeology at Simon Fraser University in British Columbia. As a graduate student, he concentrated on the human skeleton, with advanced training requiring dissection courses in primate and human anatomy. His doctoral research in physical anthropology involved two areas of study: the analysis of hundreds of prehistoric skeletons from the northwest coast of North America; and the use of chemical analysis of bone to aid in the identification of modern human remains relating to forensic investigations. After joining the University of Alberta in 1980, his primary interests continued to grow in the area of human identification studies, or forensic anthropology, a subdiscipline of physical anthropology.

Although the Franklin expedition's failure was of considerable historical importance, it was first and foremost a mass disaster, involving multiple human deaths linked to a single, catastrophic event. It represented an unresolved forensic case, a fact in no way altered by the time that had passed. (If such a tragedy were to occur today, it would be investigated along precisely the same lines as would the carnage resulting from, for example, a modern-day train wreck, fire or airplane crash, using exactly the same scientific techniques to interpret skeletal and preserved soft tissue remains.) Given this fact, Beattie planned to collect any skeletal remains found on King William Island, then try to identify physical evidence that would support or disprove the conventional view of the expedition's destruction through starvation and scurvy. He intended to look for information on health and diet, for indications of disease, for evidence of violence and for information as to each individual's age and stature. There was also a remote chance that a victim's identity could be established, through dental features such as gold teeth and crowns, or through personal belongings found in association with a body.

Because of his special training in forensic anthropology relating to human identification, Beattie had assisted in numerous investigations conducted by medical examiner's offices, the Royal Canadian Mounted Police and other police agencies, and had testified in court as an expert witness. On King William Island, he planned to apply this expertise to a far older and greater mystery.

Beattie prepared for his Arctic journeys by studying sites identified by nineteenth-century searchers, and on 25 June 1981, set out from his cramped office on the thirteenth floor of the Henry Marshall Tory Building on the University of Alberta campus in Edmonton to investigate the Franklin expedition sites for the first time. First, he boarded a Boeing 727 to Yellowknife, the capital of the Northwest Territories, then flew on past the Arctic Circle to the central Arctic transportation centre of Resolute, a tiny community of 168 people nestled on the south coast of Cornwallis Island. Travelling with Beattie was co-investigator and Arctic archaeologist James Savelle.

A truck from the Polar Continental Shelf Project picked up the two researchers at the terminal in Resolute; they were then driven to nearby barracks where they met up with field assistant Karen Digby. The Polar Shelf, an agency of the Canadian government, provides a vital service by supplying scientists and researchers in Canada's far north with logistical and air support. Beattie, Savelle and Digby soon met Polar Shelf base-manager Fred Alt, picked up a short-wave radio, a 30.06 rifle and 12-gauge shotgun, and prepared for a Twin Otter aircraft to carry them into the field.

From Resolute, the research team flew to Gjoa Haven, an Inuit community on the southeast coast of King William Island, where Inuit students Kovic Hiqiniq and Mike Aleekee joined the team as assistants. Hiqiniq and Aleekee arranged for two hunters to carry the researchers and their equipment by snowmobile the next day, south across ice-clogged Simpson Strait. There, at Starvation Cove, an inlet on the North American mainland that sprawls and meanders inland for several miles, it is believed that the last of Franklin's men perished.

On 27 June 1981, the five researchers made the gruelling twelve-hour journey over hillocks and cracks in the ice on *komatiks*, traditional sledges once hauled by dog teams, but in this case pulled by snowmobiles. Sitting atop a mound of equipment and supplies, each firmly grasped hold of both sides of the komatik, as every icy obstacle along the way threatened to dislodge them. Joining them on the journey was the wife of one of the hunters carrying an infant tucked inside her *amauti*, or hooded parka. The temperature was seasonal, hovering between zero and 41°F (-17.5°C and 5°C).

Beattie and Savelle hoped to survey Starvation Cove, looking for relics or remains of the hardiest men from the doomed expedition, but the land is extremely low, marshy and sandy, and was almost completely covered by meltwater that summer, making such work all but impossible. The snowmobiles soon continued on, carrying the researchers a short distance north to a temporary Inuit fishing camp on Richardson Point. Dining that night on raw and boiled seal meat and raw caribou, they questioned their hosts about possible European gravesites on the south coast of King William Island. One possible site was described as lying on a high crest of land at Peabody Point, along their planned route.

The first actual survey work of the field season was conducted in the early morning the following day. A mist hung over the researchers as they walked over Richardson Point, which is just ⅔ mile (1 km) wide. Besides prehistoric and historic Inuit campsites (the locations of which were mapped by Savelle), nothing was found. Disappointed that any evidence of Franklin expedition crew members on the North American mainland remained hidden, the five-member survey team parted company with the Inuit hunters and crossed back over Simpson Strait to the southern coast of King William Island near Booth Point, hauling their supplies and equipment, including a canoe, themselves.

There, 1½ miles (2.5 km) west of Booth Point, they located the partial skeleton of the single individual from the Franklin expedition referred to in the 1869 expedition account of Charles Francis Hall. The unusual scatter of bones was found outside a tent circle associated with the expedition. It was a significant discovery, and it raised hopes that other Franklin remains would be located that summer. Once work at the Booth Point site was complete, the survey party then continued westward along the south coast of the island. (The grave identified by the Inuit fishermen they had visited at Richardson Point was located at Peabody Point, but it was actually an Inuit burial from the early 1900s. Because of its more recent origin, the remains were not investigated.)

At Tulloch Point, where in 1879 Frederick Schwatka had discovered what was believed to be a Franklin expedition grave, the researchers also found skeletal remains, though Beattie and Savelle would identify anatomical and cultural features that confirmed the skeleton was actually the mid-nineteenth-century remains of an adult Inuk male. Another burial site thought to have been of Franklin expedition origin, identified by Canadian explorer William Gibson in 1931, turned out to contain the remains of an adult Inuk female, also probably from the nineteenth century. Both of the latter sites were mapped and bone samples collected for further analysis. What became clear, though, was that at least some of what were Inuit graves had been mistaken for those of Franklin's men by searchers, further confounding Beattie's attempts to piece together the circumstances surrounding the expedition's destruction.

On 5 July, as the research team surveyed the coastline west of Tulloch Point, the large white dome of the Distant Early Warning (DEW) Line Station at Gladman Point came into view—nearly 16 miles (25 km) away. It was strange to see this Cold War relic on the tundra. But such radar stations are not uncommon in the Canadian Arctic: twenty-one dot the landscape from Alaska to Baffin Island. Built in the 1950s as a line of defensive warning against air attack from the Soviet Union, the stations had been modernized in recent years and were continuing their function of maintaining sovereignty over Canada's airspace.

After hours of hiking, the party reached a reasonably large, slow-moving river that required the use of their canoe to cross. Once on the other side, and within a few miles of the station, they began to set up camp. While Digby, Hiqiniq and Aleekee went about this routine task, Beattie and Savelle walked to the station. They were warmly greeted, and over the next day the tired crew were treated to hot coffee, fresh fruit and showers.

It was while they were visiting the station that they learned of an amazing coincidence. A few days prior to their arrival, one of the station personnel had, while hiking, discovered a moss-covered human skeleton on the tundra's surface within a mile of the station. This discovery was reported to the closest Royal Canadian Mounted Police detachment at Spence Bay (today called Taloyoak). When Beattie and Savelle and their group arrived at Gladman Point, the constable stationed at Spence Bay was on his way in his small plane to investigate the discovery. When he arrived he met up with the surveyors, and Beattie and Savelle both accompanied the constable and station personnel when they went to view the bones. As it turned out, the skeleton was that of a prehistoric Inuk male. His remains had rested above ground for hundreds of years. It was remarkable that, considering the hundreds, perhaps thousands, of people who had been to the station during its construction and period of operation, the skeleton was discovered only a few days before a forensic anthropologist and archaeologist literally wandered up to the station's front door.

The Gladman Point skeleton was the last to be found that summer. Beattie returned to Edmonton in late July, disappointed that the remains of only one of the 105 officers and men who has deserted the *Erebus* and *Terror* had been located. It was possible that the physical evidence of scurvy identified on the Booth Point remains would be one of few notable accomplishments of the 1981 survey. But it had been important to learn that previous searchers had almost certainly mistaken Inuit burials for those of Franklin's sailors. In addition to the small contributions to the archaeological record made that summer, the historical record had at least been further clarified and corrected.

Tiny pieces of the bone samples collected from both the Franklin sailor's skeleton and the Inuit skeletons were soon sent to a laboratory for trace element analysis. Use of such analytical techniques on skeletal remains is common, as various elements found in bone can provide information about problems in diet and possible deficiency disorders. Then, weeks later, while Beattie and Savelle redrew maps and reviewed field notes at the University of Alberta offices, the scatter of the bones found at Booth Point returned to bother them. For nearly all of the skull fragments had been found near a group of larger stones at what was identified as the entrance to the tent structure, while bones from the arms and legs were found more loosely scattered around the outside of the stone circle. What was initially thought to have been the remains of a sailor who had been left behind at a campsite, either near death or already dead, now began to reveal more ominous secrets.

In late September, when Beattie and Savelle were preparing the first report on the summer's research, they were forced to acknowledge what had been implied by the evidence at the site from the beginning: They had found the first physical evidence to support Inuit accounts of cannibalism among the dying crewmen.

While studying the right femur found at the site, Beattie confirmed that three roughly parallel grooves measuring .02–.04 inches (.5–1 mm) in width and up to ½ inch (13 mm) in length had been cut into its back surface. The cut marks were made by a metal implement, suggesting intentional dismemberment. Fracture lines indicated that the skull had also been forcibly broken; the face, including both jaws and all the teeth, was missing. Evidence that the body had been intentionally dismembered was further supported by the selective parts of the skeleton found: the head, arms and legs.

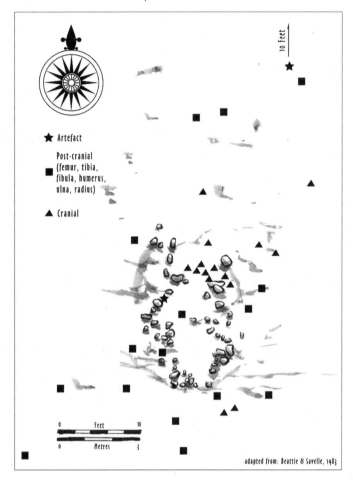

Map depicting scatter of human remains and Franklin-era
artefacts around a tent circle at Booth Point, King William Island.

Besides the face, most of the skeleton was missing, including.
the twenty-four ribs, sternum (breastbone), all twenty-four vertebrae of the back, the three large bones of the hip (sacrum and two
innominates), the two clavicles (collar bones) and the two scapulas
(shoulder blades).

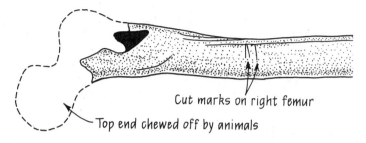

Cut marks on right femur

Top end chewed off by animals

Hudson's Bay Company searcher John Rae was the first to hear of the ghastly possibility of cannibalism among Franklin expedition crewmen. In the spring of 1854, Rae was given details of the expedition's final days by Inuit who also had in their possession a variety of artefacts. Rae recorded their descriptions of a shocking sight:

> From the mutilated state of many of the corpses and the contents of the kettles, it is evident that our wretched countrymen had been driven to the last resource—cannibalism—as a means of prolonging existence.

The response to this testimony was immediate and fierce. Many Britons simply refused to believe cannibalism was possible. Charles Dickens, who followed the Franklin search closely, spoke for them when, in 1854, he argued that Franklin expedition crewmen represented the "flower of the trained English Navy . . . it is the highest degree improbable that such men would, or could, in any extremity of hunger, alleviate the pains of starvation by this horrible means."

Dickens then attacked the source of the stories, the Inuit, as "covetous, treacherous and cruel . . . " Writing in *Household Words*, he said:

> In weighing the probabilities and improbabilities of the 'last resource,' the foremost question is—not the nature of the extremity; but the nature of the men. We submit that the memory of the lost Arctic voyagers is placed, by reason and experience, high

above the taint of this so-easily allowed connection; and that the
noble conduct and example of such men, and of their own great
leader himself, under similar endurances, belies it, and outweighs
by the weight of the whole universe the chatter of a gross handful
of uncivilised people, with a domesticity of blood and blubber.

United States Chief Justice Charles Patrick Daly, president of the
American Geographical Society, went a step further, charging that
Franklin was "murdered by the Indians, who had already imbued
their hands in the blood of white travellers." Rae fought back,
arguing,

> I consider it no reproach, when suffering the agony to which ex-
> treme hunger subjects some men, for them to do what the Es-
> quimaux tell us was done. Men so placed are no more responsible
> for their actions than a madman who commits a great crime.
> Thank God, when starving for days, and compelled to eat bits of
> skin, the bones of ptarmigan up to the beak and down to the toe-
> nails, I felt no painful craving; but I have seen men who suffered
> so much that I believe they would have eaten any kind of food,
> however repulsive.

Fifteen years later, Rae received corroboration from Charles Francis Hall, who had also heard the tales of cannibalism and reported
them in much greater detail. Even today, the stories are abhorrent.
The Inuit reported finding boots "that came up high as the knees
and that in some was cooked human flesh—that is human flesh that
had been boiled." Wrote Hall: "Some bones had been sawed with a
saw; some skulls had holes in them." Other bodies found nearby
had been carefully stripped of all flesh, "as if some one or other had
cut it off to eat."

Even three decades after the disaster, gruesome accounts continued to be collected from the Inuit of the region. Lieutenant
Frederick Schwatka's 1879 search recorded "almost unmistakable

evidences of their being compelled to resort to cannibalism." An Inuk named Ogzeuckjeuwock reported seeing "bones from legs and arms that appeared to have been sawed off . . . The appearance of the bones led the Inuits to the opinion that the white men had been eating each other." Schwatka's account was compelling and, according to one British newspaper, had finally "cleared the reputation of a harmless people from an undeserved reproach."

It is difficult for those sated in their daily demands for food and drink to believe that any civilized person would intentionally and knowingly eat human brains, consume strings of arteries or split open bones so that the marrow could be picked out and eaten. That fact is no different today than it was during Queen Victoria's reign. Yet under certain dire, life-threatening circumstances, many people would come to the realization that seems to have faced the last tattered remnants of Franklin's expedition, that cannibalism is all that stands in the way of sure death.

Modern disasters, such as the 1972 crash of a chartered plane in the Andes Mountains of South America, provide insights into the rationale for consuming other humans. One of those to survive the Andes crash explained later in an interview:

> Real hunger is when you have to eat human flesh. But when you see yourself growing thinner and thinner and weaker every day and see the bones standing out and feel your eyesight dimming— you make the decision to live by whatever means possible.

Prehistoric occurrences of cannibalism associated with starvation provide striking similarities to the Booth Point skeleton findings. An archaeological investigation of an Anasazi settlement in the American Southwest revealed 11 skeletons that had been dismembered and processed for eating: "The overall picture of skeletal destruction is that of dismemberment, crushing of long bone shafts, facial mutilation, scattering and loss of elements of the trunk (ribs, vertebrae, and pelves), and the loss of hands and feet."

So cannibalism follows a pattern: once the decision is made, the initial sections removed from the body are the meatier areas like the buttocks, thighs, lower legs and arms. Recognizably human parts, such as hands and feet, are not eaten at first. As time passes and hunger continues to tear at the survivors, the options of where the flesh comes from are reduced, and bone marrow, organs, arteries and skin are consumed. Removal of muscle tissue is usually done with a knife or other sharp object, and this can leave butchering marks on the bone. Removal of bone marrow requires the bone to be smashed open. The brain is either pulled through the base of the skull or eaten after the face is cut off. The need by members of Franklin's dying crew for a portable food supply was the reason for the only exceptions to this pattern.

A small group of the last survivors of the doomed expedition trudged eastward along the south coast of King William Island in July or perhaps August 1848. The exhausted men probably continued to hold out hope that they would reach the mouth of the Back River, from where they would attempt to travel nearly 1,000 miles (1,500 km) upstream to the safety of a Hudson's Bay Company fort located on the eastern edge of Great Slave Lake. Slowing significantly as a result of increased exhaustion aggravated by scurvy, their food supply at an end, the sailors must have desperately looked for alternative food sources. But there were too few birds' eggs to feed the group and hunting on the sparse northern island would have been unrewarding.

When their food finally ran out and they were too ravaged by hunger and disease to continue, the men sat down and prepared to die. But with the first death came new hope. The survivors must have found themselves contemplating a stark fact: starvation need not be a factor any longer.

Cannibalizing the trunk of the body would have given them enough strength to push on. The head, arms and legs, easily portable, were carried along as a food supply. Finally they came to a part of the island that turned sharply to the northeast—away from their goal. Camping on a small spit of land near Booth Point, the same spit of land later visited by the University of Alberta researchers, they ate their last meal. Disease and physical deterioration continued to drain them of energy as they turned southward across ice-covered Simpson Strait, avoiding the many long, thin slivers of black seawater slicing through the ice and the turquoise and azure pools of meltwater, making their way towards Starvation Cove. For them, the adventure and the suffering would soon be over.

— 9 —

The Boat
PLACE

I N SURVEYING the King William Island coastline the following
year, Beattie, this time with field assistants Walt Kowal, a graduate student in anthropology at the University of Alberta,
Arne Carlson, an archaeology and geography graduate from
Simon Fraser University in British Columbia and Inuk student Arsien Tungilik, planned to retrace the searches of M'Clintock in
1859 and Schwatka in 1878–79.

Although both nineteenth-century searchers had discovered
the skeletal remains of crewmen at a number of sites, the surveyors
would concentrate on Schwatka's published accounts, since the explorer had found and described more of these finds. Schwatka had
also gathered up the scattered bones and buried them in common
graves at the various sites, placing stone markers on them. Beattie
hoped these graves could be located, and, with great anticipation,
plotted their supposed position using Schwatka's journals and
maps. From the descriptions of bones buried at some of the sites,
the number of crewmen represented could be four or more.

After a three-and-a-half-hour flight south from Resolute on 28 June 1982, the Twin Otter supplied by the Polar Continental Shelf Project swept over Seal Bay on the west coast of King William Island. Spotting a dry gravel ridge near the beach, the pilot circled back, flying close to the ground and as slow as aerodynamics would allow. The co-pilot opened a door and, with the help of Arne Carlson, booted a crate filled with supplies out of the plane. All watched as the box bounced a few times and rolled to a stop on the ridge, its pink-coloured cloth wrapping visible from miles away. The aircraft then headed south along the coast to Erebus Bay, where a similar procedure took place. (The run-off from melting snow on King William Island made landings too risky that season, and the staff at the Polar Shelf base in Resolute came up with the idea of the air drops.)

The scientific team then headed on to Gjoa Haven, where field assistant Arsien Tungilik was picked up. The Twin Otter soon flew back towards the northwest coast. After a time, the pilot suddenly banked the plane to the left—he had spotted a potentially good landing site in a land otherwise covered with summer run-off. Gesturing to Beattie, he pointed out of his window to the beach ridge and nodded his head. Looking at his map, then out the window, Beattie nodded back that the site, about 3 miles (5 km) north of Victory Point, would make a good starting point for the survey. After making one more low-level pass, the pilot put the plane down with feet to spare and, with one engine left running, the scientific crew jumped out of the plane's side door and began unloading their supplies. Within five minutes everything was piled outside, and the pilot and his co-pilot pulled themselves back up into the plane. After restarting the second engine and throttling up, the plane edged forward. Seconds later it was airborne and heading north, then immediately it banked and flew past the group on the ground, the pilots waving as they set course for distant Gjoa Haven to refuel before their return to Resolute.

Although the team's food caches had been dropped along their planned route, each person's backpack was weighed down with food and supplies. Extra clothing for temperatures expected to hover around the freezing point, and other personal items, were usually stuffed to the bottom. Next came the food, consisting mainly of packaged freeze-dried goods and chocolate bars. Other important items such as matches, tent- and boot-repair kits, first-aid kits and ammunition were packed near the top. Sleeping bags were tied to the bottom of the packs, with a tent and sleeping pad strapped one to each side. The rifle and shotgun were attached to the top and could be reached easily while the pack was on. Other items that increased the weight of each load were the cooking utensils, stoves and fuel. A radio was carried, with which they would make twice-daily contact with the base camp at Resolute. Later, when leaving a cache site, their packs would be stuffed to overflowing with supplies and more things would be hanging from straps on the outside.

Each team member was burdened with one of these heavy packs (Beattie and Tungilik carried more than 60 pounds/30 kg; Carlson carried even more), but it was Kowal, a powerful man with seemingly endless energy, who served as the self-assigned workhorse for the survey party. During the first phase of the fieldwork, Beattie and Carlson had to lift Kowal's pack up to help him get it on. In it, in addition to his own belongings, he carried food, the radio, a rifle, ammunition, a sleeping bag and pad, a tent, an inflatable raft, a set of oars, two camp stoves, his camera and, strapped to the back of the pack, a full 5-gallon (23-litre) container of stove fuel—for a total weight of more than 130 pounds (60 kg). Beattie was amused and amazed at the sight of Kowal as they moved along on their survey: a huge mountain of supplies appeared to be lumbering ahead on its own, powered by two legs that would disappear as Kowal squatted to investigate something on the ground. The mountain would then slowly rise and continue along on its course.

Loaded down as they were, each researcher had to move slowly to conserve energy. The survey needed alert minds and inquisitive eyes; fatigue would steal those necessary qualities away. They took frequent rests supplemented by liquids (tea, coffee, hot chocolate) between each camp. Even with these breaks, they were able to survey between 6 and 12 miles (10 and 20 km) each day, and when searching an area out of one of their established camps, they took only the necessary supplies for one day, greatly increasing their range and speed.

Their first day on the island, even before they had a chance to set up camp, a curious Arctic fox was noticed studying them from a nearby beach ridge. Beattie thought of the brief visit by the small animal, still covered in its heavy white winter fur, as a form of welcome to the strange and exotic island they were about to explore. Although Beattie had visited King William Island's south coast the previous year, he was about to survey areas where people had not been for many years.

When the fox had scurried off into the distance, the four surveyors busied themselves setting up the tents of their first camp and preparing a meal of freeze-dried food. After settling in, despite being tired from the long plane journey, they then briefly explored the surrounding area. Walking inland soon brought them to a large lake, and they could see in every direction that the land was flat and virtually covered in a sheet of water.

The following morning, as they moved northward along the coast, the temperature gradually warmed to 41°F (5°C), the sun emerged and the wind shifted so that it was blowing off the island. The team stopped briefly to remove parkas, then continued in shirt sleeves for the remainder of the day. The warmth of the season resulted in great quantities of meltwater flowing towards the coast from inland lakes, which made surveying conditions very difficult and almost impossible along parts of the route. Each mile of coastline covered usually required two or more miles of walking.

Although their plan was to survey completely up the coast to Cape Felix, on the northwestern tip of the island, it would be physically impossible on foot. So when they reached a swiftly flowing stream at Cape Maria Louisa, 12 miles (20 km) south of Cape Felix, they decided to turn south. After searching unsuccessfully for a Franklin campsite that had been discovered in the area by M'Clintock and Hobson in 1859, they then camped for the night, returning to near Victory Point the next day.

Breaking camp on the morning of 30 June, the four men carried their supplies southward to the bank of another swollen stream. The depth of the water and speed of the current were too great to consider wading across, and they had to skirt round the outflow by walking out onto the ice of Victoria Strait. They wrapped their supplies in a large orange tarpaulin, tying the corners together. Then, dragging this large bundle and burdened with their overstuffed backpacks, they picked their way over the broken piles of ice at the waterline and out onto the smoother ice further offshore.

For the next two hours they walked, waded and jumped over fractures and cracks in the ice and areas of open water created by the stream, until they were able to angle back to the safety of the shore on the far side of the stream. After kicking off their boots and taking a well-earned rest, the survey then continued south along the shoreline to the place visited by James Clark Ross in 1830, subsequently named Victory Point.

Standing on the low rise of the point and looking south, Beattie was astonished by the accuracy of the scene, as depicted in an engraving made from a sketch drawn by Ross during his explorations—part of his uncle Captain John Ross's failed 1829–33 expedition. James Clark Ross described his visit:

> On Victory point we erected a cairn of stones six feet high, and we enclosed in it a canister containing a brief account of the proceedings of the expedition since its departure from

England . . . though I must say that we did not entertain the most remote hope that our little history would ever meet an European's eye.

Despite the accuracy of the engraving, nothing could be found of the cairn erected by Ross. Only a small cairn dating from the mid-1970s remained.

Victory Point is a low gravel projection into Victoria Strait, rising less than 33 feet (10 metres) above the high-water mark. From this spot it is possible to see Cape Jane Franklin several miles to the south, glazed with a permanent snow cover on its western rise, and to the west, the thin, horizontal dark line of Franklin Point. Ross named these features in 1830, in the case of Franklin Point writing in his journal that "if that be a name which has now been conferred on more places than one, these honours . . . are beyond all thought less than the merits of that officer deserve." (In one of those instances of tragic irony, Sir John Franklin would die within sight of Franklin Point and Cape Jane Franklin, seventeen years later.)

Two miles (3 km) south of Victory Point, Beattie and his small party came across another, much smaller, projection of land, marking the site where the crews of the *Erebus* and *Terror* congregated on 25 April 1848, three days after deserting the ships 15 miles (24 km) to the NNW. It is this place that, along with Beechey Island, forms the focal point for the discovery of the fate of the expedition, for a note of immeasurable importance was left here, providing some of the few concrete details relating to the state and action of the crews from the wintering at Beechey Island in 1845–46 to the desertion of the ships on 22 April 1848.

Setting up camp, Beattie prepared to spend two days thoroughly researching and mapping the site as well as surveying the surrounding area. The two tents were placed so that their doorways faced each other; the team could then sit and prepare meals and talk in their own makeshift courtyard. During that first evening, the sky and clouds to the south darkened to a deep purple and bolts of lightning flashed out from the clouds, reaching down towards the ground. Although orange sunlight still shone on their camp, the four watched with anxiety as the dark storm moved westward to the south of them. The site, known as Crozier's Landing, was so flat that their metal tent poles were prominent features—perhaps even lightning rods. They were relieved when the storm at last faded from view.

By 1982, few relics of the Franklin expedition remained at Crozier's Landing. Where piles of the crews' discarded belongings once lay strewn about, only scattered boot and clothing parts, wood fragments, canvas pieces, earthenware container fragments and other artefacts could now be gleaned from among the rocks and gravel. One rusted but complete iron belt buckle was found during the survey, as was a stove lid, near the spot where M'Clintock had located a stove and pile of coal from the expedition. A smashed but complete amber-coloured medicine bottle was also found, as was part of the body of a clear glass bottle, complete with navy broadarrow marking.

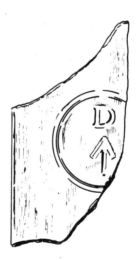

Glass fragment showing the navy broadarrow.

What struck Beattie was the paucity of the remains marking this major archaeological site. How could a place with such a history of tragedy and despair—shared by 105 doomed souls—appear so impartial to the events that transpired here during late April 1848? The artefacts that were mapped and collected in 1982 were pathetic, insignificant reminders of the failed expedition. Disturbances at the site were such that a search for the grave of Lieutenant John Irving, discovered by Schwatka, failed to turn up anything, though a series of at least thirteen stone circles indicated the actual location of the tenting site established by Franklin's men. Other tent circles attested to the visits by searchers, primarily M'Clintock and Hobson in 1859 and Schwatka in 1879, and by Inuit. Evidence of more recent visits were also clearly visible: a hole excavated by L.T. Burwash in 1930, small piles of corroded metal fragments (possibly the remains of tin canisters), a note left by a group during an aerial visit made in August 1954 and other signs of visits made within the last decade. A modern cairn is situated at the highest point of the site, representing the approximate location of the cairn in which the note was discovered by Hobson in 1859.

However, Beattie's group did make one interesting discovery as they marked with red survey tape the locations of artefacts scattered along the beach ridge. Paralleling this ridge, and towards the ice offshore, was an area of mud that, because of the time of year, had begun to thaw—and visible in the mud were coils of rope of various sizes. The anaerobic conditions of the mud and the long period of freezing each year had resulted in good preservation of the organic material, in stark contrast to the disintegrated rope and canvas fragments found on the gravel surface. One of the preserved coils was of a very heavy rope, about 2 inches (5 cm) in diameter. Yet despite this discovery, so little of the presence of Franklin's men at Crozier's Landing remained that it was almost impossible to visualize that scene of bustling activity and preparation that would have been played out in growing despair. The last marks of this most famous of Arctic expeditions were all but erased, as if scoured away by the constant, turbulent and chilling winds that blow off the ice. Beattie began to entertain the possibility that pursuing new leads into the fate of the expedition on King William Island might be a waste of time.

From the perspective gained at Crozier's Landing, where the final agony of the explorers began in 1848, perhaps the deeper mystery was not so much the fate of the 105 men who died trying to walk out of the Arctic (which had until this time been Beattie's focus), but the mystery of the twenty-four others who died (including a disproportionate number of officers) while the expedition was still aboard-ship and food stores remained. (After deserting their ships, the deaths of the 105 survivors seemed unavoidable along the desolate shores of King William Island.) To Beattie, it became increasingly obvious that the real Franklin mystery lay not here at its tragic end, but much earlier: the period from August 1845, when the expedition sailed into the Arctic archipelago, until 22 April 1848, when the ice-locked vessels were deserted off King William Island. For it was during those thirty-two lost months that nine officers, including Sir John Franklin, and fifteen seamen died. (Three were buried at Beechey Island; the graves of the others have never been found.)

Even before the ships were deserted, the Franklin expedition had been an unprecedented disaster. Its heavy losses contrasted sharply with the escape of John Ross and his crew, including James Clark Ross, after they deserted the discovery ship *Victory* on the southeast shore of the Boothia Peninsula in the early 1830s. For despite all that time in the Arctic, away from the protection of their ship and suffering the ravages of scurvy, Ross returned to England with nineteen of his twenty-two men. To Beattie, it began to appear that the most important insights into the Franklin disaster would come from the group of twenty-four who died aboard ship.

While Beattie and Carlson mapped and collected the few artefacts found at Crozier's Landing, Kowal and Tungilik built a makeshift sledge from scraps of lumber found beside the ice edge.

Round nails and the relatively fresh appearance of the wood suggested it was of very recent origin, and the two carpenters, using rocks for hammers, put it to good use. They planned to haul the camp supplies, mounted on the sledge, south across ice-covered Collinson Inlet to near Gore Point. Although the ice was fairly rotten and beginning to break, they calculated that, with some care, they could save more than a week's walking by cutting across the inlet's mouth instead of going round its wet and marshy source.

ABOVE *Carrying survey supplies out onto the ice of Victoria Strait* and BELOW *over Collinson Inlet, this time using a sledge made from twentieth-century timber and nails found at Crozier's Landing.*

Within an hour the sledge was complete and they prepared to resume their southward trek. The early evening hours were becoming cool and a silvery fog hung over the ice. The wind, usually a constant companion, had dropped to a whisper. Beattie and Carlson, who stayed behind to complete the artefact collection, watched as the other two were soon engulfed by the swirling fog. They stood silently for a few moments, listening to the receding sounds of trudging footsteps and the rasp of the sledge runners.

With Kowal pulling the sledge by a rope looped around his chest, the two weaved, struggled and fought their way across the 2½-mile (4-km) distance in four hours. Tungilik, with his superior knowledge of ice conditions, walked ahead and scouted the safest route, which Kowal followed faithfully. When they reached land they lugged the supplies up onto the beach. Although both were completely exhausted, they immediately began the arduous journey back to rendezvous with Beattie and Carlson, who had struck out across the inlet after their artefact collection was completed.

The ice was very difficult and dangerous to cross. Parts were so soft that the men would sink to their knees; large ponds of melted water blanketed the ice surface. Wide cracks were a hazard in a number of locations and innumerable smaller cracks braided the ice. Tall, massive hummocks of snow and ice dotted the route, and Beattie worried about surprising a bear hidden on the opposite side of one of these—a healthy paranoia that resulted in a wide berth being given to these small ice mountains. As well, he noted that the ice they travelled over, and had seen offshore since their arrival on King William Island, was first-year ice, often little more than 12 inches (30 cm) thick. Recently, he knew, Polar Continental Shelf Project scientists had used ice core samples taken from High Arctic ice caps to study climate conditions over time, and had concluded that the Franklin era was climatically one of the least favourable periods in 700 years. This explained the multiyear ice encountered by Franklin off the northwest coast of King William Island, ice that was sometimes more than 80 inches (200 cm) thick.

Carrying packs filled with artefacts, Beattie and Carlson laboured across the ice for an hour. The fog had finally lifted when they saw Kowal and Tungilik a mile distant, heading towards them. Within another hour they were all safely across.

On 4 July, the team searched unsuccessfully for the grave of a Franklin crewman recorded by Schwatka. They also searched for the cairn at Gore Point, where a second Franklin expedition note was discovered by Hobson in 1859. (Virtually identical to the note found at Crozier's Landing, this scrap of paper contained only information on the 1847 survey party of Gore and De Vouex. There were no marginal notes on the document, though, curiously, the error in the dates for wintering at Beechey Island was repeated.) A small pile of stones was located on the far end of Gore Point. As the pile was definitely of human origin and did not come from an old tenting structure (either Inuit or European), it seemed likely that the stones represented the dismantled cairn that had once held the note.

Moving southward along the coastline, the team encountered nothing to indicate that the area had been visited recently, only locations marking the probable campsites of Schwatka and his group. The next focal point in their survey was the supply cache that had been dropped from the air on the south shore of Seal Bay. After spending two days at this location, making good use of the stores of food and observing the dozens of seals that dotted the ice floes offshore, the team surveyed the coast down to a location adjacent to Point Le Vesconte, where Schwatka discovered and buried a human skeleton. Point Le Vesconte is a long, thin projection of land that is actually a series of islets. At low tide it is easy to walk out along the point, but, as the team discovered, at high tide the depth of water separating the islets can nearly reach the waist.

Of all of Schwatka's descriptions, the locations of two skeletons along this coast were the best documented and most accurately identified on the survey team's maps. At Point Le Vesconte, Schwatka had recorded human bones, including skull fragments scattered around a shallow grave that contained fine quality navy-blue cloth and gilt buttons. The incomplete skeleton, of what Schwatka believed had been an officer, had been carefully gathered together and reburied in its old grave and a stone monument constructed to mark the spot. Yet again, the survey team failed to locate this grave or the second one on the adjacent coastline. Beattie was disappointed. In "curating" the skeletal remains he discovered, Schwatka had apparently marked each grave with "monuments" consisting of just a couple of stones. Along King William Island's gravel- and rock-covered coastline, such graves were lost in the landscape. After scouring the area for an entire day, the frustrated party pushed on to the south.

On the morning of 9 July, Beattie turned on his shortwave radio for the daily 7 AM radio contact with Resolute. But instead of being greeted by the reassuring and familiar voice from the Polar Shelf base camp, only a vacant hissing sound was heard. No contact with Resolute could be made that morning. The aerial was checked, the batteries changed, the radio connections and battery compartment cleaned, all in preparation for the regular evening communication.

Loss of radio contact is serious in the field; within forty-eight hours the Polar Shelf will dispatch a plane to the last known location of the party, bringing an extra radio and batteries. There may be a genuine emergency, but if the reason for missing radio contact is trivial, such as simply sleeping through the schedule, the Polar Shelf will put in a bill for the air time spent on re-establishing contact, for an important function of the twice-daily radio contact is to track the status of each group of scientists working in the field throughout Canada's Arctic. It is to everyone's advantage to pass along position information and plans for camp moves to the officials in Resolute.

With their radio not functioning, the team was completely cut off from the outside world. As the group sat around discussing the consequences, they guessed it must be a radio blackout caused by solar activity—a relatively common occurrence. What worried Beattie was that, in their last radio contact with Resolute, they had indicated they were on their way to a predetermined camp location, 25 miles (40 km) south at Erebus Bay. Loss of contact with Resolute meant there was a possibility that a plane would be sent out within the next day or two to Erebus Bay. There was some urgency, therefore, to get to that location before the plane. Three thoroughly exhausting, long days of surveying and backpacking followed before radio contact was at last resumed; for those days, they felt like they were the only people on earth. The absolute isolation imposed by the radio blackout was a sobering experience, one they were not anxious to repeat.

As they approached Rivière de la Roquette across a dismally flat landscape, two small objects caught their attention. The first was a small grey lump in their path, which soon revealed itself to be a young Arctic hare, or leveret. Born fully haired, with their eyes wide open, hares are able to run just minutes after birth. This tiny, gentle animal stood out in stark contrast to the forbidding landscape. It was rigid with fright, its heart pounding. The four watched it for a time, took some photographs, then continued on. The second object turned out to be what was almost certainly an Inuit artefact, constructed from material collected in the nineteenth century from a Franklin site. It resembled a primitive fishing rod made of two pieces of wood and twine; the wood held together in part by a brass nail. It was a good example of the use made by the Inuit of abandoned European artefacts.

Surveying the coast had largely meant walking along beach ridges of limestone shingle and sloshing through shallow sheets of water draining off the island. Now, as they held up their hands to shade themselves against the sun, the team could see the other side of Rivière de la Roquette, ⅓ mile (.5 km) to the southwest; beyond that point the land was too flat to pick out any landmarks. The river itself posed a considerable obstacle, and there was discussion as to whether they should attempt to walk round it, out on the ice of Erebus Bay. However, earlier that day they had been able to see the effect of the river's flow on the ice in the bay. The volume of water had pushed it far offshore, and the ice that could be seen through binoculars did not look inviting. Finally, all agreed that to walk out on that rotten ice would be too dangerous; the river would have to be waded.

Beattie recalled the vivid description of Schwatka's group when they had stood on the same spot 103 years before: at that time the river was considered impassable down near its mouth, and the group had to hike inland a number of miles to where the river narrowed and they could cross in icy-cold, waist-deep water. Beattie wondered how he and his crew, far less rugged and experienced than Schwatka's men, would fare in gaining the far bank. Carlson and Tungilik had hip waders, which they untied from their backpacks and put on. Kowal donned pack boots that reached to mid-calf and began slowly wading out into the shallow edge of the river, searching carefully for submerged banks of gravel that would allow him to keep the water from rising above the boot tops. Tungilik struck out along the same route. Carlson and Beattie unpacked and began inflating a two-man rubber boat that they had carried (along with a set of oars) since their survey began. They planned to use it to float their supplies across the river, but Beattie also hoped to find a way to keep his feet dry. As he had only pack boots himself, it seemed reasonable to have Carlson, in his hip waders, pull him across the river in the boat. Kowal was too far away for the others to see if he was having success in keeping dry, and the wind and distance were too great to shout to him.

Carlson and Beattie had problems inflating the boat with the rubber foot pump, and when the craft was half-inflated, the pump ceased working altogether. Despite having a rather floppy, unmanageable water craft at his disposal, Beattie loaded his pack and climbed in. He quickly found himself floundering—before finally tumbling over on his back with his legs sticking up in the air. After a good laugh, he righted himself and, soaked, climbed out of the boat. He and Carlson started wading slowly across after the others, the empty and limp boat bobbing and swivelling downstream from a rope attached to Carlson's pack. The water turned out to be very shallow almost the whole distance across, though within 160 feet (50 metres) of the other side it increased to knee depth.

Resting by a rock near the river bank the four looked off to the west across a forbidding 6 miles (10 km) of mud flats. Their next stop would be the food cache that had been dropped from the plane on the first day of the season. They needed to replenish their supplies: over the past two days they had virtually run out of food and fuel, and they were looking forward to the supplies they had packed in the distant cache. So, thinking as much about their empty stomachs as the obviously difficult walk before them, they struck out onto the grey-brown featureless mud flats.

The clay-like mud had melted down 4 inches (10 cm) or more and was soft and pasty. Each footstep squeezed the mud out like toothpaste, and the friction and suction made extracting their feet a struggle. At first they sank in only up to their boot tops, but as they pushed a few more miles out onto the flats, there was more water in the mud. Now their feet sank down to the permafrost. The grip of the mud, sometimes ankle-deep but at other times more than knee-deep, was so strong that they often pulled their feet right out of their boots.

At times they would encounter an island of vegetation where the footing was good, and at each of these spots they would take a short rest before plunging into the mud again. In one of these "islands," the intact skeleton of a bearded seal was found. Virtually undisturbed by animals, it looked almost surreal against the backdrop of the mudflats.

Halfway across they began to see the slightly raised beach ridge that marked the location where they had dropped their cache, and two hours later, when they finally started up the nearly imperceptible slope of the western extent of the flats, they were within only a few miles of their next camp. When at last they reached firm ground, they threw their packs down and sat to rest their legs.

It had taken more than four hours to cross the flats. Although the cold wind blew persistently off the ice at Erebus Bay, the day was sunny and warm, nearly 50°F (10°C), and before long all were lying on their backs, soaking in the sun, thankful that they did not have to return by the same route. Twenty minutes passed with hardly a word said before one of them, Carlson, finally sat up and busied himself with his pack. Their bodies now rested, stomachs began to growl; the next goal was the cache.

Walking to the west they dropped quickly down into another flat area, but this one was only two-thirds of a mile across and had good footing. Several pairs of whistling swans, which had constructed their large nests here, could be seen nearby, and the four men paused to observe the large and majestic birds before continuing on their long walk. Then, in the middle of the flats, Tungilik stopped dead and, pointing at the ground, asked Kowal, "What's this bone?" Kowal was shocked to see a right human tibia lying on the surface of the flats. He called to Beattie and Carlson, who had been following. As the others hurried towards them, Kowal decided to have some fun. He quickly covered the bone with a piece of driftwood. When Beattie and Carlson finally arrived, both panting under the weight of their packs, Kowal said, "Look at this!" Beattie looked down at the wood and said, "You made me hurry up for this?" Then, turning the wood over with his foot, a broad smile crossed his face. All thoughts of reaching the food cache quickly vanished as the team searched the location for other bones. Five more were found nearby, as were two weathered pieces of wood planking, one of which had remnants of green paint, a brass screw and badly rusted iron nail shafts. Because the six bones were from different parts of a skeleton, it seemed likely that they were from one person. However, since none of the bones was from the skull, it was not possible to tell whether the person was a European or Inuk, though the bones were close enough to the location of the lifeboat first found by M'Clintock that they were most likely those of one of Franklin's men. The wood planking supported this interpretation.

The bones were photographed, described, then collected, and the location marked on the team's maps. Elated with their discovery and feeling renewed confidence that this area of the boat would yield new and important information, they continued on at an increased pace. When they saw the bright pink bundles of supplies in the distance, they broke into a jog and, if the packs had allowed, would probably have raced to their cache. Reaching the bundles almost simultaneously, they unslung their packs, rummaged quickly to locate their knives and within seconds were all slashing away at a claimed bundle. Each man searched for his favourite food: Kowal was looking for boxes of chocolate-covered macaroon candy bars; Tungilik, cans of roast beef; Beattie, tins of herring; and Carlson, canned tuna. With hardly a word to each other they dug into their food, sitting on the sandy beach ridge among the debris of their haphazard and comically frenzied search. The sounds of chewing, the crackle of plastic wrappers and the scraping of cans were interrupted by Kowal: "Can you believe us?" he said, looking up from a near-empty package, a chocolate macaroon poised in his right hand. "And we're not even starving. Those poor guys must have really suffered."

On 12 July the surveyors headed out from their newly established base camp. They found nothing more in the area where they had discovered the six bones, just two-thirds of a mile from their camp, but 2 miles (3 km) to the west of the camp they discovered a 100- by 130-foot (30- by 40-metre) area littered with wood fragments. As they closely searched the site, larger pieces of wood were also found. Schwatka's description of the coastline and the small islands a few hundred feet out in Erebus Bay left the men with little doubt that they had reached the boat place where the

large lifeboat from the Franklin expedition, filled with relics, was
first discovered by M'Clintock and Hobson in 1859 and later visited
by Schwatka in 1879. But the sight that had filled M'Clintock and
the others with awe so many years before had vanished: the skeletons that once stood guard over their final resting place were
nowhere to be seen. An exhaustive search of the site was conducted, and slowly, out of the gravel, came bits and pieces that
graphically demonstrated to them the heavy toll of lives once
claimed by the desolation of King William Island.

In the immediate vicinity, they eventually located many artefacts, including a barrel stave, a wood paddle handle, boot parts
and a cherrywood pipe bowl and stem similar to those found by
M'Clintock at the same site. More important, however, was the discovery of human skeletal remains. From the boat place and scattered along the coast to the north, they found bones from the
shoulder (scapulas) and leg (femurs, tibias). Several of the bones
showed scarring due to scurvy—similar to the markings discovered on the bones found a year earlier near Booth Point. (In total,
evidence of scurvy would be found in the bones of three individuals collected in 1982.) The team worked long and hard, each of the
four men combing the ground for any relic or human bone. Dusk
soon surrounded them, but no nightfall follows dusk during the
summer at such high latitudes. It was under the midnight sun that
Tungilik made the survey's most important find.

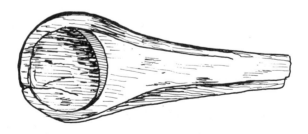

Cherrywood pipe.

While systematically searching the boat place, Tungilik caught sight of a small ivory-white object projecting slightly from a mat of vegetation. Picking at the object with his finger, out popped a human talus (ankle bone). With his trowel, Carlson scraped the delicate, dark green vegetation aside, revealing a series of bones immediately recognizable as a virtually complete human foot. Continuing his excavation, which lasted into the early morning hours of 13 July, Carlson found that most of the thirteen bones from the left foot were articulated, or still in place, meaning that the foot had come to rest at this spot and had not been disturbed since 1848. The remaining skeletal remains varied from a calcaneus, or heel bone (measuring 3 inches/8 cm in length), to a tiny sesamoid bone (no bigger than .12 inches/3 mm across). Also found was part of the right foot from the same person, which supported the interpretation that a whole body once rested on the surface at this spot.

M'Clintock had argued that, as the lifeboat was found pointing directly at the next northerly point of land, it was being pulled back towards the deserted ships, possibly for more supplies:

> I was astonished to find that the sledge (on which the boat was mounted) was directed to the N.E.... A little reflection led me to satisfy my own mind at least that this boat was *returning to the ships*. In no other way can I account for two men having been left in her, than by supposing the party were unable to drag the boat further, and that these two men, not being able to keep pace with their shipmates, were therefore left by them supplied with such provisions as could be spared, to last them until the return of the others with fresh stock.

The 1982 discoveries at the boat place supported this interpretation: the human skeletal remains were found scattered in the immediate vicinity of the lifeboat, and in the direction of the ships for a distance of two-thirds of a mile. It appears that those pulling the lifeboat could go no further and had abandoned their burden and the two sickest men. They continued on, but some had nevertheless died soon after.

In all, the remains of between six and fourteen individuals were located in the area of the boat place. In determining the minimum number of individuals from the collection of bones, Beattie first looked to see how many of the bones were duplicated. Then he examined their anatomy, such as size and muscle attachment markings, comparing bones from the left and right sides of the body to see if they were from one or more individuals.

Beattie was sure that the bones had been missed by Schwatka. From his journal, it is obvious that Schwatka was reasonably thorough in his collection of bones. He had discovered the skull and long bones of at least four individuals and buried these at the site. As in the previous searches along the coast that summer, Beattie and his crew were not able to find this grave. Of the bones discovered by the scientists in 1982, no skull bones were found.

Strangely, the most touching discovery made at the boat place was not a bone but an artefact, found by Kowal. Surveying a beach ridge further inland on 13 July, he saw, lying among a cluster of lemming holes, a dark brown object that, on closer inspection, turned out to be the complete sole of a boot. Picking it up he could see that three large screws had been driven through the sole from the inside out, and that the screw ends on the sole bottom had been sheared off. Kowal carried the artefact back to camp, where the others, who had been cataloguing the collection, examined it. It was obvious that the screws were makeshift cleats that would have given the wearer a grip on ice and snow—a grip absolutely necessary when hauling a sledge over ice.

It was this object, more than even the bleached bones of the sailors, which brought home to the four searchers the discomfort, agony and despair that the Franklin crews must have endured at this final stage of the disaster. For the research team, the piece of boot symbolized the final trek of the men of the *Erebus* and *Terror*.

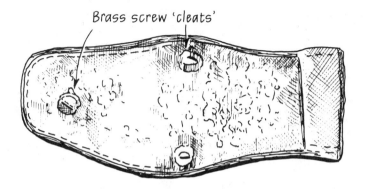

Brass screw 'cleats'

Boot sole found at the "boat place," showing screw "cleats."

The imagination can play tricks in such situations. And while sitting alone during the dusk-shrouded early hours of 14 July, with brisk winds blowing in off Victoria Strait, Beattie felt that Franklin's men did indeed still watch over the place. It was as if the dead crewmen might yet rise up for one last desperate struggle to ascend the Back River to safety.

Later, Beattie, Carlson, Kowal and Tungilik surveyed 3 miles (5 km) further to near Little Point. To the west of this location was a long inlet filled with rotten ice, which effectively formed a barrier to any further survey that season. And so, packing their precious cargo of bones and artefacts, the team readied to leave the island. With the King William Island surveys at an end, Beattie was already wondering what new insights into the Franklin disaster his small collection of bones would provide.

A Doorway

OPENS

URING THE EARLY months of 1982, bone samples collected from four skeletons discovered on King William Island in 1981—three Inuit (two males, one female) and the Franklin expedition crewman from near Booth Point—were submitted to the Alberta Soil and Feed Testing Laboratory for trace element analysis. The reason for the testing was to gain possible insights into the individuals' health and diet. The method of analysis used, called inductively coupled plasma atomic emission spectroscopy, would assess the level of a number of different elements contained in the bones. At the time, Owen Beattie believed that scurvy and starvation were the likely cause of the Franklin disaster, but the 1981 bone samples were submitted without instructions to look for a particular element.

By the time Beattie returned from the field in 1982, the findings of the trace element analysis were waiting for him. The results showed that the level of lead found in the Franklin expedition crewman's bones was extremely high, raising the possibility that some—or all—of the crew had been exposed to potentially toxic levels of lead; and that the difference between the lead levels found in the Inuit skeletons and that of the Franklin crewman was astounding. In the three Inuit skeletons, the lead levels ranged from 22 to 36 parts per million. (Such levels fall within the range identified in other human skeletons from cultures with no exposure to lead beyond that found in the environmental background.) In contrast to the Inuit skeletons, the occipital bone from the Franklin crewman registered levels of 228 parts per million. These results meant that if the Franklin crews had suffered this level of intake during the course of their expedition, it would have caused lead poisoning—the effects of which in humans have been well documented and include a number of physical and neurological problems that can occur separately or in any combination, depending on the individual and the amount absorbed. Anorexia, weakness and fatigue, irritability, stupor, paranoia, abdominal pain and anaemia are just a few of the possible effects.

Lead poisoning had plagued the ancient Greeks and Romans, who employed kettles, buckets, pipes and domestic utensils made of lead. Because the metal has a saccharine taste when dissolved (which is why the acetate is commonly called "sugar of lead"), the Romans had even used sheet lead to neutralize the acidity of bad wine. Even in 1786, when Benjamin Franklin provided the first detailed medical description of the "mischievous effect from lead," the serious, even deadly, risks that he enumerated were nonetheless not widely disseminated. Cosmetics such as face pomades and hair powder, pewter drinking vessels, tea caddies, water pipes and cisterns, children's toys and candlewicks all caused lead poisoning in the nineteenth century.

One scholar who has studied the circumstances under which lead poisoning arises, describes the outbreaks as "legion, oftentimes bizarre, and sometimes dramatic." A mystery illness, for instance, called the "York Factory Complaint," afflicted the Hudson's Bay

Company's fur trade post from 1833–36. Most of the men at the fort suffered the telltale signs of "debility," resulting in a series of unexplained deaths. Symptoms included "a total loss of reason," "great nervous weakness," weight loss, convulsions and stupor. One new arrival at York Factory in 1834 described the inhabitants as having a peculiar pallor, which made them seem "more like ghosts than men." At the time, the illness was blamed on a number of factors, including "the want of vegetables and fresh beef." Today, scientists attribute the outbreak to saturnism (lead poisoning), most likely derived from the lead-lined containers used for food or drink.

Whilst lead's dangers were little understood at the time, some warnings did enter the medical and scientific literature of the mid-1800s—an article in *Scientific American* that appeared in 1857, for instance, declared "all combinations of lead are decidedly poisonous." One particular characteristic militated against its discovery, and gave rise to lead poisoning's other name: the "aping disease." As one scientific study concluded: "So protean are its manifestations that it, like syphilis, may simulate a hundred other conditions." Lead poisoning also has a way of appearing in epidemics, so that it was often attributed to some unrelated cause. In the context of Arctic expeditions, these symptoms—emaciation, discolouration of the gums, abdominal colic, shooting pains of the limbs—would naturally suggest to medical officers and expedition commanders a well-known and feared illness: scurvy. All are, however, symptoms of lead poisoning.

Most poignantly for those dragging heavily laden sledges, "lead poisoning has a mean way of penalizing the extremity most used in muscular effort."

The unexpected discovery of elevated bone lead levels begged another question: What could have been the source? Suspicion immediately fell on the relatively new technology of preserving foods in tin containers, as used by the Franklin expedition. Nearly 8,000 lead-soldered tins containing 33,289 pounds (15,113 kg) of preserved meat were supplied to the expedition, as well as the tinned equivalent of 2,560 gallons (11,638 litres) of soup, 1,200 pounds (545 kg) of tinned pemmican and 8,900 pounds (4,040 kg) of tinned preserved vegetables. (Even today, the seams and seals of some tins are known to be a significant source of lead contamination in some developing countries, so this certainly could have been a problem.) But ignorance of its ill effects remained commonplace. Just as authorities had failed to understand the link between scurvy and reliance on tinned food, so too they failed to understand the effect of interior-lead-soldered seams on tinned foods, and thus, on those dependent for long periods on such provisions. In addition, lead-glazed pottery and tableware were used by nineteenth-century British Arctic expeditions. The storage and serving of acidic foods and beverages (which can dissolve lead salts)—such as lemon juice, wine, vinegar or pickles—in lead-glazed vessels could have been a major source of lead ingestion during the expedition. Other possible sources of lead on the expedition included tea, chocolate and other foods stored in containers lined with lead foil. In addition, food colouring, tobacco products, pewterware and even lead-wicked candles could have added to the possible contamination. As a result, lead poisoning, compounded by the severe effects of scurvy, could have been lethal for many members of the expedition's crews during the early months of 1848. Rapidly declining health might well in fact have been the major reason for the decision by Crozier and Fitzjames to desert the ships. As the note discovered by Hobson on King William Island shows, nine officers and fifteen men had already died by 25 April 1848.

This radical new theory, proposed by Beattie, would prompt debate among historians who had, for so long, relied on the theories of nineteenth-century searchers and, later, parliamentary inquiries in Britain as the basis for their investigations. While such sources are invaluable in the reconstruction of events, all the volumes written about the doomed expedition combined were not able to provide the scientific data Beattie had already gained from the scanty physical remains found on King William Island.

*A cup made from an empty food tin from one of the Franklin
search expeditions—showing that the cycle of lead contamination from the tins
could continue even after they had served their primary purpose.*

The problem with Beattie's theory, however, was that skeletal remains alone were not enough to make a conclusive case. Although the lead values found so far were undeniably high, bone does not reflect *recent* exposure so much as it does *lifetime* exposure; lead sources present in the early industrial environment of mid-nineteenth-century England could have been to blame rather than any short-term exposure on the expedition. Also, contamination over the twenty-five or so years of the unknown Franklin crewman's life could have caused physical or neurological symptoms, but they would have been much milder than those associated with classic lead poisoning and might have resulted in only slight behavioural problems. Therefore, to establish or disprove lead as a health problem on the expedition required the analysis of preserved soft tissue, which would reflect lead exposure following the departure of the expedition from England in May 1845.

The unexpected discovery of high lead levels shifted the focus away from the just-completed 1982 survey of King William Island. The gross examination of these bone materials, however, yielded two important observations: they added to the evidence for scurvy as a factor in the crewmen's health late in the expedition and, significantly, backed up the bone lead findings. Values of the bone lead analyses from the remains of sailors collected in 1982 ranged from 87–223 micrograms per gram. By contrast, lead levels in bones of Inuit of the same time period and same geographical area ranged from 1–14 micrograms per gram. This provided convincing evidence that environmental lead contamination in the Arctic was not a contributing factor to the lead exposure. But even a physical anthropologist could learn little more from these test results. The definitive answer lay elsewhere: at the only known location where Franklin crewmen had died and been buried in the frozen ground by their shipmates. That place was tiny Beechey Island, off the southwest coast of Devon Island, where three sailors, Petty Officer John Torrington, Able Seaman John Hartnell and Private William Braine of the Royal Marines, died during the first winter of the Franklin expedition and were buried in the permanently frozen ground. What if those bodies remained frozen to this time? Wouldn't they hold the key to whether Beattie's lead theory was supportable or not?

Preserved human remains have given researchers and historians untold insights into life in very different worlds from our own. They are time capsules of the history and evolution of human beings. The mummified pharaohs of ancient Egypt, for example, have added greatly to our knowledge of that distant time, just as the bog people of northern Europe have shed new light on Iron Age man. But bodies have also remained frozen for great lengths of time. Examples include Charles Francis Hall, who died in 1871, and whose partially preserved remains were uncovered in Greenland's permafrost in 1968. Prehistoric Inuit have also been found entombed, in the ice near Barrow, Alaska, and in Greenland, while in the Altai Mountains of southcentral Siberia, 2,200-year-old Scythian tombs have been discovered containing frozen and partially preserved human remains. The Arctic temperatures on Beechey Island were perfect for at least the chance of similar preservation.

Beattie first officially proposed the exhumation of the three graves to Canadian authorities early in 1983. In 1981 and 1982, he had required only an archaeology permit issued by the Prince of Wales Northern Heritage Centre of the Northwest Territories and a science permit from the Science Advisory Board of the Northwest Territories to conduct his survey for skeletal remains on King William Island. The plan to investigate the buried corpses of Beechey Island, however, was far more complicated. The site was, in effect, a graveyard, and the identities of the three Franklin expedition sailors were known. Beattie had to ensure that all proper authorities were notified and that they approved of the planned research.

Archaeology and science permits were obtained from the Territorial government, which in turn asked that the British Admiralty, now part of the Ministry of Defence, be informed and that an attempt to contact any living descendants of the three sailors be made. The scientific team sought, and eventually received, clearance from the chief medical officer of the Northwest Territories, who assessed whether there was a potential health risk involved in the exposure of remains dating to the mid-nineteenth century. Exhumation and reburial permits, issued by the Department of Vital Statistics of the Northwest Territories, were also applied for. Permission from the Royal Canadian Mounted Police was also required, and, with its assistance, Beattie notified the British Ministry of Defence of the planned excavations. The Settlement Council of the Resolute Bay community also granted permission to conduct research on the site, which falls within their local jurisdiction. Finally, in an effort to contact any descendants of the three Franklin crewmen, Beattie wrote to the *Times* asking that a request for descendants to contact him be published as soon as possible. The short article produced no response.

Because of the nature of the work on Beechey Island and what might be contained in the graves, the research team was then expanded to include an archaeologist and a pathologist. At last, in August 1984, the team of scientists from the University of Alberta left Edmonton for Resolute, en route to Beechey Island. They shared the same hope: that the very cold that once worked to destroy the Franklin expedition would now help them unlock the mystery of its destruction.

PART TWO

The
ICEMEN

Down in the hold, surrounded by the creaking of the wooden hull and the stale odours of men far too long enclosed, John Torrington lies dying. He must have known it; you can see it on his face. He turns towards Jane his tea-coloured look of puzzled reproach.

Who held his hand, who read to him, who brought him water? Who, if anyone, loved him? And what did they tell him about whatever it was that was killing him? Consumption, brain fever, Original Sin. All those Victorian reasons, which meant nothing and were the wrong ones. But they must have been comforting. If you are dying, you want to know why.

MARGARET ATWOOD, "The Age of Lead"

Mr Franklin smiled upon them all; he had a marble-white smile, like a tombstone angel, like a shot beluga whale on the beach; he slowly stretched the white rubber-marble skin of his face; as the lead-sugars and lead-garnishes of Mr Goldner worked themselves more thoroughly into his system, he came by degrees to bear more resemblance to another kind of whale, a grey one, gravel on its heavy skin . . .

WILLIAM T. VOLLMANN, *The Rifles*

— 11 —

Across the

PRECIPICE

I T IS CLEAR that all went exceedingly well for Sir John Franklin
during the first months of his expedition. The *Erebus* and the
Terror dodged through the ice of Baffin Bay in 1845 and quickly
passed through Lancaster Sound, the eastern entrance to the
Northwest Passage. Finding their westward progress impeded by a
wall of ice in Barrow Strait, Franklin turned his ships north into the
unexplored Wellington Channel for some 150 miles (240 km), penetrating to 77°N latitude. A second barrier of ice probably forced
the expedition to retreat along the west and south coasts of Cornwallis Island (thus making clear that the land mass was an island)
before finding a winter harbour at Beechey Island. Here, they settled into their first winter campsite, doubtless filled with a sense of
purpose. They had not yet found a passage, but the coming summer held every hope of success.

But first, Franklin and his 128 men—most of whom were without previous polar experience—had to contend with the approaching twenty-four-hour darkness and bitter cold of the Arctic winter.

They would be completely isolated from all other human beings
and beyond hope of rescue for many months should something go
wrong; then came the deaths of John Torrington, John Hartnell
and William Braine.

Speculation as to the cause of death of those three men dominated Owen Beattie's thoughts, when, on 10 August 1984, he and a
scientific team consisting of pathologist Dr. Roger Amy and research assistants Walt Kowal, Joelee Nungaq and Geraldine
Ruszala lifted off in their Twin Otter from Resolute and turned
eastward for the flight across the choppy waters of Wellington
Channel to Beechey Island. As the aircraft approached the distant
cliffs of their destination and nearby Devon Island, there was little
to provide a sense of scale. But as the plane descended, rounding
the northern spit of Beechey Island, then closed in on the sloping
area of Franklin's winter camp, Beattie was astonished at how insignificant the islet looked alongside massive Devon Island.

Beattie had never visited the historic site before and, peering
out of the window as the plane passed by the graves about 100 feet
(30 metres) above the ground, he was deeply moved by the site's
vulnerability. Along the whole eastern slope of the island, the
headboards of John Torrington, John Hartnell and William Braine
were the tallest features visible, framed by towering, vertical cliffs
to the west and the shore of Erebus Bay to the east.

Adjacent to the graves was a landing area, scored by long parallel wheel marks in the gravel where other planes had landed, some
perhaps earlier that summer, others many years before. The pilot,
flying by the graves, checked out the makeshift landing strip and
the wind direction. He then powered the Twin Otter up and out
over Erebus Bay, turned sharply towards the cliffs and, pulling out
of the turn, lined up with the landing area. Skimming only a foot or
two over mounds of gravel, the plane, flaps now fully extended,
was committed to a short field-landing. With the graves directly off
the left wing, the main wheels touched down into the gravel.
Immediately the pilot brought the nose wheel down, applied the

brakes and reversed thrust on the propellers. The plane came abruptly to a full stop.

After half an hour spent unloading a huge pile of supplies, the team stood back and watched the plane lift off and fly out over Union Bay, then into the distance, the droning of the engine gradually replaced by quiet. For the first few minutes, the crew strolled around the site. They were struck by the absolute isolation. Apart from the Antarctic and perhaps a handful of other places, there is nowhere in the world where a person can face solitude as in the Canadian Arctic. Even the presence of a few workmates does not compensate for the emptiness and loneliness of the far north.

The first task was to construct a temporary home, much as Franklin's men had done here many years earlier. Everyone helped to pitch two large communal tents, and, as soon as these were ready, five sleeping tents were set up. Two large long-house tents, measuring 12 by 18 feet (3.7 by 5.5 metres), would provide much-needed living space for a crew whose sleeping tents were large enough only for a sleeping bag and backpack. Each long-house tent had a strong tubular aluminium skeleton, covered by a canvas outer skin; another canvas cover was tied on the inside. These two layers would provide excellent protection from the wind, rain and snow. A heavy canvas floor covered the sharp gravel. The door consisted of a double flap that could be tied tightly shut. When the tents were in position, the radio aerial and a weather station were assembled and raised.

Beattie spent time that first day on Beechey Island studying the tiny Franklin graveyard where he hoped some answers lay buried. The three graves lay side by side, about 26 feet (8 metres) above sea level. He planned to begin by exhuming Petty Officer John Torrington, who was probably the first on the expedition to die. Interred alongside Torrington were Able-bodied Seaman John Hartnell and Private William Braine.

Torrington's headboard was simple, but both Hartnell and Braine had inscriptions taken from the Bible carved on theirs.

The Beechey Island gravesite: The graves, from right to left, are of Thomas Morgan of the Investigator (d. 1853); and from the Franklin expedition, Private William Braine RM (d. 3 April 1846), Able Seaman John Hartnell (d. 4 January 1846), Petty Officer John Torrington (d. 1 January 1846); and a fifth, unidentified grave.

Hartnell's included the following passage: "Thus saith the Lord of Hosts, consider your ways." Haggai, i,7.', while Braine's read, "Choose ye this day whom ye will serve" Joshua, xxiv, 15.' These unusual inscriptions have prompted some searchers and historians to suggest that foul play or mishap marred that first winter. One of the jobs of a forensic anthropologist is to interpret whether foul play could have caused or contributed to the death of an individual. Before the work started on Torrington's grave, Beattie wondered what he might find.

Two days after the first members of Beattie's scientific team arrived, a second Twin Otter flew in carrying project archaeologist Eric Damkjar and research assistant Arne Carlson. Damkjar brought news of a family emergency to Nungaq, and the young assistant left on the same aircraft.

Torrington's grave was carefully staked out, mapped, sketched and photographed so it could be restored to its original state upon

The grave of 20-year-old John Torrington after the removal
of the gravel mound. Notice the row of small limestone shingles that form
a fence-like feature around the grave.

completion of the exhumation. Each stone covering the grave, from the tiny 2–4-inch-high (5–10-cm-high) stone fence made of limestone shingle that surrounded it to the stones that covered the burial mound itself, were numbered with water-soluble ink to assist the scientists in reconstruction.

They worked surrounded by the permanence of the stark and seemingly ancient land. But for the lonesome graves, a few remaining Franklin relics and their own small cluster of tents, there was nothing human in the place. The hard, angular coastline of Devon Island juts out in the distance east of Beechey Island, with cliffs rising some 660 or more feet (200-plus metres) out of Lancaster Sound and Barrow Strait. When the land is covered with snow, the stratigraphy of the cliffs produces marked horizontal stripes of white and grey that appear like a chart of the ages. Beechey Island itself is actually a very small appendage to the southwest corner of Devon Island, to which it is connected by a narrow filament of gravel barely 13 feet (4 metres) across in parts and within the reach of windblown ice. It was first seen by Europeans on a cold August day in 1819. Captain William Edward Parry briefly described landing on Devon Island:

> The first party landed at the foot of a bluff headland, which forms the eastern point of this bay, and which I named after my friend MR RICHARD RILEY, of the Admiralty.

(It was on that point of land, Cape Riley, that searchers would find the first traces of the Franklin expedition thirty-one years later.) Then Parry looked to the west, across a bay that now bears the name of Franklin's ship, *Erebus,* at what would eventually become one of the most important and recognized sites in Arctic exploration:

> . . . on the side of the bay, opposite to Cape Riley, was an island; to which I . . . gave the name of BEECHEY ISLAND, out of respect to SIR WILLIAM BEECHEY.

Parry never set foot on the tiny island he named.

The northeast corner of Beechey Island slopes first gently upwards from the shore of Erebus Bay through a series of level beach ridges ideal for the construction of small buildings, or a graveyard. Upslope from the area used by Franklin and his crews, the land rises more steeply, culminating in high cliffs that overlook the campsite and the bay where the two ships would have been locked in the ice. The top of the island is remarkably flat, and in the southwest corner of the plateau, overlooking Barrow Strait, Franklin had the large rock cairn built. From this vantage point, 590 feet (180 metres) above sea level, it is possible to see Somerset Island 40 miles (70 km) to the south; Cornwallis Island is easily visible 30 miles (50 km) west across the entrance to Wellington Channel.

A small stream cuts down to the south of Franklin's camp area, past the grey gravel covering the three graves, before emptying into Erebus Bay. Only in July and August does the stream come to life, providing a source of water for visitors to the site. In July, when the sun has warmed the rocky ground, hardy flowers bloom, filling the landscape with tiny random pockets of bright colour. But in August, as the team worked, the blooms had already fallen away.

On 12 August 1984, having erected a tent shell over the grave to protect it from the elements, the University of Alberta researchers began to dig through the ground of Torrington's grave. It took them less than an hour to remove the top layer of gravel using shovels and trowels, but when the excavation reached 4 inches (10 cm) into the ground, the men encountered cement-like permafrost. After a short, unsuccessful experiment in melting the permafrost with hot air, they resorted to pick and shovel to attack the frozen ground.

Soon after the uppermost levels of the permafrost had been chipped, broken and shovelled away, a strange smell was detected in the otherwise crisp, clean air. At first it wafted upwards intermittently, mingling with the smell from the smashing, sparking contact of pick with gravel, but as the excavation deepened the smell gained in strength and persistence and soon dominated the work. Although not totally the smell of decay, it served to remind Beattie of what he might encounter. But not until much later, when the coffin was fully exposed, would the true origin of the smell be determined.

Two long days were spent struggling through almost 5 feet (1.5 metres) of permafrost before the researchers got their first glimpse of the coffin. At the deepest part of the excavation, field assistant Walt Kowal, carefully clearing off a thin layer of snow at the foot-end of the grave, exposed a small area of clear ice. Beneath the ice casing he could see dark blue material. Until this discovery, there was speculation as to whether anyone was actually buried in the grave. Torrington's body might have plunged through the ice into the freezing waters and been lost; other expeditions of the period had constructed dummy graves as a form of memorial. Or maybe the body would be simply missing, removed sometime during the past 138 years—a possibility that first occured to the exasperated team when they had dug about 1½ feet (.5 metre) below the top of the permafrost. As the researchers struggled deeper and deeper into the ground and still found no sign of a coffin, the thought that the grave really might be empty began to seriously trouble them. So when Kowal saw the blue material, he shouted, "That's it! We've got it!" and stood back with a sense of accomplishment and relief.

Beattie and the others quickly gathered and knelt in a close circle around the discovery. With such a small area exposed it was impossible to determine what the fabric represented. Beattie thought it might be a section of the Union Jack. Others speculated it might be part of a uniform, a shroud or the coffin itself. But for a time the material was left under the thin cover of ice. Although the researchers had obviously discovered something in the grave and were anxious to continue, Beattie was still awaiting the exhumation and reburial permits from the government of the Northwest Territories, notification of permission from the Royal Canadian Mounted Police and clearance from the chief medical officer. What had been done up to that point was considered archaeological work and was covered by a separate permit. Having established the exact location of the body, Beattie was now forced to call an end to the excavation until the required permissions arrived.

Abundantly clear to Beattie after removing more than 3 feet (1 metre) of permafrost, was that Torrington's preservation would probably be excellent because of the ice. Originally there had been some doubt, as 138 Arctic springs and summers had passed. But even at the height of summer the season's heat had had little or no effect on the upper reach of the permafrost—and Franklin's men had gone to a good deal of trouble interring Torrington deep in the frozen ground. Then, as the researchers waited for the permits, they were confronted with a problem that could have ruined the whole project. Water began to flood the grave.

The water was subsurface run-off from the melting snow and permafrost of the slope and cliffs inland from the excavation, further fed by periods of rain and sleet. Everything was at stake. What had lain undisturbed for more than a century could be severely damaged or destroyed by water within hours if they didn't act quickly.

It was decided that a shallow V-shaped ditch 130 feet (40 metres) long would be dug directly upslope of the graves (the three crewmen were buried alongside one another, with Torrington closest to the sea). This ditch, shovelled and scraped only a few inches into the permafrost, would act as a collecting canal, effectively diverting the water away from the graves. Within a matter of hours, the water seeping into Torrington's grave had slowed to a trickle; eventually it stopped.

With still no news about the required permits, Roger Amy and Geraldine Ruszala made use of the down time to explore the spit of land connecting Beechey Island to Devon Island. Well into their hike, Amy, casting his eye along the spit, noticed a dirty-coloured snowbank about ⅛ of a mile (.2 km) away. His eyes were drawn by its unusual colour, but, as he looked more closely, he saw it move. Amy stopped dead in his tracks as the realization hit him: they were walking directly into the path of a polar bear. These huge and powerful animals, which can weigh 1,985 pounds (900 kg) and stand 11½ feet (3.5 metres) on their hind legs, often avoid human contact. However, periodic polar bear attacks do take place in the Canadian Arctic.

Amy whispered to Ruszala to start slowly backing up as the bear began sauntering towards them. They were at least ⅓ of a mile (.5 km) from camp, but they continued this cautious retreat almost the whole distance, with the bear following along at the same speed.

Finally, with the camp within earshot, they turned and ran. "A bear, a bear," Ruszala shouted, wildly pointing back towards the spit. The bear was still about one eighth of a mile away when Kowal and Damkjar fired several shots into the air to frighten the animal. These first blasts simply increased the bear's curiosity, but the two men continued firing and, after ambling a few feet closer, the bear wisely decided it might be better—if not simply quieter—to alter its course and move on to other business. The crew followed the majestic animal's retreat until it was last seen swimming speedily across Union Bay towards Cape Spencer. Amy and Ruszala, however, were badly shaken by the experience of being stalked.

As the wait for the final permits continued, Beattie and Damkjar decided to explore the remains of Franklin's winter camp, then the historic sites along the east coast of the island.

Most of the relics left behind by Franklin's expedition had already been collected and taken away by the search expeditions that followed. Those that remained were subjected to continual disturbance right up to 1984. Despite this, a number of important artefacts could be seen in the areas adjacent to the graveyard. Most prominent among them was a large gravel-walled outline, believed to have been a storehouse. Also nearby the graves were the remains of a smithy, a carpenter's shop and, further away, depressions where tent structures or observation platforms once stood. (Between 1976 and 1982, Parks Canada had conducted detailed archaeological investigations of a number of important historical sites in the Arctic. Beechey Island was one of the sites studied. The only artefacts from Franklin's expedition remaining at that time— besides the structure outlines—were clay pipe fragments, nails, forge waste, a stove door fragment, wood shavings and tin cans.)

Beattie also looked over two graves dating from the searches of the 1850s that had been dug alongside Torrington, Hartnell and Braine. One of the graves was that of Thomas Morgan, a seaman from Robert McClure's ship, the HMS *Investigator*. The owner of the other grave is unknown, though one journal from the 1850s indicates that it may be a dummy grave serving as a memorial to French Navy Lieutenant Joseph René Bellot. Both of these men had died heroic and tragic deaths. Morgan had been among the scurvy-wracked from the *Investigator* who—before the Franklin expedition achievements were discovered—had been credited with being the first to cross the Northwest Passage. Having abandoned the ice-locked *Investigator* with the rest of McClure's crew at Mercy Bay on the north coast of Banks Island, Morgan had made the difficult trek by foot over the ice first to Dealy Island, then later reached Beechey Island, only to die aged thirty-six in May 1854 on board the HMS *North Star*. Bellot, who had served in the French Navy with distinction, later volunteered to join in the Franklin search. Bellot visited the Arctic first under Captain William Kennedy aboard the *Prince Albert*, then later aboard the HMS *Phoenix*. On 18 August 1853, while carrying dispatches to searcher Sir Edward Belcher up icy Wellington Channel, Bellot was caught by a gust of wind and swept into the frigid water. His body was never recovered.

Beattie and Damkjar, leaving the graves and adjacent Franklin campsite behind them, walked south along the beach ridge above the waterline. The first artefacts found along their route were tins, scattered individually or in small clusters. Close inspection of the cans identified them as being from the supplies of the search expeditions. Not only had Captain Horatio Thomas Austin and Captain William Penny—the searchers who had first discovered Franklin expedition relics on Beechey Island—spent time here, but others later used the island as a base for their searches. Walking along, the number of tins increased and wood fragments also became evident. Visible around a curve in the coastline was the mast of one of several vessels left at King William Island during the 1850s—jutting at a steep angle out of a gravel beach ridge. The vessel, which was probably left on the island to serve as a depot, was still largely intact in 1927 when Sir Frederick Banting, codiscoverer of insulin, and Canadian painter A.Y. Jackson visited the

ABOVE *Owen Beattie standing at the ruin of Northumberland House, the supply depot built in 1854 by the crew of the* North Star, *part of the fleet commanded by Belcher.*
BOTTOM *Eric Damkjar inspecting the monument erected by Sir Edward Belcher to commemorate all those who died searching to discover the fate of Franklin's expedition.*

island on a sketching trip. The mast, and a small section from the hull of the vessel, which lay flat on one of the lower beach ridges, were all that remained for Beattie and Damkjar to inspect.

Along one of the highest beach ridges was a series of recent markers and cairns dating from the 1950s to the 1970s. Also at the site: a memorial combining the monument left by Leopold M'Clintock in 1858 and a cenotaph erected by Belcher as a memorial to all those who died during the Franklin search.

Belcher, commanding a British naval fleet of five ships from 1852 to 1854, ordered that one of these ships, the *North Star*, under the command of William John Samuel Pullen, remain off Beechey Island as a base for the other vessels. Directly in front of the cenotaph, on a much lower ridge, is the skeleton of Northumberland House, the supply depot built by the crew of the *North Star* in 1854. It had been in a reasonable and useful state of repair even into the early 1900s, but no longer. Only parts of the wood walls were still visible, though a stone wall had held up quite well. Scattered in and around the structure were hundreds, possibly thousands, of artefacts from the structure itself and the food containers (primarily wooden barrel staves and metal barrel hoops) once housed inside. On 6 August 1927, when Banting and Jackson visited Northumberland House, significant damage had already been done to the structure, though Jackson noted in his journal that "there are a lot of water barrels, thirty or forty of them, that could be used today." Banting, however, also noted that "Bears had chewed holes in the side of some of the barrels, large enough to admit the head and neck so that they could get the last drop of the contents." Still, the scattered relics on Beechey Island do not attest to the hundreds of men, from various expeditions, who spent time at the site over the course of the searches of the early 1850s. Even on such a small island, their artefacts are lost among the forbidding landscape.

Peering off the south shore of the island during his survey, Beattie thought of the wreck of the *Breadalbane*, sent from England with fresh supplies for the ships under Belcher. Crushed in the

HMS Breadalbane *(left) and HMS* Phoenix *landing provisions at Cape Riley.*

ice, the *Breadalbane* sank off the island on 21 August 1853. In 1980, Canadian underwater explorer Dr. Joe MacInnis located the remains of the remarkably preserved ship under 330 feet (100 metres) of water and, in 1983, led a diving team to visit the wreck.

Returning to camp from his hike, Beattie saw that the wait for permissions was taking its toll on everyone's nerves. Feeling that the permissions would not be granted in time to complete the project that summer, Amy finally decided to return to Edmonton, where he had a number of pressing professional obligations. He left Beechey Island on 15 August.

At last, on 17 August, Beattie received a radio transmission from the Polar Shelf offices in Resolute giving permission to proceed with the exhumation, autopsy and reburial of John Torrington. Hearing the letters of permission read over the radio caused a great sense of relief and fuelled a new surge of energy and enthusiasm. The last letter also detailed the procedures to follow should contagious disease be detected in the Franklin crewmen. Everyone in the Arctic could have picked up the transmission and heard the Polar Shelf radio operator read in part: "If, in the course of the excavations, Dr. Beattie discovers any evidence of infectious disease in the artefacts or corpses exhumed, further digging should be discontinued."

Work on clearing off the last layer of ice and gravel began almost immediately, and the source of the noxious odour soon became apparent. It was not partly decomposed tissue, as had been expected, but rather the rotting blue wool fabric that covered the coffin.

As they reached the coffin lid, the wind picked up dramatically and a massive black thunder cloud moved over the site. The walls of the tent covering the excavation began to snap loudly, and, as the weather continued to worsen, the five researchers finally stopped their work and looked at one another. The conditions had suddenly become so strange that Kowal observed, "This is like something out of a horror film." Some of the crew were visibly nervous and Beattie decided to call a halt to work for the day. That night the wind howled continuously, rattling the sides of Beattie's tent all night and sometimes smacking its folds against his face, making sleep difficult. Ruszala, unable to sleep, stayed in one of the long-house tents. All were concerned about the stability of the tent that had been erected over Torrington's grave and, through the night, anxious heads would peer out of their tents to check on it. Towards morning, a violent gust slashed its way under the floorless tent, lifting it up and over the headboard before slamming it down on the adjacent beach ridge. Only a single rope held to its metal stake, preventing the tent from blowing into Erebus Bay. In the morning, the weather finally calmed and they dismantled the tent, remarkably only slightly damaged, and continued their excavation in the open.

Time was not a major consideration during the work, and, with continuous daylight, all soon lost track of the actual time of day. Eating when hungry, sleeping when tired, a natural rhythm developed, resulting in a work "day" stretching up to twenty-eight hours in length. The only reminders of the regimented, time-oriented

The tinned wrought iron plaque nailed to the lid of John Torrington's coffin. The inscription reads: "John Torrington died January 1st 1846 aged 20 years."

outside world were the daily 7 AM and 7 PM radio schedules with the Polar Shelf operators. During these broadcasts they would pass along weather information and messages and listen to the messages and weather reported in turn from the other Polar Shelf-supported camps strewn across the Arctic.

As the last layer of ice and gravel cemented to the top of the coffin was removed, Damkjar thought he could see something different in the texture of the fabric on the upper central portion of the lid. "Look at this," he said, while continuing the thawing and cleaning. "It looks like something is attached to the lid or maybe carved into it." Damkjar's slow and meticulous work eventually revealed a beautiful hand-painted plaque that had been securely nailed to the coffin lid. Roughly heart-shaped, with short, pointed extensions along its top and bottom edges, it was made of tinned wrought iron, perhaps part of a tin can, and looked as though it was hand-cut. It was painted dark blue-green and on it in white was a hand-painted inscription: "JOHN TORRINGTON DIED JANUARY 1ST 1846 AGED 20 YEARS."

The coffin containing John Torrington. The arrow points to true north.

The plaque was a touching last gesture made by Torrington's shipmates, and Damkjar spent a lot of time studying and sketching the discovery. Frozen for 138 years, the paint was showing signs of peeling, and rust had accumulated around its outer edges. The rust was carefully cleaned away and the plaque's surface lightly brushed with water to remove the accumulated crust of silt.

The coffin itself was also impressive. It was obviously well made and its mahogany lid and box had been individually covered by wool fabric dyed dark blue. White linen tape had been tacked to the lid and box in a geometric, military, yet decorative manner that contrasted with the personal nature of the plaque. Bolted to the sides of the coffin were brass handles, the one on the right still in the "up" position, and bolted to the foot- and head-ends were brass rings. But what was most remarkable was the size of the coffin—it appeared almost too small to contain an adult, though this may have been an optical illusion created by the box being in a narrow hole.

During the hours spent removing the permafrost adhering to the coffin, the researchers would occasionally tap on the lid, expecting to hear a hollow sound each time, but this was never the case. Rather, it was like striking a large block of marble, a strange sound given the circumstances. This result obviously meant a heavy mass was enclosed. It couldn't be just a body.

The removal of the lid was surprisingly difficult. It was very strongly secured to the box by a series of square shafted nails, and, as the researchers were soon to find out, it was "glued" down by ice within the coffin. The options for removing the lid were to pry it up, pull the nails or shear the nails at the junction of the lid with the box. Prying the lid would almost certainly destroy it: the wood was soft and delicate. For a similar reason, the team decided not to attempt to pull the nails out of the coffin. The best method, in Beattie's mind, was to shear the nails. He placed the chisel edge of a rock hammer against the lid/box junction at each nail location and struck the rock hammer inward with another hammer. The chisel head drove into and through the nail without damage to the coffin.

Finally, after all the nails had been sheared and the ice holding down the lid had thawed, Beattie took the foot-end and slowly lifted it up, revealing the shadowy contents of the coffin. A partially transparent block of ice lay within, and, through the frozen bubbles, cracks and planes in the ice, something—some form—

could be seen. But the more closely they looked, the more elusive the contents became.

This block of ice was the most serious obstacle yet. They had come to within inches of the body, only to be confronted with an apparently insurmountable obstacle. Work stopped while Beattie brooded over the next step. The options were few.

An aircraft engine preheater on the site, a noisy, temperamental and dangerous machine, could not be used to thaw the ice because hot air would put the biological matter and any artefacts enclosed at considerable risk. The outside air temperature was always at or slightly below freezing and in the grave lower still, so natural thawing was not a possibility. Chipping away the ice was not practical and probably impossible.

Ruszala suggested pouring water, some heated, some cold, onto the ice block. It worked better and faster than could have been hoped for. The researchers heated buckets of stream water on the camp stoves, lugged them bucket-brigade-style to the grave, then poured the water over the ice, from where it eventually ran out of the bottom join of the coffin onto the floor of the grave. The run-off was then scooped into a pail and dumped away from the gravesite. The team worked hard, spurred on by the knowledge that they would soon come face to face with a man from the Franklin expedition, and progress was swift.

The first part of Torrington to come into view was the front of his shirt, complete with mother-of-pearl buttons. Soon, his perfectly preserved toes gradually poked through the receding ice.

Most of the day was spent at this initial stage of exposure. All the while, the face remained shielded, covered by a fold of the same blue wool lain over the outside of the coffin. This created an eerie feeling among the researchers; it was almost as if Torrington was somehow aware of what was happening around him. But for artists' portraits and a few primitive photographs, who living today has ever seen the face of a person from the earlier part of the Victorian era, a person who took part in one of history's major expeditions of discovery? It would not be long before they were to gaze upon the face of this man from history.

Beattie was fascinated by the almost perfect preservation of the toes. The realization that a completely preserved human was attached to them had not yet sunk in. This was a strange period during their work: they were extremely close to a frozen sailor from 1846, and yet, they were concentrating so much on small details of thawing that the eventual exposure of the complete person was totally unexpected.

Arne Carlson was painstakingly thawing the section of coffin fabric covering the face area. Using a pair of large surgical tweezers, he pulled the material up carefully as it was freed by the melting ice. It was a difficult and meticulous task; as Carlson wanted to prevent any tearing of the material, he had to work hunched closely to it. Then suddenly, as he pulled gently upwards on the right edge of the material, the last curtain of ice gave way, freeing the material and revealing the face of Petty Officer John Torrington. Carlson gasped and sprang to his feet, allowing the fabric to fall back on Torrington's face. Pointing with the tweezers, Carlson said in a strangely calm voice: "He's there, he's right there!" The others quickly gathered at the graveside, and, while everyone peered at the fabric covering, Beattie pulled it back.

All stood, numb and silent. Nothing could have prepared them for the face of John Torrington, framed and cradled in his ice-coffin. Despite all the intervening years, the young man's life did not seem far away; in many ways it was as if Torrington had just died.

It was a shattering moment for Beattie, who felt an empathy for this man and a sadness for his passing—and as if he were standing at a precipice looking across a terrifying gulf into a very different world from our own. He was a witness to a tragedy, yet he had to remind himself that the tragedy belonged to another time.

The sky on the day of the autopsy was overcast, the grey clouds merging with the grey waters of Erebus Bay. The temperature was

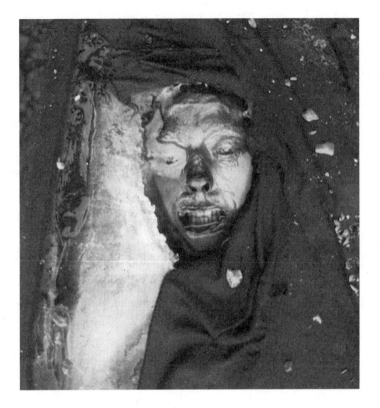

*The first photograph of John Torrington, taken moments
after the wool coffin covering was pulled back.*

30°F (-1°C), the wind a steady 12 miles per hour (20 km/h) from
the south. Standing at the graveside and looking into the coffin, the
gloom seemed to be reflected in Torrington's simple grey linen
trousers and his white shirt with closely spaced thin blue stripes.
The shirt had a high collar and was pleated from the waist down-
wards, where it was tucked into the trousers. Under Torrington's
chin and over the top of his medium-brown hair was tied his kerchief, made of white cotton and covered in large blue polka dots.

John Torrington looked anything but grotesque. The expres-
sion on his thin face, with its pouting mouth and half-closed eyes

gazing through delicate, light-brown eyelashes, was peaceful. His nose and forehead, in contrast to the natural skin colour of the rest of his face, were darkened by contact with the blue-wool coffin covering. This shadowed the face, accentuating the softness of its appearance. The tragedy of Torrington's young death was as apparent to the researchers as it must have been to his shipmates 138 years before.

Torrington would have stood 5 feet 4 inches (163 cm) tall. His arms were straight, with the hands resting palm down on the fronts of his thighs, held in position by strips of cotton binding. These bindings were located at his elbows, hands, ankles and big toes. Their purpose was to hold the limbs together during the preparation of the body for burial. It was discovered later that his body lay on a bed of wood shavings, scattered along the bottom of the coffin, with his head supported by a thicker matting of shavings. He wore no shoes or boots, and there were no other personal belongings beyond his clothing.

Yet by far the strongest and most vivid memory Beattie has of this remarkable event centres not around the final thawing of Torrington's body in the coffin, but on the lifting of the body out of

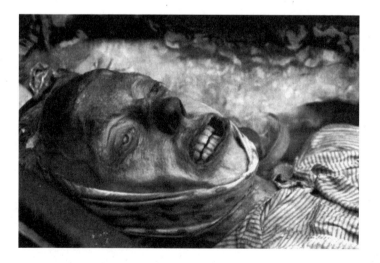

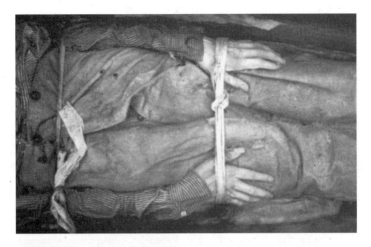

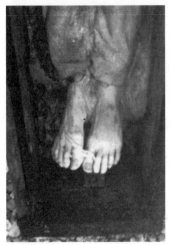

ABOVE & BOTTOM *John Torrington: The body was bound with strips of cotton to hold the limbs together during preparation for burial.*

OPPOSITE *The dark stain on his forehead and nose marks where his face came into contact with the blue-wool coffin covering, which was folded inside the coffin lid.*

the grave in preparation for autopsy. It was a remarkable and highly emotional experience, with Carlson holding and supporting Torrington's legs, Beattie his shoulders and head. He was very light, weighing less than 88 pounds (40 kg), and as they moved him his head lolled onto Beattie's left shoulder; Beattie looked directly into Torrington's half-opened eyes, only a few inches from his own. There was no rigidity of his body, and rigor mortis would have disappeared within hours of his death. Although his arms and legs were tightly bound, he was completely limp, causing Beattie to comment, "It's as if he's just unconscious."

The two men carefully lowered Torrington to the ground outside the grave. There he lay, exposed to the Arctic sky for the first time in 138 years. If he had miraculously stirred to consciousness after his long sleep, Torrington would have thought that he had missed just two changes of season—a sleep of but eight months.

The bindings were removed and the body undressed. Away from the reality of the research project, an observer might suggest that the undressing of the body was an indignity to Torrington. But given the situation, both the need for medical evidence as to the fate of Franklin's expedition and the team's own feelings, which were very personal and intense, no indignity could exist.

Looking at Torrington lying naked on the autopsy tarpaulin, Beattie saw for the first time the condition of the young sailor and was shocked by the emaciated appearance of the body. All wondered aloud at what could have been the cause. Had he died of starvation? Was he suffering from some serious disease that had robbed him of his physical strength? It was immediately evident that foul play was unlikely; what they saw was a young man who had been extremely ill when he died. Of course, Torrington's emaciated appearance was to a small extent due to the loss of moisture that occurs over a prolonged period of freezing, and in that sense, the preservation of the body could not be described as perfect. But every rib in the body was visible. And later, during the autopsy, no fat would be found, confirming that the weight loss before death was real and significant.

His hands, which Beattie commented "look like they are still warm," were extremely long, delicate and smooth, "like you would expect a pianist's to be." There were no calluses on the palms or fingers, which would have been expected on an active participant in the expedition. Torrington had been the leading stoker on the

Terror, and his hands would normally have shown evidence of his work if he had been recently active. Yet there was none, and for that reason Beattie was convinced he must have been too ill to work for some time before he died. Also, his nails were quite clean and he had recently been given a haircut, either in preparation for his burial or perhaps in the period just before his death.

The first part of the examination was a meticulous search for external signs of the cause or causes of death (wounds, markings, disease) or of medical treatment (signs of medicinal bleeding). None was found except for the deep and discoloured marks on the elbows, hands and ankles made by the cotton bindings. Then Beattie conducted a standard autopsy. Tissue, organ, bone, fingernail and hair samples were taken for analysis by Roger Amy at his laboratory at the University of Alberta.

The autopsy took more than four hours to complete. Beattie and Carlson wore surgical aprons, their hands double gloved with rubber surgical gloves. The procedure involved making a Y-shaped incision in the chest and abdomen, retracting the skin and musculature, the temporary removal of the front portion of the rib cage and exposure of the thoracic and abdominal organs. Yet when the autopsy began, all internal structures were completely frozen. It was necessary to thaw each organ with water before samples could be collected. Using a scalpel, .3–.7 ounces (10–20 grams) of tissue were then collected from each organ. Carlson and Damkjar prepared and marked the sample containers with identification information and numbers. A preservative was poured in them and Beattie dropped each collected sample in the appropriate container, which was then sealed. Damkjar also took pictures of the various stages of the autopsy while Kowal took notes dictated to him by Beattie. One of the most difficult aspects of the whole procedure was keeping their hands warm, and one bucket of hot water was kept nearby so that Beattie and Carlson could immerse their hands in it.

From the beginning, Beattie could see features that could be of medical importance. The lungs, when exposed, appeared completely blackened and were attached abnormally in a number of locations to the chest wall by a series of adhesions (scar tissue). Torrington's heart also appeared abnormal. No food could be found in the stomach or bowel.

Torrington's right thumbnail was collected, as were samples of his hair, rib bone and radius bone. These would be subjected to various forms of analysis in later months in an attempt to construct a diary of his health during the time he spent on the expedition prior to his death, as well as a short period of time prior to the expedition.

A difficult but necessary procedure during an autopsy is the exposure of the brain. With a surgical hand saw, and with assistance from Carlson and Damkjar, Beattie removed the skull cap and collected samples of brain tissue and made observations of the brain anatomy. All of the samples collected and observations made would be pieced together later after Amy's analysis of the data and microscopic evidence from the samples.

During the autopsy, Beattie saw that, even though preservation of the body was excellent, post-mortem degenerative changes in the structure of the tissues had taken place. Later, Amy would confirm that the microscopic details showed that virtually all cellular structures were badly or completely damaged. The brain had also shrunk, as had some of the other organs, to about two-thirds' normal size, and had completely autolyzed (the cells had been destroyed by their own enzymes). Beattie would later be approached a number of times by people with the idea that perhaps one day in the future, Torrington could have been revived by some elixir or as yet unimagined technology, but the evidence of massive cellular damage found in every organ precluded this possibility.

Throughout the autopsy, Beattie kept Torrington's face covered; somehow, this gave the reassurance that his privacy was maintained, illustrating how strongly the face is perceived as the window of the soul and the reflection of our identity.

After the autopsy, Torrington was re-dressed, lifted back into his grave and into the coffin. After carefully positioning the body, the lid was then replaced. Water would soon begin to fill the grave again and freeze, ensuring Torrington's lasting preservation. Ruszala placed a note in the grave, giving the names of the seven researchers and a description of their feelings and purpose at the site. It was a private offering to John Torrington that, along with his body, would quite likely outlast all of the team's own physical remains after their deaths. The group then quietly gathered together at Ruszala's suggestion, for silent prayers and some individual thoughts, before John Torrington was again assigned to the frozen depths, maybe this time forever. For these moments, Beattie contemplated Torrington's life and the events of late 1845 and early 1846, then the events of his own life in the summer of 1984, and how the years separating the two had somehow vanished.

After filling in the grave, Beattie stopped to peer down the beach towards Erebus Bay. It was almost possible to see the two ships held in the ice just offshore, Franklin's men moving ghost-like in small groups on the ice and across the island. The crews would have paused for John Torrington on those bitter January days of 1846, but none could have guessed what horror his death foretold. Their adventure was young and the Northwest Passage, which had long haunted men, beckoned somewhere across the icy waters to the west.

The Face of

DEATH

THE ARCTIC SUMMER of 1984 was nearing an end. Although the weather had been generally good (except for the occasional light dusting of snow), the warmth of the summer sun was lost towards the close of August and the nights had turned cold. As each day brought winter closer, nightfall gradually crept into the twenty-four-hour light of the Arctic summer, and a generator had to be used to power a photoflood lamp inside the cook tent in the evenings.

The weather became so unpredictable that, if the team had radioed for an airplane from Resolute to come for them, the half-hour required to fly that distance could have seen a complete change in weather. A simple change in wind direction or a quickly dropping cloud ceiling would also have made a landing on Beechey Island impossible.

Beattie had originally hoped to uncover all three of the Franklin expedition graves on the island that summer, but, worried about the weather and drained by the experience of exhuming John Torrington, his thoughts turned instead towards the laboratory work that awaited him in Edmonton. Three days had been spent on Torrington's final exhumation and autopsy and the scientific team was exhausted, physically and emotionally. Beattie wanted to pack it in for the season, as did the others. Just one radio call to the Polar Shelf and they could be away from the island. But something had bothered Beattie and the others about the appearance of Hartnell's grave. Before completing the autopsy on John Torrington, Walt Kowal had begun to dig into the permafrost covering John Hartnell.

A close inspection of the graves of John Hartnell and William Braine soon revealed that their construction by the crew of the *Erebus* had been very similar, if not identical. But they were no longer so: it was clear that Hartnell's grave had been disturbed at some point in the 138 years since his death. The large limestone slabs, once part of a grave structure like Braine's, which has an almost crypt-like appearance, had been simply piled on top of the burial place, as if they had been lifted away and later hastily replaced. Inspecting the surface of the grave and looking closely into the nooks and pockets produced by the large rocks, the researchers found small fragments of wood and some tiny scraps of blue material similar to that which covered Torrington's coffin. Beattie had no idea when the grave had been disturbed. The team discussed the situation, as well as the difficulty of completing an autopsy on Hartnell within the time remaining. If there had been one or more previous openings of the grave, they would have to take great care in gathering evidence—and the time required for this could be considerable. Beattie decided to look for clues that might explain the history of the damage and determine the state of preservation, but to conduct the autopsy another year.

Before the excavation of Hartnell's grave was complete, Beattie visited a site that would add important insights into his research. Located nearly ⅔ mile (1 km) north of the gravesite, at the narrowest point of the island near the spit, is a large oval mound with a

The grave of 25-year-old John Hartnell.

central depression filled with the fragments of hundreds of rusted and disintegrating food tins from Franklin's expedition. When this location was discovered in August 1850, searchers found a neat arrangement of 700 or more tins piled "like shot" into low pyramids about 1½ feet (.5 metre) high. The tins were empty of food and had been filled with gravel. The reason for the "cairn," as it was described, is not clear. But not wanting to miss any possible clue left behind by Franklin's people, the searchers of 1850 thoroughly investigated each of the tins, dumping out the gravel. Literally leaving no stone unturned, they also dug into the ground underneath the tins with the hope of finding a buried document. It is this excavation that produced the oval mound and depression that mark the site today.

There has been much debate about the significance of these tins. It was thought that the "cairn" was evidence of problems with the preserved food. Certainly, by the 1850s, Stephan Goldner, who had supplied the Franklin expedition, was encountering problems with the quality of the tinned foods he delivered to later expeditions. And more than one of the searchers in the 1850s observed that a number of the tins at Beechey Island had bulging ends, evidence that some of the food had putrefied. Still, one searcher, Peter Sutherland, wrote that the tins "were carefully examined without anything being discovered that could lead to the remotest idea that the preserved meat which they contained had been in an unsound state." And one twentieth-century historian has argued that the number of tins present at the site was not in excess of what was expected to have been used by the expedition during their stay on Beechey Island. In other words, there was no evidence for large quantities of bad food being dumped on the island.

Beattie had seen photographs of food tins from various British Arctic expeditions and had handled a few, but as he picked through the tins from Franklin's expedition, he saw that they were different. The lead soldering was thick and sloppily done, and had dripped like melted candle wax down the inside surface of the tins. Beattie wondered if this could be the source of the lead in the Booth Point skeleton and in the human remains collected elsewhere on King William Island. This idea became more credible to him as each piece of tin he picked up demonstrated the same degree of internal contamination from the solder. Samples were collected for further examination and plans made to return for a comprehensive study of the site.

Meanwhile, Kowal was finding the excavation of Hartnell's grave much more difficult than had been experienced with Torrington. The permafrost was harder and more consolidated than was encountered in the other grave, and he constantly commented on this difference. The increased difficulty in the pick and shovel work hinted that the grave had been disturbed, then refrozen. As digging continued, more fragments of wood and blue material were pulled from the grave fill itself, reinforcing Beattie's view that the previous disturbance had been considerable and may have involved the exposure of the coffin, and probably Hartnell's body as well.

Shortly, Kowal announced that he had found the foot-end of the coffin. To everyone's surprise it was not deeply buried, only

33 inches (85 cm) into the ground. They had expected a burial at least as deep as Torrington's.

The white tape decoration on it was in poor condition, and, as Kowal continued to clear the permafrost from the top of the lid, he uncovered other areas of damage. "Someone sure did a number on this grave," he said, as he finished exposing the lid. The right-hand side at the forearm level had been smashed through, leaving a gaping hole. It was possible to identify each blow of the pickaxe that had done the damage. A large rectangular piece of the blue fabric adjacent to the hole was missing. The lid, originally nailed to the coffin, was slightly ajar, the nails having either been removed or broken. There was no doubt that the coffin had been exposed and opened before. The condition of the white fabric tape decoration was in stark contrast to the symmetrical dignity of Torrington's coffin, and Beattie was shocked by the damage, which at first appeared to have been caused by a wanton act of vandalism. But as work continued it became obvious that, though there had been considerable damage done during the previous excavation, it was not the work of vandals or pot hunters. The lid had been replaced and the nails appeared to have been carefully removed. Vandals would have simply pried the lid off the coffin, causing major structural damage.

Beattie jumped into the grave and bent over the hole in the lid. Pulling some of the gravel out of the hole, he said, "Look at this— Hartnell's shirt!" A small piece of fabric, nearly identical in design to John Torrington's shirt, had come free from the ice. The fabric, obviously part of the right shirt sleeve, was torn, and the thought entered Beattie's mind that, if the clothing had been damaged in the area of the hole in the lid, perhaps there was damage to Hartnell's body as well.

Unlike Torrington's, there was no plaque on the lid of Hartnell's coffin, and Beattie believed the plaque was removed by the people who had exposed the coffin. A close inspection of the wood in the area where a plaque would have been fixed did not reveal any nail holes, though it is possible they could have closed since the

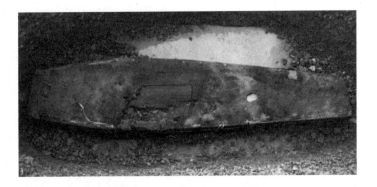

John Hartnell's coffin, damaged in 1852 when his body
was exhumed by Commander Inglefield and Dr. Sutherland.

time of the plaque's removal. A less satisfactory interpretation was that, being an able seaman, Hartnell did not warrant a plaque. But considering that his messmates (including his younger brother Thomas) would normally have been responsible for the preparation of a plaque, it seemed likely there had been one. Not only had Hartnell been buried at only a little more than half the depth of John Torrington, the coffin also did not seem to be aligned with the headboard. As the researchers intended to expose no more than the coffin lid, an assessment of the damage to the rest of the coffin would have to wait until their planned return.

When Kowal lifted the coffin lid on 23 August, everyone was crouched round the graveside. Inside Hartnell's coffin there was again a solid block of ice. "There is no doubt that he will be as well preserved as Torrington," Beattie said. However, unspoken was a fear that Hartnell's body, as well as the coffin, had been damaged. There was only one way to confirm these fears.

Exhumed, John Torrington was a frail, innocent-looking young man. He did not fit the image of a sea-toughened sailor and adventurer, but simply of a young man who died too soon. Because of this, not one of the scientists was prepared for what awaited them a few inches below the ice in Hartnell's coffin.

Kowal poured water over Hartnell's face area and soon spotted the outline of a nose through the receding ice. While John Torrington's face had been slightly discoloured by contact with the coffin covering and by exposure to a pocket of air, Hartnell's nose appeared natural in colour. Gradually, Kowal could see a ghostly image taking shape through the ice—a frightening, shimmering face of death.

"This guy is spooky," Kowal said while continuing the exposure of Hartnell, "the quintessential pirate. This guy is frightening."

The others watched in silence as the face was finally completely exposed. Perhaps the emotional drain of their work with Torrington was only now taking its toll. As with Torrington, they were shaken by the second face that was emerging from the rock-hard ground of the island. Shaken, but in a different way.

Whereas Torrington had embodied a youthful, tragic innocence, John Hartnell reflected the harsh realities of death and suffering in the Arctic: his was the face of a sea-hardened nineteenth-century sailor. His right eye socket appeared empty and his lips were rigidly pursed, as if he were shouting his rage at dying so early in his adventure. John Hartnell's last thoughts and the intensity of the pain he suffered during those final moments of life had been captured—literally frozen—on his face.

His features were tightly framed by a cap, a shroud drawn up under his red-bearded chin and the contours of melting ice on either side. A lock of dark hair could be seen below the rim of the cap; unlike the right, his left eye appeared normal. "I wonder why there is such a difference in the preservation of the eyes," Beattie mumbled, as each took a turn to examine Hartnell. "Was the eye injured before his death? Was it diseased?" Answers to the countless questions would have to await their planned return to Beechey Island.

Besides the face, only the clothing covering the right forearm was exposed. The body had been covered in a shroud, or sheet. A portion of the shroud and the underlying shirt sleeve of his right arm had been torn by the pickaxe used during the original exhuma-

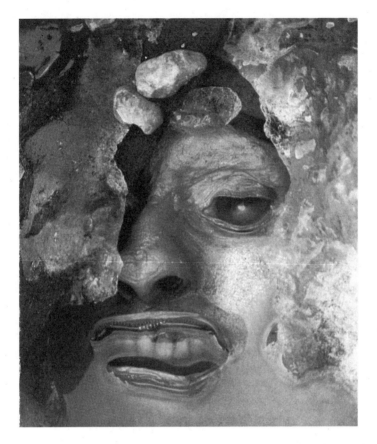

The first view of John Hartnell.

tion. There also appeared to be damage to the arm itself. The total time of Hartnell's exposure was close to twelve hours.

Later, back in the labs and libraries of Edmonton, Beattie would begin piecing together a solution to the mystery of Hartnell's disturbance. Sir Edward Belcher was the first to dig into the graves in October 1852, but, discouraged by the resistant permafrost, his men gave up after excavating only a few inches. A month later, members of a privately funded search expedition exhumed Hartnell. The leader of the expedition was Commander

Edward A. Inglefield, and he was accompanied by Dr. Peter Sutherland, who had suggested such an exhumation while serving with Captain William Penny's search expedition two years earlier. Inglefield's Arctic exploits were considerable and, in 1853, he was awarded the Royal Geographical Society's Arctic medal. During the award speech, Sir Roderick Murchison (head of the society) described the exhumation. The transcript of the speech reflects a number of errors and embellishments:

> . . . Commander Inglefield, being in a private expedition, resolved to dig down into the frozen ground, for the purpose of ascertaining the condition in which the men had been interred. The opening out of one coffin quite realized the object he had in view, for at six feet [1.8 metres] beneath the surface, a depth reached only with great difficulty, by penetrating frozen ground as hard as a rock, a coffin, with the name of Wm. Heartwell, was found in as perfect order as if recently deposited in the churchyard of an English village. Every button and ornament had been neatly arranged, and what was most important, the body, perfectly preserved by the intense cold, exhibited no trace of scurvy, or other malignant disease, but was manifestly that of a person who had died of consumption, a malady to which it was further known that the deceased was prone.

Inglefield's expedition was one of those supported by Lady Franklin. With a crew of seventeen on board the screw schooner *Isabel*, they were at Beechey Island on 7 September 1852. In his published journal, Inglefield described his first sight of the graves:

> That sad emblem of mortality—the grave—soon met my eye, as we plunged along through the knee-deep snow which covered the island. The last resting place of three of Franklin's people was closely examined; but nothing that had not hitherto been observed could we detect. My companion told me that a huge bear was seen continually sitting on one of the graves keeping a silent vigil over the dead.

Inglefield did not describe the exhumation of Hartnell in this journal, but there is a blank period in it covering the time between
when he and Sutherland finished dining with the officers of the
North Star and the departure of the *Isabel* from Beechey Island
shortly after midnight " . . . with as beautiful a moon to light our
path as ever shone on the favoured shores of our own native land."
An unpublished letter written by Inglefield to Rear-Admiral Sir
Francis Beaufort on 14 September 1852, fills in this gap:

> My doctor assisted me, and I have had my hand on the arm and
> face of poor Hartnell. He was decently clad in a cotton shirt, and
> though the dark night precluded our seeing, still our touch de-
> tected that a wasting illness was the cause of dissolution. It was a
> curious and solemn scene on the silent snow-covered sides of the
> famed Beechey Island, where the two of us stood at midnight.
> The pale moon looking down upon us as we silently worked with
> pickaxe and shovel at the hard-frozen tomb, each blow sending a
> spur of red sparks from the grave where rested the messmate of
> our lost countrymen. No trace but a piece of fearnought half
> down the coffin lid could we find. I carefully restored everything
> to its place and only brought away with me the plate that was
> nailed on the coffin lid and a scrap of the cloth with which the
> coffin was covered.

A remarkable letter and, as the 1984 research showed, accurate in
its description of what had happened, even down to the removal of
the piece of fabric. This was all the evidence that was needed to explain the history of the grave's disturbance, the cause of the damage and the mystery of the missing plaque and fabric.

Another letter written by Inglefield on 14 September, this one
to John Barrow Jr. at the Admiralty, differs from that to Beaufort,
explaining that he had engaged not just Sutherland but six officers
in the work, concealing the exhumation from his able seamen as
he was wary of "the superstitions feelings of the sailors." Most
notably, where the letter to Beaufort professes detection of a

"wasting illness" as Hartnell's cause of death, Inglefield's letter to Barrow is equivocal:

> I was most anxious to have examined the body that the cause of death might be ascertained, but our utmost efforts had been exhausted and to lay bare the middle of it to take off the copper plate that was nailed on the lid and to discover that no relic had been laid with him that could give a clue to the fate of his fellows was all our strength and the intense cold that had set in with midnight permitted our doing.

Inglefield ends his letter to Barrow with a request for his discretion on the subject, "as the prejudices of some people would deem this intended work of charity sacrilege." There can be no doubt, when their activities of that day are plotted out, that Inglefield would have been at the gravesite for only three or four hours prior to midnight, the appointed time for the *Isabel* to set sail, though he reported it was actually 1 AM when they got on board.

By this stage in the 1984 field season, there was no hope that the medical investigations of Hartnell and William Braine could be completed. It was obvious the scientific team would have to return to the Arctic island again to complete the research.

After photographs were taken of Hartnell, they began reconstructing the coffin and the gravesite. The lid was replaced on the coffin in the slightly askew position in which it had been discovered. A thin layer of gravel was lightly shovelled over the lid, and, in anticipation of their return to the site, a bright orange tarpaulin was placed over the gravel-covered coffin. Standing around the grave, shovels in hand, they remarked on how garish the fluorescent tarp looked in contrast to the grey surroundings of the quiet grave. "There will be no trouble in locating the coffin next year with that protecting it," Kowal said.

With the reconstruction of the surface features of Hartnell's grave complete, the crew readied to leave the island. The plane would come for them in two days—plenty of time to pack, clean the site and do some more exploring. It was also a time to take in all that they had experienced. Kowal and Ruszala left for a 22-mile (35-km) hike to Cape Riley and back, while Damkjar and Carlson headed up onto the headland of the island.

Beattie spent the time alone, staring out at Erebus Bay. He remembered an account he had read about an earlier visit to Beechey Island, a visit made by the explorer Roald Amundsen in August 1903. Amundsen, on his attempt to sail the Northwest Passage, had stopped at Beechey Island to pay tribute to Franklin. Amundsen later wrote in his narrative, *The North West Passage,* that he experienced a "deep, solemn feeling that I was on holy ground." He imagined the bustle of activity that had transpired as the *Erebus* and *Terror* prepared to winter here, and also pondered the causes of the deaths so early on in the expedition: "The dark outlines of crosses marking graves inland are silent witnesses before my eyes as I sit here. The spectre of scurvy showed itself for the first time, and claimed, if not many, yet several lives." Amundsen's party then "re-erected the only gravestone that had fallen down." With his small vessel *Gjoa* anchored in Erebus Bay, Amundsen grappled with the decision of what route to take. He made the correct one, becoming the first man to successfully sail the elusive passage, though he wrote of the Franklin expedition: "Let us raise a monument to them, more enduring than stone: the recognition that they were the first discoverers of the Passage." As Beattie reflected back on his summer's experience, he did so with a growing feeling that the very freshness of the Franklin sailors' bodies guaranteed the success of his own expedition. Little doubt remained that important new insights into the fate of Franklin and his crews would surface during the months of laboratory work ahead.

The team's final day on Beechey Island, 26 August 1984, was warm and sunny. The tents came down quickly and the gear was carried down by the graves. The gravel in the camping area was smoothed over and some final bits of paper picked up. Beattie then radioed the Polar Shelf base manager in Resolute Bay, and the plane departed to pick them up. Some final photographs were taken of the site and they set up a tripod to take a group picture. As they were doing this they could just make out the sound of a plane to the west. In the Arctic, there is a sixth sense about airplanes: people will suddenly look up and say, "There's a plane," and everyone will stop what they are doing and listen intently. Usually nothing is heard, but no one doubts that an aircraft is coming. Within a few brief seconds, the unmistakable sound of the engine is heard by all.

Soon a Twin Otter hissed by overhead. Everyone waved, the cameras came out and all watched as the plane made one pass, then circled and landed.

Sitting on the left side of the plane, Beattie looked out at the graves. During the previous two weeks, he had taken hundreds of photographs of all three and had looked into two of them, yet he felt strangely compelled to take one more photograph through the fogged and scratched window and spinning propeller of the Twin Otter. After pressing the shutter, and before he could wind the camera for a second picture, the plane began to roll. And with a roar and two jarring bumps, the plane was up and away. Seconds later, they were out over Union Bay, turning towards Cornwallis Island, visible to the west. Within forty-five minutes they were all sitting in the eating area of the Polar Shelf facilities in Resolute Bay, sipping coffee and eating a splendid home-cooked meal the staff had put aside for them. The security and hospitality of the Polar Shelf in Resolute was in marked contrast to the small campsite that had been their home. Already, the emotions attached to Beechey Island were fading. Priorities now turned to showers, laundry and news of the outside world. The jet from the south would arrive the next day, and that meant going home. The season had been a success, but still more exciting discoveries awaited them in their laboratories in Edmonton.

— I3 —

The Evidence

MOUNTS

E ssentially, the body of John Torrington was that of a
mummy. What made it so different from mummies recovered
from other archaeological sites in the world, however, was the
amazing quality of preservation.

When archaeologist Howard Carter opened the three coffins of
the Egyptian pharaoh Tutankhamen in the Valley of the Kings,
he found the monarch's body in a very bad state of preservation.
Dr. Douglas Derry, the anatomist who examined Tutankhamen's
mummy, wrote a detailed report describing the charred and discoloured remains. The report outlined the damage done through
the embalming process and through time: "the skin of the face is of
a greyish colour and is very cracked and brittle . . . the limbs appeared very shrunken and attenuated."

Even mummies better preserved than Tutankhamen, whether
embalmed in preparation for burial or intentionally desiccated by
exposure to sun or air, have still suffered major alteration to the appearance, colour and detail of their soft tissues.

Of course, the nature of burial can, on rare occasions, result in the unintentional whole or partial preservation of an individual. Some of the best-preserved human remains from antiquity have been found in peat bogs in several locations in northwestern Europe. In some cases the acids of peat bogs have kept human bodies largely intact not for hundreds but for thousands of years. But those same acids badly discoloured the "bog people," as they are known, leaving skin "as if poured in tar" and hair bright red, and helping to decalcify the bones. Another natural means of preservation can result from cold temperatures and lack of moisture. In 1972, 500-year-old mummified human remains, including that of a child, were discovered at Qilakitsoq, Greenland. All of these mummies, however, were rigid and inflexible, the drying and hardening of the tissues having locked the body forever into the position in which it was buried.

Undoubtedly the most amazing aspect of the Beechey Island research was the discovery of the near-perfect preservation of soft tissue. In effect, the unbroken period of freezing from early 1846 to 1984 suspended any major outward appearances of decay, allowing John Torrington to look very much as he had in life, right down to the flexibility of the tissue. Even when samples of Torrington's tissues were studied by microscope, some of them looked recent in origin. Other clues, however, did reflect the lengthy period of freezing. Details of internal cellular structure were commonly missing, and in most tissues the cells were also partly collapsed. Preservation seemed also to vary within the individual. For example, microscope slides made from bowel samples collected from Torrington appeared as if they were taken right out of a textbook on modern human histology or pathology, while slides made from his other organs showed considerable post-mortem change and loss of detail.

Still, Torrington's condition was highly unusual, even for a body preserved in ice. Normally, the fats in the organs and muscles of humans or animal cadavers (whether encased in ice, submerged in water or located in a high-humidity environment) are transformed into adipocere, the so-called "fat wax" or "grave wax." This ivory-white-coloured adipocere has a soapy, cheese-like consistency and a pungent, pervasive and unforgettable smell. While the superficial shape of the organ is maintained under the right conditions, over decades the adipocere changes, ending with desiccation as a firm, though crumbly, body mass, without internal structure. However, Torrington displayed a totally different morphology.

Equally intriguing, a similar level of preservation was later observed in the 5,300-year-old iceman found in the Otztal Glacier of the Italian Alps in 1991. And in meetings and discussions between Beattie and Dr. Konrad Spindler of the University of Innsbruck, the lead investigator of the Tyrolean iceman project, it was verified that there is a relationship between the mummification process and the temperature at which the bodies are stored. As Spindler wrote of his discovery: "Transformation into fat wax takes place at temperatures around 0°C [32°F]; mummification with gradual dehydration, on the other hand, occurs at lower temperatures, from about five degrees below zero on, in which case permafrost conditions represent the decisive requirements."

LABORATORY RESULTS of the autopsy on John Torrington painted a picture of a young man wracked with serious medical problems. Unfortunately, despite careful study of the organ samples by Roger Amy at the University Hospital in Edmonton, a specific cause of death could not be established.

What was most obvious at the time of the autopsy were Torrington's blackened lungs, a condition called anthracosis—caused by the inhalation of atmospheric pollutants such as tobacco and coal smoke and dust. Also, his lungs were bound to the chest wall by adhesions, a sign of previous lung disease. Microscopically visible destruction of lung tissue identified emphysema, a lung disease normally associated with much older individuals; evidence of tuberculosis was also seen. Amy's interpretation of the adhesions, and of the presence of fluid in the lung associated with pneumonic infection, suggested to him that pneumonia was probably the ultimate cause of death.

However, it was in the trace element analysis of bone and hair from Torrington that the probable underlying cause of death was found. Atomic absorption analysis of Torrington's bone indicated an elevated amount of lead of 110–151 parts per million (the modern average ranges from 5–14 parts per million). Although not as high as those found in the Franklin crewman from Booth Point, the level of bone lead was still many times higher than normal. Torrington would have suffered severe mental and physical problems caused by lead poisoning and, so weakened, finally succumbed to pneumonia. (One theory as to why the Booth Point skeleton had greater lead contamination is that the Franklin sailor found in 1981 lived more than two years longer than John Torrington, and was thus exposed to lead on the expedition for a longer period.)

Most vital to Beattie's investigation, however, were the results of a trace level analysis conducted on hair. (Four-inch-/10-cm-long strands of hair from the nape of Torrington's neck had been submitted for laboratory analysis to determine if Torrington had been exposed to large amounts of lead. The hair was long enough to show levels of lead ingestion throughout the first eight months of the Franklin expedition.) For Beattie was astounded by the results of the carefully controlled test. Lead levels in the hair exceeded 600 parts per million, levels indicating acute lead poisoning. Only over the last inch or so did the level of exposure drop, and then only slightly. This would have been due to a drop in the consumption of food during the last four to eight weeks of Torrington's life, when he was seriously ill.

By combining information gathered from the manner of Torrington's burial, the new information about his physical condition and illnesses and period accounts of similar burial services conducted in the Arctic, it was now possible for Beattie and his research colleagues to re-create Torrington's final days, death and burial with some accuracy.

There is no question that during the last couple of weeks of life, John Torrington would have known his time had almost come. Beattie's studies revealed that the petty officer's health had never been good, but in late December 1845, it was different. John Torrington was dying. He had boarded the *Terror* eight months earlier, doubtless filled with high hopes. He must have been outwardly healthy when the expedition made its last contact with whaling vessels in late July and early August, or he would have been sent home. Indeed, sickness seems to have struck in September, about the same time that Franklin's two ships anchored for the winter some 660 feet (200 metres) off the northeast section of Beechey Island.

It was a slow-moving and lingering illness. The early symptoms of the deadly combination of emphysema and tuberculosis with lead poisoning would have included loss of appetite, irritability, lack of concentration, shortness of breath and fatigue. Torrington probably continued to work until mid- to late-November, when he would have been sent to the sick bay. The lack of any bed sores on his body shows that during much of December, on the advice of the ship's physician, Torrington would have taken slow walks below deck several times a day. There he could talk with friends and, from time to time, before the illness became acute, look out through the gloom of the Arctic winter at the barren, snowswept rock of Beechey Island.

Torrington's physical condition would have worsened dramatically over Christmas. His behaviour would have grown unpredictable, with dramatic mood swings that must have caused grave concern to surgeons Alexander Macdonald and John Peddie. For there was no way that these men, with the knowledge and equipment of their time, could have known the true nature of his illness. All they would have been able to do for Torrington through most of the course of his disease was to keep him well-fed, likely relying more heavily on tinned provisions as the preferred food. Yet, despite their attention, his weight would have continued slowly dropping to the point of malnutrition. Then, probably during the last days of 1845, Torrington developed pneumonia, a serious blow considering his already diminished state of health. He would never again look out into the Arctic night.

Sometime in the days immediately preceding death, Torrington would have given his few possessions to someone who would promise to return them to his father and stepmother when the expedition had sailed through the Northwest Passage into the Bering Strait and returned triumphantly to England. Towards the end, the twenty-year-old sailor would have fallen into a delerium, then suffered a series of convulsions before dying on New Year's Day.

News of the expedition's first loss would likely have spread quickly through the crew of the *Terror,* and the surgeon would have notified Captain Francis Crozier. Within minutes, the men of the *Erebus,* including Franklin, would have been informed of John Torrington's death. The surgeons probably debated the cause, going over the protracted and progressive nature of his disease before concluding it was pneumonia complicated by a history of tuberculosis. There was no call for an autopsy. Torrington's body was then carefully cleaned and groomed below deck, where the temperature probably hovered continually around 50°F (10°C). It was 1 January, and his death surely cast a shadow over any New Year celebrations.

After Torrington's body was washed, he was dressed in his shirt and trousers. The two surgeons took care in binding his limbs to his body: one of them wrapped a cotton strip round the body and arms at the level of the elbow, tying a bow at the front; the other quickly tied cotton strips round the big toes, ankles and thighs.

Above deck, where the ship had been draped with a canvas cover to keep out the snow and some of the cold (the temperature would still be around 14°F/-10°C), the carpenter Thomas Honey and his mate Alexander Wilson began carefully constructing the coffin, Macdonald having provided them with Torrington's measurements. They used a stock timber, mahogany, measuring ¾ inch (1.9 cm) thick by 12 inches (30 cm) wide. The lid and coffin bottom were each constructed of three pieces: a long central piece with shaped sections attached by dowels to each side. The box was constructed of the same type of wood; the curves at the shoulder produced by kerfing (a series of parallel cuts made across the inside width of the board, allowing it to be bent without breaking). Square iron nails were used to secure these sections together.

The coffin lid and box were then carefully wrapped in navy blue wool material, held in place by narrow white ribbons nailed to the coffin and outlining its contours. Torrington's messmates had taken great care in preparing the labelled metal plaque that was to be attached to the outside of the coffin lid. Another task of the carpenters, under the direction of one of *Terror*'s lieutenants, was the preparation of an inscribed headboard.

Carrying picks and shovels, a small group of seamen from the *Terror* then walked from the ship to a location on the island just up-slope from the armourer's forge. Here, they used their feet and shovels to sweep away a thin layer of snow from a small area of beach gravel. In the bitter cold, where the earth seemed like iron, they must have wondered about the seemingly backbreaking work they'd been assigned. But Franklin had ordered a proper burial, as close as circumstances would permit to that which John Torrington would have received in his native Manchester. After perhaps a few brief words, several of the seamen grabbed a pickaxe each.

The digging would have been treacherous and difficult, illuminated only by lamplight. In the near darkness, the pickaxes would have sent up showers of sparks as they struck against the icy earth. As the sailors took turns hacking at the ground in the deepening grave, they finally reached a depth of 5 feet (1.45 metres).

Preparations for the burial of John Torrington would have taken a day or two, but finally the small, slender coffin was lowered on ropes over the ship's side down to the ice, several feet below. It was probably then secured to a small sledge and no doubt draped with a flag. A party of seamen picked up the ropes secured to the front of the sledge and began to drag it slowly over the ice and snow towards the gravesite. If Beattie's own experience of King William Island was any indication, it must have been a tortuous trail, with small hummocks of ice preventing them from dragging the coffin in a straight line. Instead, they would have had to zigzag towards the shore.

A small procession would have followed, probably made up of Torrington's messmates and friends from the *Terror* and led by Sir John Franklin, Captain Francis Crozier, Commander James Fitz-james and some of the *Terror*'s officers. Someone carried the wooden headboard, a monument not only to Torrington but, as events turned out, to the whole expedition.

A layer of snow found on the coffin lid by Beattie and his team shows that a light snow was falling that day, early in January 1846. The men who stayed on the ships probably watched as, man by man, the procession was swallowed by the snow. Soon all that would have been seen were the lamps, flickering and swaying like fireflies around the shadows of the invisible party. Then they too disappeared.

Franklin probably presided at the burial. He was a deeply reli-gious man who, eight months earlier, had asked the British Admi-ralty to furnish one hundred Bibles, prayer books and testaments for sale at cost aboard the ships.

The snow, a spiralling yellow curtain in the lamplight, swirled around the group standing at the graveside. Some sifted and settled into the grave, obscuring the last view of Torrington's coffin. Each breath of Franklin's would have been made visible by the gripping cold, the sound of his voice blending with the icy, penetrating wind that always seems to blow at Beechey Island. His words were prob-ably brief, but presented with obvious reverence and sincerity. Quickly, the ceremony was over, and thoughts turned away from the young man who, just months before at Woolwich, near Lon-don, had joined Franklin's carefully selected crew a relatively healthy man.

IN MANY WAYS, Torrington's was an uneventful death, yet the confirmation of high lead levels in his body was of great significance in the context of the entire expedition. Beattie had stepped beyond the conventional theories about the expedition's end. It now seemed clear that the startling proof of lead poisoning in Torrington, coupled with the results from the Booth Point skeleton and the bone remains gathered in 1982, demonstrated that lead had played an important, if not pivotal, role in the Franklin disaster. Lost was the accepted explanation of scurvy and starvation alone carrying off the expedition. Beattie's medical findings from Torrington opened the door on a whole new way of looking at this and other nineteenth-century expeditions. But such a radical new theory about the underlying cause of the destruction of one of history's great voyages of discovery needed to be backed up by as much evidence as possible. The more bodies demonstrating lead contamination, the more credible the case that the theory applied to the entire expedition.

Therefore, the laboratory discoveries made during 1984 only served to underline the importance of returning to Beechey Island and establishing the cause of death of Hartnell and Braine. Another important part of the investigation would be to establish what conditions must have been like on the expedition during 1845–46, and to reconstruct the last months and days in the lives of the three men buried on Beechey Island. Their bodies would provide an unprecedented and privileged opportunity to look into British and Canadian history—but a three-dimensional history, represented by the only true "survivors" of Franklin's expedition.

After the 1984 field season ended and news of the preservation of John Torrington and John Hartnell was announced, two indirect descendants of Hartnell contacted Beattie. Donald Bray of Croydon, England, was astonished to see coverage of Beattie's expedition and to hear the name of his ancestor mentioned. Bray, a retired sub-postmaster, had devoted years to tracing his family history and was in possession of rare letters and documents that added haunting insights into Hartnell's family and life. Most touching were two letters to John and Thomas Hartnell, one sent by their mother, Sarah, and the other by their brother, Charles, both of which were intended to greet the sailors upon their completion of the Northwest Passage. The two men never received the letters, dated 23 December 1847. John Hartnell had already been dead for nearly two years and Thomas's death probably came the following summer on King William Island.

"My Dear Children," Sarah Hartnell's letter began, "It is a great pleasure to me to have a chance to write you. I hope you are both well. I assure you I have many anxious moments about you but I endeavour to cast my prayers on Him who is too good to be unkind." After a reference to her own illness and other news about family and friends, the letter ended: "If it is the Lord's will may we be spared to meet on earth. If not God grant we may all meet around His throne to praise Him to all eternity." Perhaps Sarah knew, as parents sometimes do, that her sons were facing their deaths.

Another descendant of John Hartnell would, along with three other specialists, join Beattie's scientific team when he returned to the field in 1986. Brian Spenceley, a professor at Lakehead University in Thunder Bay, Ontario, and a great-great-nephew of Hartnell, would soon be able to experience that which no other man has: to look into the eyes of a relative who has been dead for more than a century.

14

Hartnell

REDUX

J UMPING OUT of the Twin Otter onto the snow-blanketed
ground of Beechey Island on 8 June 1986, Beattie was tem-
porarily blinded by the bright, sunny sky and the sun's rays
reflecting off the white ground. Only gradually did major geographical features and the three tiny headstones that poked their
way through the snow become visible, assuring him that he was
once again on the island where so many memories lay.

This time Beattie planned to complete his examinations of the
Franklin graveyard; part of his research team had already arrived
with him from Resolute. That group, consisting of archaeologist
Eric Damkjar, project photographer Brian Spenceley, historical
consultant Dr. Jim Savelle (who was a co-investigator with Beattie
during the 1981 season and now served as a research scholar at the
Scott Polar Research Institute) and field assistants Arne Carlson,
Walt Kowal and Joelee Nungaq would set up camp and then conduct
the detailed archaeological work and exhumations. A team of
specialists consisting of pathologist Dr. Roger Amy, radiologist

Dr. Derek Notman, radiology technician Larry Anderson and Arctic clothing specialist Barbara Schweger would arrive one week later.

Beattie was starting his 1986 field season earlier than in 1984, in order to avoid the problem of water run-off from melting snow. But as the temperatures remained below freezing in June and a brisk wind swept across the island for a good number of days, heightening the cold, the investigators had to endure additional hardships.

Each of the crew quickly set to work establishing camp, consisting of the usual array of individual and communal tents, with one new addition, a 16-foot-tall (5-metre) flagpole, where the bright red-and-white Canadian flag snapped in the near constant winds alongside the flag of the Northwest Territories. During this work, however, Beattie's mind was fixed on something else. For two years, one question had nagged him. It was a question posed by almost everyone he had talked to about the research on Beechey Island: Was there any guarantee that the bodies of John Torrington and John Hartnell were again encased in ice after their 1984 reburials? The theory that the summer meltwater would trickle down into the filled-in excavations, seep into the coffins and subsequently freeze was a good, logical one. But Beattie wondered if the process were so simple. The 1984 exhumation of John Torrington was final and complete; there could be no verification of the theory there. However, uncovering John Hartnell, exposed once in 1852 and again in 1984, would soon answer the question.

A tent was again erected over Hartnell's grave to protect the exhumation process from the elements. As before, digging was extremely difficult. The exposure of Hartnell's coffin required twenty-four hours of continual digging by Kowal, Carlson, Savelle and Nungaq, a process that had now become almost mechanical. One person would labour with the pickaxe until either the pain in his hands or the exhaustion in his arms required rest. The loosened ice and gravel would then be shovelled into buckets by one or two of the excavators, lifted out of the grave to another of them and finally dumped on the growing pile of "back-dirt." Conversation between the excavators began with recollections of previous archaeological digs, especially those of 1984, but as the hours passed, the relentless sound of the pickaxe, broken regularly by the rasping, fingernail-on-blackboard sound of the shovel pushing into resistant gravel and ice, eventually won out.

When the coffin lid was finally exposed and the limits of the coffin identified, the group took a long overdue rest and waited for the arrival of the team of specialists. To this point, the excavation was a replay of 1984. But the next step, the removal of the coffin lid, though also done in 1984, would this time provide an answer to the question of the refreezing of the bodies. They were therefore poised at the true beginning of the 1986 investigation.

During the break in the exhumation work, Beattie and Damkjar returned to the food-tin dump for a more detailed survey than the one they had conducted in 1984. Two days were spent thoroughly documenting what was left of the tins. Out of the original 700 or so, fragments of fewer than 150 remained. Tins are a very transportable, recognizable and desired artefact for amateur archaeologists and collectors, and, over the decades, people had been depleting the information pool represented by the containers. None of those remaining was complete and most were badly fragmented. But all portions of the tins were represented, including the soldered seams.

The area of the tin scatter was gridded with string and tied in to a datum point. Each square of the grid was photographed and searched, and every tin fragment located and described. All of the larger pieces and those with particularly good features were individually photographed. Samples of "ordinary" tins were collected for later study, along with some tins that were particularly good examples of poor soldering and manufacture.

On the second day of work at the can dump, Beattie and Damkjar were interrupted by Nungaq, who had been out hiking on the ice of Union Bay during the break in the digging. He came walking quickly along the spit towards them, his dog Keena held tightly by her chain. "There's a bear coming," he said, as he trotted up the rise of the mound. Pointing west, he continued: "Look, over there, it's coming right for us." Little interest in the tins remained, as Beattie and Damkjar squinted out over the bright field of ice. Then Beattie saw it. The bear's head was lowered and it did not appear to be moving at all, though its body was swaying slightly from side to side. From this quick glimpse, Beattie recalled an important lesson. He remembered when he was a student pilot and his instructor had lectured him: "If you spot another airplane coming your way and it appears to be moving, you're safe—just keep your eye on it. But if that plane looks like it is standing still, watch out, because it's coming straight for you." A strange thing to recall at this particular time, but the rule still applied. Although the bear was a good distance away, perhaps a mile, it looked awfully big. And within minutes they were all heading back to camp, cameras swinging from their necks, clutching notebooks, tripods and rifles. They did not want to leave either expensive camera equipment or their collected data at the tin dump for the bear to play with, so they had filled their arms with everything taken to the site. Halfway back to camp, they turned to see the bear crossing the spit with a slow, purposeful gait. They breathed easier when they watched the bear stop for a moment to test the air, then move on, heading across Erebus Bay to Devon Island.

The Twin Otter carrying Amy, Notman, Anderson and Schweger at last swept over the camp. Beattie noticed right away that skis had been strapped onto the tundra wheels of the aircraft. The thin layer of snow on the island made landing there impossible; the plane would have to land offshore, on ice-covered Erebus Bay. That meant that the heavy load of equipment on board, over half of the 3,300 pounds (1,500 kg) of equipment to be used during the research, would have to be carried across the ice and up the beach to their camp. After brief greetings, the eleven-member team watched the Twin Otter leave, then spent the next two hours at that difficult task.

Exhumation work resumed with the digging of a work area adjacent to the right side of the coffin. This exposed the coffin's side for the first time, and immediately, something of interest was discovered: three "handles" were found spaced along the side of the coffin wall. However, these were not real handles like the ones on Torrington's coffin, but symbolic representations made out of the same white linen tape that decorated the edges of the coffin.

As in 1984, the team used heated water to accelerate the thawing process. There was no running water on the island, so Kowal developed a highly efficient method of melting snow, providing a constant, though meagre, water source. The water was heated, two buckets at a time, on naphtha stoves located in the adjacent autopsy/X-ray tent. When ready, Kowal carried the buckets across to Carlson and Nungaq, who would slowly pour the water over the dark-blue-wool-covered coffin. When too much water had accumulated in the bottom of the grave, making work virtually impossible, an electric sump pump was lowered in. The water drawn out of the grave was then directed through a hose away from the excavation area. It seemed to Beattie that the thawing was much more difficult than it had been in 1984; the time of year probably accounted for the difference. Although they did not test the temperature of the permafrost in 1984 or 1986, it seemed that at every depth it was colder in June than in August.

After photographs of the cleaned coffin were taken and it was measured (79 by 19 by 13 inches/203.5 by 48 by 33 cm deep), the delicate task of loosening and removing the already damaged lid was started. When at last it was lifted, Beattie and Carlson could see immediately that Hartnell's right arm area and face, both exposed in 1984, were again completely encased in ice. "Well, the water flowed back in, didn't it?" Beattie said. The question had been answered. Standing by Hartnell's ice-protected body, Beattie thought about the condition of John Torrington only a few steps away. He was now satisfied that the young petty officer was again suspended in time by the very process that had allowed them a brief, privileged glimpse in 1984.

Damkjar, standing alongside the upper edge of the grave with the others, pointed out that the ice around Hartnell appeared quite discoloured. The ice in the centre of the block, about where Hartnell's chest should be, was not an opaque white as with Torrington, but very brownish, even mottled.

Soon the work of exposing the body began, the warm water quickly unveiling the features of the seaman's face. This was an overwhelming experience for Spenceley, Hartnell's great-great-nephew, who stood close by the grave's edge, gazing in silence at his own family history over a distance of 140 years.

There did not seem to be any major deterioration in the tissues during the two-year hiatus. One observation made in 1984 was that Hartnell's left eye was well-preserved while his right eye appeared to be damaged, and it had been unclear whether this had happened while he lived or somehow shortly after his death. Inglefield's reports on the exhumation that he and Sutherland had conducted in 1852 had not indicated any problem with Hartnell's right eye. But in 1986, Beattie noticed immediately that, in addition to the shrunken right eye, Hartnell's left eye showed some shrinkage as well. He concluded that it is likely that exposure, for even a brief period, causes changes peculiar to the eyes, leaving the rest of the external features unaffected. In other words, the exposure of Hartnell in 1852 probably induced changes in the right eye—the fact that the left eye appeared normal to the researchers in 1984 indicated that Inglefield and Sutherland probably did not expose the left side of the face. The shrinking of the left eye over the two years that had passed since its exposure in 1984 supported the theory.

As the ice surrounding Hartnell thawed, it became apparent that he was wrapped in a white shroud from his shoulders down. The damaged shirt sleeve on his right arm was exposed through a tear in the sheet and pieces of the coffin lid appeared to have been driven forcibly into his right chest wall during the 1852 exhumation. When the obscuring ice was melted higher up the arm, the tears in the shroud, shirt sleeve and undergarments were visible as scissor or knife cuts. Obviously, to fully expose Hartnell's arm, Sutherland had had to make cuts in the shroud and clothing. This evidence showed that the investigation of Hartnell's body in 1852 was limited to his face and right arm. It would have been too difficult and taken too much time for Sutherland to do more.

On Hartnell's head was a toque-like hat, which in turn was resting on a small frilled pillow stuffed with wood shavings. Thawing of the ice surrounding the body continued until Hartnell was completely exposed. Nothing was moved by the group until the shrouded body had been thoroughly described and photographed. The next stage was the folding back of the shroud, which took a very long time because only the very thinnest layer of the exposed shroud and body was actually thawed and additional thawing of the fabric was required.

As Hartnell was unwrapped from the shroud his left arm was exposed, followed by his right arm. Immediately, Amy and Beattie could see that the arms had been bound to the body in the same manner as was seen on Torrington, though this time the material used was light brown wool. However, his right hand was lying on an outside fold of the binding. It was clear that his right arm had been extracted by Sutherland, who, when his examination was complete, had not tucked the hand back underneath the binding but left it lying on top.

Hartnell's blue-and-white-striped shirt was of a similar pattern to that seen on Torrington, though the stripes were not printed but woven (a more expensive material than that found on Torrington) and the design was also different from Torrington's. It was a pullover style, and some of the front buttons were missing, the buttonholes being tied shut with loops of string. The lower portion of the shirt had two letters embroidered on it in red and the date "1844." The letters appeared to be "TH," and it may be that the shirt had originally belonged to John Hartnell's younger brother and expedition companion, Thomas.

Underneath the shirt was a wool sweater-like undergarment, and beneath that a cotton undershirt. He was not wearing trousers, stockings or footwear. Beattie and Schweger were puzzled that Hartnell should have had three layers of clothing covering his upper body and nothing on below the waist. They suspected that there may have been a viewing of the body aboard the *Erebus* prior to burial, with the man's lower half covered by the shroud.

ABOVE & OPPOSITE *John Hartnell: He was wrapped in a shroud, wearing a cap which, when removed, revealed a full head of dark brown hair.* BOTTOM *The bottom of Hartnell's shirt was embroidered with the date 1844 and the initials "TH," suggesting that the shirt may have belonged to his brother, Thomas.*

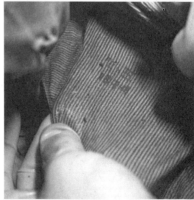

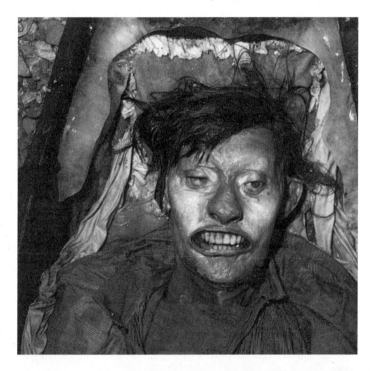

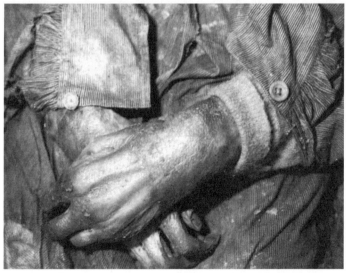

Hartnell's legs and feet were slightly darkened and very shrunken and emaciated by illness and in part by the freezing. Like Torrington, his toes were tied together. In preparation for the temporary removal of Hartnell's body for the X-ray examination and autopsy, the shroud was completely pulled back and Hartnell's cap removed, revealing a full head of very dark brown, nearly black, hair, parted on his left. Without his hat, Hartnell lost much of the sinister look that first confronted the scientists in the summer of 1984. Instead, he appeared to be simply a young man who, for some mysterious reason, had died at the age of twenty-five on 4 January 1846.

Now began the most difficult and unpleasant phase of the exposure. Even as Hartnell lay in the coffin, apparently ready to be gently lifted out, his body was still part of the permafrost, solidly frozen to the mass of ice below. Slowly and carefully, water had to be directed underneath the body, freeing it a fraction of an inch at a time. The permafrost had a grip that would not let go without a fight. But finally, the scientists won the battle and the body was freed.

Before lifting Hartnell from his coffin, his right thumbnail was removed and samples of hair from his scalp, beard and pubic area were collected for later examination and analysis. Beattie, Carlson, and Nungaq then lifted the body out of the grave onto a white linen sheet, where it was immediately wrapped. Hartnell was carried a distance of 10 feet (3 metres) to the autopsy/X-ray tent, where Notman and Anderson prepared to take a series of X-rays while he was clothed. Still frozen to the bottom of the coffin were Hartnell's nineteenth-century shroud, and beneath that, a folded woollen blanket. Damkjar, over the next day, struggled to remove these two items. When they were finally freed, they were handed over to Schweger for analysis and sampling.

Notman and Anderson had already set up their X-ray "clinic" inside the autopsy tent. The next order of business was the assembly of the darkroom tent. Beattie had provided them with the inside dimensions of the long-house tent months before and, using these, they had designed a unique, collapsible and portable dark-room. The structure consisted of a tubular metal frame that was screwed together; over this, a double layer of thick black plastic (cut, formed and taped together) was pulled and tucked in along the floor. On one side they had fashioned a door from a double overlap of the plastic cover, forming a light trap. Inside the dark-room, Anderson had just enough room to stand and manoeuvre around the chemical tubs. A mechanical timer was hung inside as well as a battery-operated safe light.

Kowal gave them a hand in melting the 110 gallons (500 litres) of clean, strained water required for the X-ray film development. Four large Coleman stoves were running in the tent constantly, and Kowal would bring in buckets of snow to melt. When a bucket was ready it was poured through a fine strainer directly into the large plastic garbage bins they had brought as chemical holders. When the tubs were finally filled with water (which took a whole day), Anderson mixed his chemicals. He then made wood-framed structures

Larry Anderson in the autopsy/X-ray tent. He is leaning on the portable X-ray unit; the black structure is a portable darkroom.

to hold the film sheets in their development frames, and these were lowered into the tubs. A 200-watt aquarium heater was then immersed in the liquid, which would bring the temperature up to the 68°F (20°C) thought necessary to provide controlled development.

The X-ray unit was a remarkably compact yet powerful instrument mounted on four tubular steel legs. Too fragile to risk being sent from their clinic at the Park Nicollet Medical Centre in Minneapolis as normal freight, Notman and Anderson had bought an airplane ticket for it, and everyone had a good laugh when they told how the machine, named Fragile Bulky Notman on its ticket, had "sat" in the first-class section at the front of the plane during the flight into Canada while they had to sit back in economy class.

When in use, the machine would be lifted over the body, its legs positioned firmly in the gravel. A focusing light beam on the bottom of the unit would then be turned on to illuminate and define the area to be X-rayed before a film plate was slid under the body.

Notman and Anderson tested their X-ray set-up on a polar bear scapula, found lying on one of the beach ridges near the gravesite. The results were very encouraging: holding the X-ray up, Notman described the bony details of the scapula to the others. Although they had been told by a number of experts that they were not likely to succeed in getting satisfactory X-rays under such difficult field conditions, his voice betrayed a note of gleeful triumph and self-satisfaction. Anderson's face also seemed to say, "Well, they were all wrong! I knew we could do it!"

With this air of success, Notman and Anderson began the difficult job of X-raying the clothed John Hartnell. The X-ray area on the ground adjacent to the door was the same as where the autopsy was to be performed. When an exposure was to be made, either Notman or Anderson would put on a heavy, full-length lead apron and all other people in the tent would line up behind their protector. A loud call of "exposing" would be made for the benefit of people working outside the tent, so that they could move away to a distance of at least 100 feet (30 metres) before the exposure was made.

Anderson would then take the film plate into the darkroom for processing. Ten to fifteen minutes later he would emerge with the dripping film, which he hung by pegs to clotheslines stretched across the length of the tent. He and Notman would then examine the quality of the film and decide if there was any need to change their technique.

When the initial X-raying of Hartnell had been completed, Notman, Anderson and Amy stood in front of the row of hanging film to begin the preliminary examination. Anderson quickly pointed to the first X-ray: "He's got a solid block of ice in his head." The frozen brain tissue obscured the X-ray image, meaning they'd have to X-ray again after further thawing. Looking at the chest X-rays, Notman pointed to a small feature near Hartnell's neck. "We've got our first metallic object," he said. "It looks like a ring on its side." (In fact, the metal was the frame of a decorative, embroidered button.) The chest X-rays were also confusing in that the internal organs appeared uncharacteristic and of unusual and varied densities—an unexpected series of observations on the first X-rays ever to be taken under such circumstances.

The bone structure was largely unremarkable, with the exception of a suspected compression fracture of one of the vertebrae in the lower part of the neck, representing a subacute injury that would not have been fatal. Hartnell may have fallen on the expedition. Some degenerative bone changes were also identifiable in the left shoulder and left elbow; found in someone so young, these sorts of bone changes (spurring and lipping) usually indicate a response to some form of injury. Also, one of the small long bones of the left foot showed evidence of osteomyelitis, or a bone infection, which could have made Hartnell susceptible to systemic infections (blood poisoning). Any of these injuries or conditions could have resulted in Hartnell being confined to sick bay, where he would have been given tinned foods as a medical comfort.

However, except for the details of the bones, little could be determined, let alone identified, from these first X-rays. Beattie wondered if the soft tissue preservation, which appeared so good to the eye, was in fact not good enough to allow X-ray information to be collected. Notman was frustrated with these first findings for, even in the desiccated and eviscerated Egyptian mummies he had studied in the past, there had always been some recognizable details in his X-rays. Only the autopsy would provide the answers.

It had been difficult to position the body with the clothing still on, and, spurred on by the confusing results of the first X-rays, Notman and Anderson wanted to try again after the clothing had been removed. Beattie, Amy, Nungaq and Schweger began the difficult task of unclothing Hartnell. "What we'll do is ask the patient to sit up," Amy said, a request for Beattie and Schweger to support the body while he attempted to remove the outer shirt. Trained in the medical field, Amy, Notman and Anderson always referred to the sailors as patients, reflecting their strictly professional attitude towards medical procedures and research, even in these extraordinary circumstances. After some initial attempts to slip the clothes over Hartnell's head and off his limbs, it was decided that it would be necessary to cut the fabric. To minimize damage to the clothes, Beattie made a single vertical cut up the back of each garment. Doing this avoided the over-extension of the limbs and prevented any stress being placed on the material, which could have caused tearing both in the fabric and along the seams.

As the clothes slipped off the body the scientists made a truly astonishing discovery.

"Son of a bitch, he's already been autopsied! Son of a gun!" said Amy. "We've got an upside down 'Y' incision. This sort of thing has not been seen before, this is absolutely unique."

Running down John Hartnell's chest and abdomen was a sutured incision that left no doubt that, in the short hours after his death, a surgeon on the *Erebus*, probably assistant-surgeon Dr. Harry D.S. Goodsir, an anatomist by training, had attempted to establish the cause of death. It's no wonder Amy was so excited at this discovery. Here he had an unprecedented opportunity to view the handiwork of a medical predecessor of long ago. By conducting his own autopsy, Amy would actually be assisting this long-dead doctor. The surgeon of the *Erebus* certainly anticipated that he would bring the information from his autopsy back to England. Now the full extent of that information would finally be known.

Dr. Harry D.S. Goodsir.

This important discovery begged the question: Why had the surgeon conducted an autopsy? To find out the cause of death, obviously; but what had prompted the decision? Perhaps the death of John Torrington of the *Terror* only three days before was part of the reason. There may also have been some symptoms associated with Hartnell's death that left serious doubt in the minds of the surgeons as to the cause of death. A challenge faced Amy, who had to sort through the riddle.

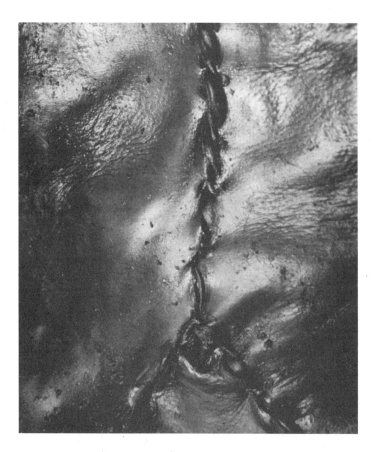

The sutured autopsy incision found on John Hartnell, dating to the autopsy conducted on his body during the expedition in early January 1846.

The standard incision in an autopsy performed today is "Y"-shaped, with the arms of the "Y" extending down from each shoulder and meeting at the base of the sternum (breastbone). From this point, the incision continues down to the pubic bone. In the case of Hartnell's autopsy, however, the incision was upside down: the arm of the "Y" originated near the point of each hip, meeting near the umbilicus (belly button) and extending up to the top of the sternum. Given that the procedures for autopsy technique in the mid-nineteenth century are not well represented in today's scientific literature, Beattie wondered if the incision indicated that the surgeon was concentrating on the bowel or whether this was the habitual procedure for autopsy followed by the surgeon. Amy was later able to reconstruct, step by step, what the original pathologist had done. The extent and direction taken during this first autopsy would provide clues to the suspicions held by the surgeon relating to the cause of death.

That an autopsy had been done solved the mystery of the strange X-rays: the surgeon of the *Erebus* had removed the organs for examination, then replaced them in one mixed mass. Not surprisingly, this disrupted anatomy resulted in a meaningless collection of soft-tissue detail in the first X-rays taken by Notman and Anderson. Also, the brownish discolouration seen in the ice when the lid was first removed probably resulted from blood and other fluids seeping out of the incision when water filled the coffin during the summer of 1846.

After Notman and Anderson had completed a second series of X-rays, a process that took another six hours (for a total of fourteen hours of X-raying), they retired for a well-deserved rest, but not before a slightly hair-raising experience. The X-raying had continued into the late hours, and most of the crew had retired to their tents. Savelle and Nungaq were sitting in the kitchen tent talking. Beattie was in the autopsy/X-ray tent, more as company for Notman and Anderson than as help. Keena, the dog brought along to serve as a watch for polar bears, was tethered outside the kitchen tent and could be heard whining in her familiar, annoying way. Suddenly Keena stopped whining—unusual in itself. But then she barked madly. The three men in the autopsy/X-ray tent looked at each other. They had never heard her bark before and they knew that there had to be a good reason: a bear. Then they heard the "pop pop pop" of rifles being fired and, off in the distance, voices shouting, "Bear, bear in camp!" Beattie reached for the rifle he had brought down to the tent and slowly stuck his head out. The tents over the graves and the autopsy/X-ray tent were separated from the main grouping by about 330 feet (100 metres), and, peering round the edge of Braine's tent back towards the main camp, he saw a bear standing in the open space. Notman and Anderson were now beside Beattie, sizing up the situation. Beattie had Kowal's gun, one with which he was not familiar—and sure enough the bolt jammed twice, but the third and final bullet went into the chamber cleanly. Notman, looking around for some other weapon, grabbed a shovel. Anderson had his camera. So armed, the three stayed behind Braine's tent out of sight of the bear, which soon became annoyed at the noise of guns and people. It ambled off, angling towards the beach. Passing downwind of the graves, just 65 feet (20 metres) away, it then caught the scent of the three and of John Hartnell. As it paused with its nose in the air, Beattie thought, "Oh, brother, it's gonna come this way." But then he heard "twang twang twang," as three bullets ricocheted off the gravel beside the bear, forcing it back in slow retreat, and the crisis ended as the bear ambled down the beach and out onto the ice. From that point on during the summer, someone always stayed outside keeping watch with the dog. From the bear tracks in the snow, Nungaq was able to determine that it had come in off the ice close to the kitchen tent, chased some gulls, wandered up to the food cache beside the kitchen tent and then saw the dog and decided to sniff it out. No wonder Keena had barked: when people started to pop their heads out of tents to see what the commotion was all about, the bear and the dog were nose to nose. Keena was lucky. Notman, Anderson and Beattie were lucky. It may have been close to the end of a long day, but none of the crew was ready for sleep now.

With the X-raying complete, Amy and Beattie, dressed in green surgical gowns, white aprons and blue surgical caps, began the autopsy. Hartnell was first measured and weighed. He was taller and heavier than Torrington, at 5 feet 11 inches (180 cm) and 99 pounds (45 kg). Amy then reopened the inverted "Y" incision by cutting the original sutures. He noted that several knife cuts were made on the surface of the chest plate before the ribs had been successfully divided during the original autopsy. It soon became obvious that Franklin's surgeons had not focussed their attention on the bowel, as their incision suggested; it seemed they believed the cause of Hartnell's death concerned the heart and lungs. In the earlier autopsy, Dr. Goodsir had removed the heart with part of the trachea. He would first have held the heart up to look at its apex for signs of disease; then he made two cuts, one each into the right and left ventricles, to look at the valves. When he had finished with the heart, he dissected the roots of the lungs to look for evidence of tuberculosis and made a few cuts into the liver looking for confirmation of the disease. Hartnell's bowel was untouched. On completion of the autopsy, Dr. Goodsir replaced Hartnell's chest plate (the anterior portion of the ribs and the sternum) upside down. The original autopsy turned out to have been a cursory one that could have been conducted in less than half an hour. During his investigations, the surgeon of the *Erebus* would have found confirmation of tuberculosis of the lungs. Once observations about the original autopsy had been completed, Amy began his own much more detailed investigation. Beattie labelled the sample containers and sealed the samples handed to him by Amy, while Spenceley photographed the proceedings.

First, any frozen water from inside the body was collected, as these fluids would have come from the tissues. Then, after sterilizing his surgical instruments in the open flame of a naphtha stove,

Amy cut a frozen piece from each of the organs and placed these samples in a sterile container that was promptly sealed and kept frozen in a cooler. The samples would later undergo bacteriological analysis in the laboratory. Other samples of organs and tissue were then taken and placed in preservative, to be later studied under a microscope. Amy occasionally made observations about the condition of Hartnell, such as the state of blood vessels: "Vessels don't contain blood, they contain ice and the ice is clear." Many of the organs were found to be in a fair state of preservation, though the brain had turned to liquid. Finally, bone was cut with a surgical saw from the femur, rib, lumbar vertebra and skull. From start to finish, when Amy resutured the original 1846 incision, the autopsy took the three men nine hours to complete. It had been very thorough.

Everyone was exhausted, yet work was continuing nearby in Braine's tent in preparation for his exposure. Hartnell's body was tightly wrapped in the autopsy sheet and carried into his own tent. When Schweger finished documenting the Hartnell fabrics, the group arranged for his reburial. The blanket was repositioned in the bottom of the coffin and the original shroud laid back in position. His body was passed down into the grave and placed in the coffin. The shroud was then closed over him, and it was soon time for their final moment with the young sailor.

Just before midnight on 18 June, they all gathered in Hartnell's tent. Schweger had brought the clothing—wrapped in mylar, an inert material that would protect the clothes. Spenceley and Beattie jumped down into the grave, and Schweger passed them each item of clothing, which they placed carefully alongside the shrouded body. Once this was complete, the lid was lowered down, but, as they tried positioning it on the coffin, the two men could not get it to fit as they had found it—a layer of ice had formed on the top edge of the coffin, and this had to be chipped away before the lid would fall into its proper place. Beattie took the small chisel hammer and removed the ice within a few minutes, and the reburial continued. Spenceley and Beattie, helped out of the grave by the others, now joined the ring of researchers standing at the graveside. A spontaneous moment of silence was punctuated by the sound of the wind snapping the tent flaps and the sorrowful howling of Keena. "One hundred and forty years ago, his brother was standing in this same spot," Beattie said at last, breaking the silence.

Slowly, the group filed out of the tent and, with hardly a word spoken, they all began to fill buckets with gravel and complete the process of reburial. At this time, none of them could fail to feel the transience of human existence and the reality of death. Exhuming Hartnell had been a hard thing to do, something very difficult to deal with. But now it was finished and, for the moment, there was relief that this one door was closing on their project. But in the tent next to them, the excavation of Private William Braine of the Royal Marines had already uncovered a surprise.

15

The Royal

MARINE

A s with torrington and Hartnell's graves, a string grid was placed over Braine's grave. Damkjar made scale drawings of the surface features in each square of the grid, while Spenceley, hovering on a ladder over his tripod-mounted camera, took a series of Polaroid photographs to be used during the reconstruction.

On the snow beside the grave, the crew assembled another long-house tent. This was lifted over the headboard and positioned over the grave, allowing some manoeuvring space at each side of the structure. The tent was then tied to Hartnell's tent and the corners secured to large metal pegs driven into the permafrost.

The gravel covering the grave and filling the spaces between the limestone rocks was removed by trowelling, and, during this cleaning process, a few artefacts were found that had, over the decades, worked their way into the cracks and corners of the grave. The exact positions of these objects, mainly wood fragments and bird bones, were recorded in reference to the string grid that still covered the grave. One of the large, slab-like limestone rocks was covered with a mat of gravel consolidated by a well-established colony of mosses, and the crew did not disturb this tiny islet of vegetation. They lifted the huge rock so that the eventual reconstruction of the grave would include the micro-garden.

One of the distinctive features of Braine's grave was the highly structured nature of its surface features. The overall impression was that it represented a crypt, and the detail of parts of the structure seemed to confirm this. A major challenge to the excavators would be the accurate reconstruction of the grave. So the rocks were removed, identification numbers and orientation indicators were penned on their undersides. These were then carried outside the tent and placed in rows on the snow, the larger rocks being used as anchoring weights for the edge of the tent.

Two hours were spent in identifying and removing nearly one hundred rocks from the surface of the grave. One of the more interesting of the large rocks was the roughly circular slab lying on the surface at the foot of the grave. Two-thirds of the exposed surface had a black colouration, which Savelle said had been applied to the grave by Penny in 1853–54. When the rock was upended, they saw that the underside was nearly completely painted black. It was apparent that this rock had at one time been standing at the foot of the grave and had functioned as the footboard seen in some of the engravings and paintings made at the site during the 1850s.

The next step, after all the rocks had been removed, was to begin the now familiar task of removing the permafrost. Kowal, Carlson, Savelle and Nungaq began digging and, eighteen hours later, encountered the first signs of Braine's coffin. The excavation of Braine's grave exemplified the determination of the crew, as they worked virtually non-stop for a total of 37 hours until the goal had been reached and the coffin completely exposed. Braine had been buried very deeply, down 6½ feet (2 metres) in the permafrost, and his coffin turned out to be the largest of the three—82 by 19 by 13 inches (211 by 49 by 33 cm) deep. This combination

Beginning the excavation of William Braine's grave.
Left to right are Walt Kowal, Arne Carlson, Jim Savelle and Joelee Nungaq.

resulted in the removal of considerably more permafrost than
from either Torrington or Hartnell's graves: all four sides of
Braine's grave excavation had to be extended as the size of the
coffin became obvious.

As the final inches of permafrost were picked away, the texture
softened, signalling the approach of the coffin. Aware that both
Torrington and Hartnell had been buried with plaques attached to
their coffin lids, Kowal explored carefully the position on the lid
where a plaque would have been placed. One of the thrills of archaeology is that discoveries, even those that are predictable because of previous experience, are invariably a surprise. The
discovery of Braine's plaque was no exception: the first, small exposure of the plaque revealed its completely unexpected appearance. It was copper-coloured and, as the exposure was enlarged,
Kowal could see that it was metal, with the green-blue patina of
copper oxidation showing on the small portion of the edge that had
been carefully exposed. Kowal continued to widen the window

*The copper plaque
found nailed to William
Braine's coffin lid.
It reads: "W. Braine
R.M. 8 Co. W.D.*
H.M.S. Erebus
*Died April 3rd 1846
Aged 33 years."*

over the plaque, which seemed to be extensive. The words punched into the metal began to emerge, and eventually the whole plaque was uncovered. It was huge, 13 by 17 inches (33 by 44 cm), and great care had obviously been taken in its preparation. The plaque read: "W. BRAINE R.M. 8 CO. W.D. H.M.S. EREBUS DIED APRIL 3RD 1846 AGED 33 YEARS."

The "4" in 1846 was backwards. Everyone was thrilled by the preservation and quality of the plaque, which, while constructed differently from Torrington's, was just as touching. With a lot of digging still to do, the plaque was covered by a piece of plastic and a thin layer of gravel to protect it during the continuing exposure of the whole coffin.

The coffin lid appeared to be in excellent condition, and Carlson felt that he could remove the lid without shearing the nails, but instead by carefully prying it with a crowbar. He began slowly, but the nails pulled free quickly and within twenty minutes the lid was loose and ready to be lifted. Carlson and Beattie, one at each end, lifted the lid slowly and gently straight up, supporting it on their arms as they passed it up to Nungaq and Damkjar, who immediately took it out of the tent.

"I see some bright red," said Carlson, as all the researchers peered at an area of blood-red ice covering Braine's face. Beattie glanced along the length of the coffin. He could see part of a shroud over the chest area. In direct contact with the coffin lid, it had not been obscured by the opaque ice that filled the rest of the coffin. When the thawing was started, the red colour over Braine's face quickly took on texture and shape. It was a kerchief of Asian design with a pattern of leaves printed in black and white. As the ice melted in the rest of the coffin, the outline of the whole shroud was soon determined.

Within a few hours, the upper half of the enshrouded body was exposed. It was the most arresting vision the researchers had experienced at the site. The outline and contours of the body could be perceived in the ivory coloured shroud, but the sight was dominated by the bright red kerchief lying over Braine's face. The vivid colour seemed so out of place deep within the grave, and the filmy nature of the material caused it to cling tightly to the face it covered, accentuating the outlines of Braine's brow, nose, chin and cheeks; in the centre, behind small tears in the kerchief, the black

ABOVE *William Braine's shrouded body, his face covered by a red kerchief.*
OPPOSITE *The kerchief is drawn back to reveal Braine's face.*

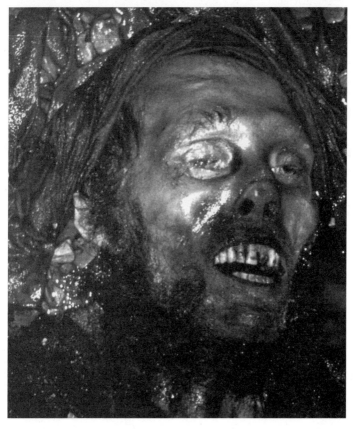

oval of his partly opened mouth was visible. Poking through the tears were some incisor teeth, producing a frightening, scarlet grin that left every one of the crew transfixed.

The edges of the kerchief were still frozen deep in the recesses of the coffin; it was not yet possible to remove it to reveal Braine's face. By pouring water into the corners of the coffin, the material slowly loosened and could be partly rolled back. As it was retracted, the face took on character and an identity.

By now, the team had been working for sixteen hours without rest. Beattie, aided by Damkjar, described the scene to the others as it became visible to him: "There's a beard, curly and dark . . . got to be careful. There are the teeth, there's an ear. It looks like he's balding a bit." Then Beattie stepped back to take in the view of a man who appeared severe and life-toughened, very much a nineteenth-century Royal Marine private. "Look at that. After a long day's work it's really something to see," he said quietly, as if to himself.

Braine's teeth were in very bad condition and one of his front teeth had been broken in life, causing the exposure of the pulp cavity. His lips, unlike Hartnell or Torrington's, were pulled tightly over his teeth—perhaps the kerchief had prevented the lips from curling outwards. His nose was slightly flattened. He would have stood nearly 6 feet (181 cm) tall, and the large coffin seemed too small for him. When he had been originally placed in the coffin and the lid attached for the first time, it had pressed down onto his nose.

His eyes were deeply sunk into the eye sockets and were only one-quarter open. The eyeballs did not appear to be very well-preserved but he still had a sleepy, nearly alive appearance. A scar on his forehead indicated that he had been struck or had cracked his head against an object several years before his death. Finally, it was possible to remove the rest of the kerchief from the face, and they saw that his hair was nearly black, long and partly curly, and that he was indeed balding.

After pulling the shroud away, his shirt and right arm and hand were also exposed. "Look at that hand, it's very well-preserved,"

Beattie said. "Nice shirt, there's not a mark on it, it looks brand new." No sign of his left arm could be found, and the possibility that it may have been amputated was discussed. As thawing progressed, they discovered that his left arm was frozen underneath his body. Beattie at first thought Braine had been too big to be placed in the coffin with his arms in their natural position. But they later saw that it would have been just as easy to have placed his arms over the sides of his chest and still have room for the coffin lid. His body and head, too, were not positioned carefully, and one of his undershirts had been put on backwards, leading them to conclude he was placed hastily in the coffin.

Thawing the body was again a matter of pouring warm water over the frozen sections. In the cold of the grave the warm water would send up clouds of steam filled with the pungent smells of wet wool and cotton. Hours of this smell took its toll on some of the crew and the emotional strain of the work drained them all. Braine, being buried so deeply, was in colder ground, and the ice would not yield without a battle. They had tremendous difficulty in thawing the portions of the clothing and shroud frozen to the bottom of the coffin, which trapped Braine within it. Warm water poured directly onto the material seemed to have little effect, and the team struggled for eighteen more hours before they were able to free him from the ice. Even then, they had to cut the clothing up the small portion of exposed back and lift him, not only out of the coffin, but out of his clothes as well. Beattie and Amy then eased him up to the side of the grave, handing him to Savelle and Kowal, who positioned him on a plastic sheet.

Immediately noticeable was the extremely emaciated appearance of this man—literally a skin-covered skeleton. Braine would have weighed less than 88 pounds (40 kg). He must have been extremely ill during his final days. Every rib could be counted and it was possible to identify features on his hip bones. His face also reflected his condition, the skin drawn taut over the cheeks and eye sockets. His limbs had a spidery appearance; so thin were his arms that his hands appeared very large. For Beattie, lifting this frail and lifeless man up and out of his grave, coming as it did after such tremendous effort to free him, was the most difficult aspect of his work on Beechey Island. The strained faces of the others illustrated that he was not alone in these feelings.

Exhausted though the team was, Braine was immediately wrapped in a sheet and carried across to the X-ray tent. Notman and Anderson, who had been sleeping after their difficult work on Hartnell, were roused so they could begin their work. The X-raying of Braine was carried out much as it had been with Hartnell, though the situation was quite different as Braine had not had a previous autopsy. Both worked continuously for nearly twelve hours until the X-raying was completed.

Before the others could rest they still had to remove Braine's clothing from the coffin for Schweger to analyze. With the body removed, thawing accelerated and the job was completed in an hour. During the initial thawing of the foot-end of the grave, Carlson thought he detected a different kind of fabric peeking out just below the shroud-wrapped feet. Not until the body had been removed and further thawing of the shroud had taken place was his observation confirmed. Rolled up and placed under Braine's feet were a pair of stockings. These were quite large and appeared to be of a heavy material, and one had a hole in it. The thawing and removal of the shroud and kerchief were left for the following day. Beattie, Kowal, Savelle, Amy and Damkjar wandered back to the cook tent, had a wash outside and went in for food and drink. They were then able to have a brief rest before returning to conduct the autopsy.

When they gathered again, all suffered terrible headaches and dizziness. Some felt they would be physically ill. They came to the conclusion that they were suffering the effects of carbon monoxide poisoning from the two stoves that burned continuously during the removal of Braine from his coffin. Although the tent flap had been tied open and a breeze had blown through during the work, the fumes had gathered in the grave pit, creating the problem.

When Amy and Beattie entered the X-ray/autopsy tent to begin their work, Notman pointed out a series of lesions on Braine's body: on the left and right shoulders, in the groin area and along the left chest wall. These lesions involved the skin and in some cases the tissue and muscle below. Close inspection revealed teeth marks. Notman and Amy agreed that rats must have attacked the body while it had rested aboard the *Erebus,* prior to burial.

Rats were a common problem on nineteenth-century ships and caused difficulties even among Arctic expeditions. Elisha Kent Kane, the United States Navy officer, had experienced severe problems with the vermin while commanding the *Advance* in the Franklin search from 1853 to 1855:

> They are everywhere . . . under the stove, in the steward's lockers, in our cushions, about our beds. If I was asked what, after darkness and cold and scurvy, are the three besetting curses of our Arctic sojourn, I should say RATS, RATS, RATS.
>
> . . . it became impossible to stow anything below decks. Furs, woollens, shoes, specimens of natural history, everything we disliked to lose, however little valuable to them, was gnawed into and destroyed.

Even efforts to fumigate the ship with the "vilest imaginable compounds of vapours—brimstone, burnt leather, and arsenic" failed to get rid of the rats.

Notman had compared the X-rays of Hartnell with those just taken of Braine and described one interesting difference to Beattie: "With Hartnell's skull we could not penetrate to see bony details with X-rays because of the solid block of ice inside. That's what is creating this uniform whiteness," he said, pointing at the X-ray. "In contrast, Braine's skull could be penetrated quite easily. I really don't have any explanation for that because they were buried under similar circumstances."

Further examination of the X-rays revealed some degenerative arthritic changes in the hands, possibly related to occupational stresses. The feet also showed arthritic changes, in particular, the big toes had a condition called *hallux rigidus*. These observations would be consistent with a man of Braine's age and occupation. In addition to arthritic changes, small bony projections, probably benign bone tumours *(osteochondromas)*, were seen in the bones of the knees (on the tibias).

The autopsy took seven hours and was extremely comprehensive. Like Hartnell's, it was performed on the ground with the body resting on a sheet of white plastic. Written and recorded accounts were made during the whole period, and a thorough photographic record taken. Beattie assisted Amy during the autopsy, labelling storage containers and collecting tissue samples.

Unlike either Torrington or Hartnell, Braine was partially decomposed, demonstrating that some time had elapsed after William Braine's death before the burial actually took place. An explanation for this apparent delay is difficult to find, though two possibilities were discussed. During the spring of 1846, parties were sent away from the ships to survey parts of nearby Devon Island. Franklin campsites had been discovered by searchers north of Beechey Island on the west coast of Devon Island and at Cape Riley. It is possible Braine had been with one of these parties when he died; after suffering a rapid decline in health in the manner of later sledge crews, some members of which became so ill that they had to be hauled back as passengers on the sledges they were meant to be pulling. There was even physical evidence to support this: The presence of ulcerations over the anterior surface of both shoulders indicated the likelihood of abrasion from sledge hauling. With two graves already located at Beechey Island, his body would have been returned for burial at the tiny cemetery. Wrapped and secured to a sledge he would have frozen within a few hours, though decomposition would have already set in. When the sledge party arrived at the ships, he may have been taken on board for examination by the doctors, followed by preparation for burial. During the time spent on ship, the rate of decay would have accelerated. Another possibility was related to poor weather. Braine may have died when the weather conditions did not allow his immediate burial. This seems a less reasonable explanation, as the body could easily have been placed in a cool or even freezing part of the ship, where the amount of observed decomposition would have been far less likely to occur. Whatever the reason, the decomposition was at least a possible explanation for Braine's body being placed quickly and without care in the coffin.

During this final autopsy, Beattie wondered what Torrington, Hartnell and Braine would have thought about his research. The three men were explorers in their own time, either through conscription or by choice, involved in dangerous exploits that embodied the Victorian ideals of adventure, imperialism and self-sacrifice. Now, at least in body, they had emerged from the ice to briefly visit the 1980s. They could not have foretold such an odyssey.

With the autopsy and X-rays complete, a plane arrived on 20 June to pick up Amy, Notman, Anderson, Schweger and Spenceley. Those remaining on site wrapped Braine's body tightly in cotton and lowered it to Beattie and Savelle, who were standing in the grave. Gently, they laid the body in the coffin and positioned it carefully. Minutes before, Beattie had spread the shroud along the bottom of the coffin and, once the body had been placed on it, the left side of the shroud was brought over the body, followed by the right side, which was tucked underneath. The kerchief, undershirt, sweater, shirt and stockings, each wrapped in protective mylar, were then placed in the coffin and the lid lowered into position. The north side of the tent was pulled back, and the sun, low in the northern sky at 11 PM, illuminated the headboard and inside walls of the tent. Standing beside the grave, bathed in brilliant yellow sunlight, the team silently gave a moment of reflection and respect to William Braine. Beattie then jumped into the grave, and a bucket of gravel was passed down to him. He slowly emptied the bucket over the plaque, spreading the gravel in a protective layer on its surface.

The filling of the grave began immediately. The huge pile of gravel, resting beside the grave, attested to the depth of the burial. Two people shovelled gravel into buckets while the others took turns carrying the buckets to the grave and pouring them in. Soon the gravel pile began to shrink, and within three hours the grave had been filled to a point where the large rocks could be repositioned on the surface—but mental and physical exhaustion had taken hold, and this task would be completed the following day.

Several days were spent completing the restoration of the site, and, after dismantling their camp, the remaining researchers left in two groups: Beattie, Nungaq and Kowal on 24 June, with Carlson, Savelle and Damkjar following on 27 June.

Other than the Franklin search expeditions of the 1850s, no one else had spent so much time at the site where the crews of the *Erebus* and *Terror* had experienced their first Arctic winter, and the early searchers had departed with many questions still unanswered. But Beattie left Beechey Island convinced that Petty Officer Torrington, Able Seaman Hartnell and Private Braine would provide some answers, for it seemed they had lived again for a few brief hours during the Arctic summers of 1984 and 1986.

— 16 —

Understanding a

DISASTER

THE FROZEN TISSUE, hair and bone samples from both John
Hartnell and William Braine were carried back to Edmonton in
a small insulated cooler, and, within two days of leaving
Beechey Island, were stored in a deep freeze at the University of
Alberta Hospital. So much depended on this tiny box of samples.
This was the evidence that would either confirm or defeat Beattie's
theory about the impact of lead on the Franklin expedition.

If trace element analysis of the samples revealed lead levels dramatically lower than had been obtained from Torrington and the
Booth Point skeleton, then the source of lead exposure for those
previously tested would have to be re-examined. The question
would then be: Why only Torrington and not the others? But if elevated levels of lead were identified during the testing of the remains
of Hartnell and Braine, then a much more substantial argument
could be made for the underlying impact that lead would have had
on the expedition. Five years of research now hinged on the extraction and analysis of the information locked in the tissue samples.

Such analysis, however, takes careful planning, and, in the following months, while Kowal prepared to test the human samples, Beattie spent his time studying the ten tin cans collected at Beechey Island.

Again, there was no question that lead contamination from the solder would have been considerable, but, on closer examination, the tins also revealed something unexpected, something Beattie and Damkjar had overlooked while plotting and describing the artefacts on the island. The side seams of some of the tins were incomplete. In fact, it appeared as if the tinsmith who made them had failed to properly seal the end part of the seams. The significance of this missed step in the manufacturing process cannot be overemphasized, as it would have resulted in spoilage of the food contained in the tins. It is, therefore, important to understand the design of the tins supplied to Franklin's expedition, both for the location of solder and the reason for the flaws.

In 1845, tinned preserved food was still a relatively recent innovation, one that would have an immediate and major impact on maritime exploration. The tin container itself, patented in England in 1811, was immediately embraced by the British for use in its Royal Navy in most parts of the world. It was an invention that presumably would allow expeditions to winter successfully in the Arctic and make an assault on the Northwest Passage seem destined for success.

The first containers were constructed from a tinned wrought-iron sheet bent round a cylindrical form, with the edges allowed to lap over one another. The tinsmith then placed his soldering iron on each formed seam (internal and external), where he floated a bead of solder along most of its length. The seams were left unsoldered at the top and bottom ends.

The top and bottom end pieces were then bent to form a flange. When the ends were placed on the cylinder body, the flange slid over either the outside or the inside of the cylinder, depending on the tin type. (The flange was the reason why the tinsmith did not

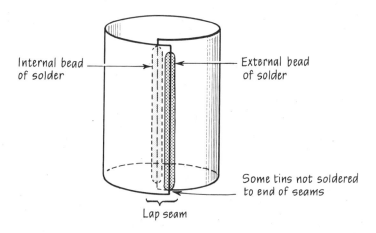

Internal bead of solder — External bead of solder

Some tins not soldered to end of seams

Lap seam

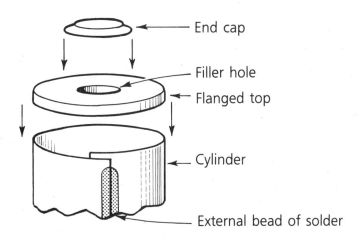

End cap

Filler hole

Flanged top

Cylinder

External bead of solder

solder the body lap-seams all the way to the top and bottom: the end pieces could be slipped onto the cylinder body without being blocked by seam solder.) However, when the ends were soldered on, the small gaps between the lap-seam and the flange were not always sealed with a drop of solder. The incomplete seam very likely resulted in the spoilage of some of the expedition's food supply, which supported the conclusions of some of the leading Franklin searchers.

The top end piece of each tin also had a filler hole that varied in size, depending on the size and type of canister. The top end piece was attached first, then heavily soldered on the inside. The bottom end piece was then attached, and it too was soldered internally through the filler hole in the top end piece. Solder was then applied round the outside of the end seams.

Food was pushed through the filler hole and the tin then almost completely immersed in boiling water (sometimes containing calcium chloride to increase the cooking temperature.) When cooking was complete and while the food was still at temperature, the filler hole was covered by a cap, secured with solder. The tins, now completely sealed, formed a partial vacuum upon cooling. The next step was to paint the outside of the tins to protect them against damage and corrosion. (The solder itself was made up of more than 90 per cent lead, with the balance being tin. This high lead level produced a solder that had poor "wetting" characteristics— in other words, it did not flow readily when in a liquid state. This meant it did not migrate easily into the spaces formed between two pieces of metal, as would solder with a higher tin content.)

The contract for the tinned preserved food was given to Stephan Goldner on 1 April 1845. On 5 May, the day Franklin received his sailing instructions, the superintendent of the Victualling Yard at Deptford reported that only one-tenth of the contract had been supplied. This was followed three days later by a promise from Goldner that by 12 May, all the meat would be delivered and the soups by 15 May, though he did ask for and receive permission to pack the soups in tins larger than in the original specification. There is a good chance that in the rush to complete the order, quality control suffered and some food that would later spoil was included among the 8,000 tins supplied to the expedition. If a significant proportion of the food went bad, it would have added a considerable burden to the expedition.

As Beattie continued his research into the problem tins, Roger Amy submitted the tissues collected under sterile conditions for bacteriological assessment. The preliminary results of this research identified tuberculosis in the lung tissue of William Braine, though there had been no success in culturing the organism. However, bacteria collected from the bowel of William Braine (an uncommon form of the genus *Clostridium*, associated with the human bowel) *was* cultured. Remarkably, bacteria dating to 1846, and once part of William Braine, is still alive today.

Then, in early 1987, Walt Kowal and experts at the Alberta Workers' Health and Compensation laboratory in Edmonton began to test hair samples collected from Torrington in 1984 and Hartnell and Braine in 1986. Again, the method of testing involved the combustion at high temperatures of solutions made from samples of the hair. (The resulting emissions are characteristic of a particular element, such as lead, and can be identified and quantified.) The first tests were run on hair collected from the crown and nape areas of Torrington's head. They revealed levels ranging from 413 to 657 parts per million (ppm), very similar to the extremely high levels previously identified in hair samples taken from Torrington.

It wasn't until April that Kowal called Beattie with results of the first tests on Hartnell and Braine: "Not a thing, didn't find a thing. There's nothing in the other two," Kowal said.

Beattie was quiet for a moment, then said: "Well, now it gets more complicated." His mind was already at work trying to figure out this new twist. But Kowal, now laughing, quickly added: "Wait a minute, I was pulling your leg. The levels are high, there's no denying it."

Hair from Hartnell had yielded lead levels ranging from 138 to 313 ppm, while hair from Braine was very similar at 145 to 280 ppm. Although not as high as the lead levels measured in Torrington, the results exceeded the contemporary hair standard by well over twenty times. Subsequent testing would eliminate the possibility of external twentieth-century contamination, and further tests on bone and tissue from Torrington, Hartnell and Braine underscored the accuracy of the hair results.

Furthermore, the fact that the information on lead exposure came from hair meant that the contamination occurred during Franklin's voyage—not from industrial pollution in the British environment of the day. Possible sources of lead exposure on the expedition were numerous, including tea wrapped in lead foil, pewterware and lead-glazed pottery vessels. But it was the reliance of Franklin's expedition on tinned food that was the root cause. It has since been calculated that each sailor would have been allotted about ½ pound (.25 kg) of tinned food every second day, resulting in regular and considerable ingestion of lead. And while there can be no exact explanation of the differences in the level of lead between Torrington on the one hand and Hartnell and Braine on the other, it is quite likely related to differences in the food consumed by the three men and their jobs aboard ship. For example, Torrington, as leading stoker, may have picked up added contamination from lead in coal dust.

What is very clear from the findings, however, now based on more than four (including the Booth Point skeleton and other bones gathered on King William Island in 1982) separate individuals and using the facilities of a series of different labs, is that lead played an important role in the declining health of the entire crews of the *Erebus* and *Terror*—not only in their loss of physical energy but increasingly in their minds' despair. Loss of appetite, fatigue, weakness and colic are some of the physical symptoms of lead poisoning; it can also cause disturbances of the central and peripheral nervous systems, producing neurotic and erratic behaviour and paralysis of the limbs. But it is the effects on the mind that may have been of greatest importance in isolating the impact of lead on the expedition. Under the continuing and prolonged stressful conditions of long periods in the Arctic, even very subtle effects of low lead exposure could have had significant impact on the decision-making abilities of the men, particularly the officers. Only clear minds can hope to make correct decisions.

There is no single reason why the expedition failed, of course; it was a deadly combination of factors. That is why there is no one answer to the question of what caused the Franklin expedition disaster. Perhaps the best that can be done today is to isolate the reasonable possibilities and fit them into the broad circumstances as identified from the scattered remains found at archaeological sites. This is what Beattie was able to do.

In some cases, such as the three sailors from Beechey Island, the effects of lead poisoning were catastrophic. Amy's autopsy results showed that, like Torrington, both Hartnell and Braine suffered from tuberculosis and died of pneumonia. In addition, radiological evidence obtained by Derek Notman identified a collapsed eleventh thoracic vertebra in William Braine, a condition caused by Pott's disease, which in turn is usually caused by tubercular infection. But it was the insidious and poorly understood poison, lead, entering their bodies at high levels over the course of the first months of the expedition, that weakened these three young men to the point that they were easily killed off by supervening diseases. Other crewmen would have been as severely affected by the poisoning, which probably explains at least some of the other twenty-one deaths experienced by the expedition in the early period before the ships were deserted on 22 April 1848.

As for the high ratio of officer deaths prior to the death march (nine out of twenty-one), Beattie found possible explanations consistent with the lead findings. If the officers, a rigidly separated and very aloof class, even during long and confined expeditions, were using their pewter tableware and eating a preferential food source (that is, proportionately more tinned food), they may have ingested much higher levels of lead than the other seamen. It is at least possible that Sir John Franklin himself died directly or indirectly from the effects of lead poisoning.

As for those men who died during the tragic death march in the spring and summer of 1848, some may have exhibited classic symptoms of the poisoning, such as anorexia, weakness and fatigue and paranoia, which would have compounded the effects of starvation and scurvy. Other crewmen may not have shown any obvious effects of the poison, perhaps because of differing diets and physical responses to the lead.

It is sadly ironic that Franklin's expedition, certainly one of the greatest seafaring expeditions ever launched, carrying all the tools that early industry and innovation could offer, should have been mortally wounded by one of them. Yet Beattie now believed he had the scientific evidence to say that this was the case.

When Sir John Franklin sailed from the Thames in May 1845, an entire nation believed that the honour of conquering the Northwest Passage was within his grasp. None could have known that inside the tins stored in the ship's hold there ticked a time bomb that helped not only to deny Franklin his triumph but to steal away 129 brave lives. And while good hopes decayed in a relatively short time for the expedition crews, the physicians aboard the *Erebus* and *Terror* would have been helpless to intervene. The health risks imposed by the use of lead-tin solder were simply not appreciated at that time. (It was not until 1890 that government legislation in Britain finally banned soldering on the insides of food tins.)

THERE IS OFTEN a terrible price to pay in human exploration reliant upon new technology. That fact was vividly demonstrated again in recent years by the failure of the space shuttles *Challenger* in 1986 and *Columbia* in 2003. Indeed, our explorers of space share a bond with past explorers of the unknown frozen shores of the earth. In many ways, there is no difference between the Franklin and space shuttle disasters. Time, technology, social conditions and politics have changed, but the spirit and motivation underlying both endeavours remain. Both used the most advanced technology of their time and both paid the ultimate price. An article published in an 1855 edition of *Blackwood's Edinburgh Magazine* laments those dangers:

We confess we have not heart enough, in the general enterprise of knowledge, to view such a sacrifice as that of Franklin and his crew without a chill of horror: there is something frightful, inexorable, inhuman, in prosecuting researches, which are mere researches, after such a costly fashion . . . and when we hear of the martyrs of science, whether they perish among the arctic snow or the sands of the desert, we begin to think of science herself as a placid Juggernaut . . . with benevolent pretensions, winning, by some weird magic, and throwing away with all the calmness of an abstract and impersonal principle, those generous lives.

These thoughts, published even before M'Clintock made his grisly discoveries, could have been written in response to Beattie's. But such conclusions dwell only on the failure of science and technology and deny the achievements. For after Franklin, others followed. They too used the latest technology available to them, and they succeeded not only in tracing a Northwest Passage but in conquering the last and most forbidding land on earth.

Epilogue

The Age of Lead

FOR DECADES, the elaborate historical constructs fashioned by students of the Franklin disaster provided a grimly satisfactory explanation of the tragedy, one that neatly adhered to prevailing expectations. Fundamentally, the expedition was viewed as a momentous test of endurance against the malignant forces of nature; Franklin's defeat, alas, confirmed the hideous risks that that entailed. Subsequent investigations rarely strayed from the well-worn path—reliance on the cumulative wisdom of early searchers, written records and accepted truths—to consider physical clues, such as first-hand observation and analysis of food sources. Even then, the work was encumbered by the limitations of the existing technology for scientific analysis.

When a Franklin expedition tin, retrieved by M'Clintock, was opened and examined in 1926, the beef contents were declared to be "perfectly satisfactory." In light of the catastrophic health consequences of ingesting the lead-contaminated contents of such tins, they would seem to have proven rather less than satisfactory

to those reliant on the tainted provisions. Results from the contemporary analyses of the human soft-tissue samples by Walt Kowal,
Owen Beattie and their colleagues, published in 1991 in the *Journal
of Archaeological Science,* only served to underscore the dramatic
nature of the lead poisoning identified in the bodies of Beechey
Island. Comparison with lead levels in modern populations, even
in instances of occupational exposure, confirmed the devastating
effects. Lead levels in the soft tissues of the crew members aver-
aged ten to thirty times higher than in modern unexposed
individuals. The pattern was similar in all soft tissues examined,
including the aorta, stomach, kidney, liver, lung, spleen, bladder,
muscle and intestine.

Examination of preserved soft tissues and previously analyzed
hair excluded the possibility that the lead exposure was simply a
product of non-expedition factors, such as the environment of
nineteenth-century industrial Britain. While the three crewmen
died early on, within only seven to eleven months of sailing,
sufficient time had elapsed to have eliminated most lead absorbed
into the soft tissues before their departure. Lead resides in different
body tissues for different periods of time after cessation of exposure. In the case of soft tissues, half of the lead present in an organ
or tissue would have been eliminated in approximately twenty-one
to forty days, with levels continuing to decline at a predictable rate.
It is clear that the source of lead exposure originated not from factors or conditions encountered in England, but from those encountered aboard the discovery vessels themselves—aboard the *Erebus*
and *Terror.* Here, too, contemporary scientific methods provide
confirmation.

The tissues and solder were subjected to lead isotope ratio
analysis, a means of "fingerprinting" the source of lead. The results indicated that the lead in the tissues was identical to that in the
solder used in the food cans. These findings, published in the journal *Nature,* in 1990, concluded that the lead contamination came

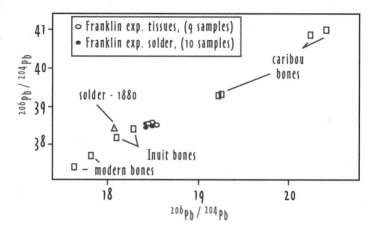

Diagrammatic representation of the lead isotope analysis.

not from a variety of sources, but, without exception, from a single European geological location. Had the body lead resulted from chronic personal exposure to a variety of local and environmental sources before the crews' embarkation, or even afterward, it is unreasonable to suppose that all the individuals would have demonstrated the same isotopic ratios. Unless the sampled sailors had literally lived under the same roof (a possibility discounted by British Admiralty records that show the crews were drawn from regions throughout the United Kingdom), the ratios of lead found in the tissues of each crew member would have been skewed differently. What's more, while representing short-term exposure, the lead in the soft tissues was indistinguishable from lead in the bones. This evidence confirms that the lead stored in the bones of crew members before the expedition was swamped by the subsequent massive exposure resulting from the solder in the tins. There is no question of the source of the lead found in the bodies of Franklin's men: it came from the tinned foods. The devastating impact on their health followed.

Furthermore, research conducted on skeletal remains discovered at a previously unrecorded site discovered on King William

Island in 1992 served to provide independent corroboration of Beattie's research. The results of this new investigation, published by Anne Keenleyside et al in the *Journal of Archaeological Science* in 1996, stated that the "pattern of distribution of lead between bones indicates excessive intake of lead during the period of the expedition. Predictions of blood lead levels based on the measured bone lead concentrations, suggest that the current upper limit for occupational exposure recommended to prevent neurological changes was exceeded." In 1997, a second publication arising from this research stated that "elevated lead levels in the remains are consistent with previous measurements and support the conclusions of Beattie and colleagues that lead poisoning had greatly debilitated the men by this point."

Tinned foods came into widespread use among the general population by the late 1800s, becoming "almost a necessity," and this popularity was mirrored by a dawning sense of the danger posed by the use of solder containing lead. These suspicions are recorded in the medical literature of the time. Documented instances of "metallic poisoning," or lead poisoning, attributed to consumption of tinned foods, began to appear in the 1880s, and reference is made to the common complaint regarding drops or fragments of solder found mixed with the food contents within the tins. The *Medical News* in 1883 warned: "In cases of obscure nervous affections look out for lead-poisoning, and bear in mind the use of canned food as a source of such poisoning." Physicians started to raise questions as to the desirability of tinning as a means of food preservation. Changes to the design of food cans were subsequently introduced, addressing the most obvious lead-contamination sources, but not before the world's most prestigious medical journal, *The Lancet,* asked why bottles were not substituted for tins. The answer surely lay with an industry that had an enormous capital stake in the trade, and the jobs associated with it. Nor are the serious consequences of lead relegated to the nineteenth century. Only in recent decades has lead been removed from house paints, gasoline and food tins (though tinned goods and lead-glazed ceramics in developing countries continue to be problematic); as well, drinking water is monitored to identify and manage the hazard.

Microbiological research into Hartnell and Braine also produced another curious, perhaps ominous, discovery. Not only have bacterial strains of the genus *Clostridium* survived the prolonged period of freezing, but some of the strains have shown resistance to modern antibiotics, a remarkable characteristic considering that the bacteria originated nearly a century before the development of antibiotics. It has been suggested that strains of bacteria more tolerant of pollutants can also show resistance to antibiotics. Medical researchers are only beginning to investigate the significance and implications of this evidence, especially in relation to the role of environmental pollutants in exacerbating the development of such resistance. There is a certain irony in the possibility that men who lived during the reign of Victoria should be the ones to alert scientists to such an insidious effect of the poison, lead, in our own time.

It is certainly not easy—and for some, doubtless impossible—to entertain the notion that so basic an instrument of human convenience as a tin can could have been a major factor in the loss of the Franklin expedition. From a purely emotional standpoint, it should have been *anything* else. If rigid adherence to conventional interpretations of the disaster is not to be followed, with scurvy, starvation, stress and hypothermia judged the relevant health factors, then at least it would be more palatable to know that any new evidence to arise did so from investigation of more glamorous sources of information, such as the *Erebus* and *Terror*, still at rest in the icy deep. The fundamental lesson of the forensic investigation into the Franklin expedition is the very recognition that so great an undertaking as the most celebrated of all Arctic voyages could be vulnerable to so apparently minute a factor. Profound questions arise from the investigations of the simple evidence represented by the tins, questions not limited to the role of lead as a factor in the fate of the Franklin expedition, but rather the health consequences of European food-preserving technology of the nineteenth century on an entire era of exploration.

Before Franklin, there were the curious references to an unexplained illness that appeared in the narrative of Captain George Back from 1836–37. Immediately following Franklin, there was the official report of Sir James Clark Ross regarding his unsuccessful 1848–49 search expedition. It is notable that Ross, like Franklin, was supplied with tinned provisions by Stephan Goldner. The outbreaks of "debility" amongst Arctic expeditions did not end there, however; another outbreak is germane to this discussion.

Commander George Washington De Long, captain of the 1879–81 Arctic voyage of the U.S. steamer, *Jeannette,* had taken specific precautions against "debility." Whilst unconvinced about lime juice's efficacy, he well understood "the importance attached to it by Arctic medical authorities and Arctic voyagers generally [and] did not care to depart from an established custom." De Long had three barrels of lime juice loaded aboard the *Jeannette.* The expedition also carried large stores of canned meats, soups and vegetables.

De Long sought the North Pole, failing which he intended to navigate the Northwest Passage. It would be a privately backed expedition; De Long's benefactor was a newspaper proprietor, James Gordon Bennett, owner of the *New York Herald* and the man who also assigned correspondent Henry Morton Stanley to travel to Africa to locate the British missionary Dr. David Livingstone. Bennett's influence was such that he was able to secure an Act of the United States Congress declaring the *Jeannette*'s voyage a "national undertaking."

De Long had been involved in an earlier cruise into the eastern Arctic, and had written, "I never in my life saw such a dreary land of desolation, and I hope I may never find myself cast away in such a perfectly God-forsaken place." He was not an Arctic lion either, in appearance (balding, pince-nez) or temperament (he was sensitive and studious), but he had caught a bad case of what his wife termed "the polar virus."

The *Jeannette* sailed from San Francisco on 8 July 1879, with a scientific staff that included an astronomer, meteorologist and naturalist from the Smithsonian Institution. Beset by ice on 6 September, she then drifted for two years in the polar pack as sickness gradually tightened its hold on her 33 crewmen. The men were largely dependent on tinned foods, and, as their symptoms worsened to include severe abdominal pain, fear spread that something in their diet was poisoning them. The crew was already in a severely weakened state when the *Jeannette* was finally crushed by the pack-ice in the Laptev Sea in 1881, though the men escaped, dragging three boats and supplies over hundreds of miles to open water. There was no fresh meat to be had out on the ice, only what provisions they could carry with them. One boat foundered in the icy sea, the other two were separated before they reached land at Siberia's Lena Delta.

Wandering across the marshy and featureless land of the delta, the crew of one boat stumbled across a native village and was saved. The men in the other boat—including De Long—faced a terrible ordeal. They located small huts, but found they had been abandoned: "We can see traces of Russians or other civilized beings. A rude checker-board, wooden forks, pieces of pencil, etc." They struggled on for a month, killing several reindeer, but it was not enough. De Long made the painful decision to kill and eat the ship's mascot, a dog named Snoozer. Soon his party was reduced to eating the animal hides the men had worn for warmth, their boot soles and, finally, moss dug from the frozen ground.

Their final days were recorded in pitiful detail by De Long, the delirious howls of the starved men "a horrible accompaniment to the wretchedness of our surroundings." In his journal, he also recorded the strange dream of the ship's surgeon, James Ambler: "He seemed to be accompanying the survivors of Sir John Franklin's last expedition on their journey to the Great Fish River." Certainly the appalling nature of their suffering had a great deal in common with that of the Franklin crewmen, and Ambler's dream proved portentous: he suffered the throes of just such a death. When his body was found, there was a trickle of blood from his mouth, into which his fingers were stuffed.

With the ground frozen, the first men to die were carried out on the ice of a nearby river and crude markers were carved and erected on its bank in their memory. Soon the survivors were too weak to carry the dead out to the ice, so they dragged them behind the corner of their makeshift shelter so the bodies were out of sight. De Long continued to read divine service, but his diary entries, which once consumed pages with scientific observations and exacting accounts of their lives amidst the polar pack, were spare. As with his strength so went erudition. De Long made a last diary entry on 30 October 1881. There was no stirring sentimentality or evocation of patriotism, simply this: "Boyd and Gortz died during the night. Mr. Collins dying." In all, twenty of the thirty-three expedition members perished. Wrote a searcher after coming across De Long's last camp: "The world is richer by this gift of suffering," though he could only offer in evidence the following: "A slight gain was made in the solution of the Arctic problem." Ironically, the *Jeannette,* or at least relics of her, completed the Northwest Passage, drifting from west to east without her crew; and wreckage from the ship appeared on the southwest coast of Greenland in 1884, borne there by the polar tides.

There was a public clamour for an accounting for De Long's tragic failure. Naval and congressional investigations followed, and, in 1883, a writer in *Medical News,* drawing from the Report of the Court of Inquiry, published evidence that something other than scurvy or starvation might have been a factor in the disaster. In response to direct questions from the Court regarding the "character of the provisions" supplied to the expedition, a survivor, Lieutenant John Danehower, said: "In May, 1881, a number of the people became affected with stomach disorders, which were attributed to tin-poisoning. It had been observed that the inside of the tomato cans had turned dark, as though acted upon by the acid . . . " When asked by the judge advocate about the physical condition of the men when they landed on the ice, in June 1881, the same witness said: " . . . Lieut. [Charles] Chipp was disabled and prostrated by what was supposed to be tin-poisoning . . . A number of men . . . were also affected by the tin-poisoning, and were prostrated a few days later."

In the Report of the Court of Inquiry, the sickness was judged to be "the result of eating canned provisions." In his 1883 account, the medical writer W.E. Magruder declared: "I have no doubt the so-called 'tin-poisoning' was really lead-poisoning, resulting from the use of cans coated with the alloy of tin and lead." As the *Medical News* went on to report: "The danger of contamination from the lead contained in the solder depends upon the way in which the can is made . . . In a hand-made can by a careless workman, a square inch or more of solder surface may be present on the inside of the can. Drops of solder may also fall into the can in the process of sealing, and most of our readers must have seen such fragments of solder. If they have not, their cooks have."

While De Long did not survive, his journal did, and it describes with remarkable clarity the effects of lead on the *Jeannette's* crew. For the first time, a contemporaneous account by an explorer identified lead poison as a health factor on an expedition:

> June 1st [1881], Wednesday.—What next? The doctor [Ambler] informs me this morning that he is of opinion that several of our party under his treatment are suffering from lead poisoning . . . No less than six people, and the sledge party yet to hear from. Suspicion was first directed to the water, for as all joints about the distiller are red leaded to make them tight, we fear that some of the lead was carried over with the steam and deposited in the receiver. This, unfortunately, cannot be entirely avoided, though it may be reduced. Then I examined all vessels in which drinking water is carried or tea and coffee made, and I put out of commission all having any solder patches, substituting iron vessels lined with porcelain. But upon examining our tomatoes, they were found to

show traces of lead in larger amounts than the water, and the doctor thinks that the distemper, if I may so call it, is due to our large consumption of that vegetable. The acid of the tomato acts chemically upon the solder used in the tins, and the dangerous mixture is formed; and since we have had tomatoes every day for dinner subsequent to May 4th, it is assumed that we have become largely dosed with lead, and some of us have had to succumb . . . It has transpired that the steward, who is the worst case, is remarkably fond of this vegetable, and eats of it unsparingly . . . A very interesting question here comes in. Our canned fruits have, I believe, similar chemical action upon the lead soldering, and no doubt we are absorbing more or less lead all the time. Now does this chemical action begin at once or at the end of two years? A very important question to an arctic expedition, for of what use is it to secure exemption from scurvy for two years if disabling lead poisoning finishes you in the third year? The doctor says each severe attack may be mitigated by medicine, but a continued absorption of the lead will produce palsy, and that would certainly be a perplexing disease to deal with in an arctic ship. If the chemical action begins as soon as the tomato is canned one is in danger at all times . . .

Certainly no exemption from scurvy was secured for many of the Arctic expeditions of this era, despite the claims made for the antiscorbutic properties of tinned foods, though in that respect De Long's seems to have fared better than most. But the ancient scourge now had company from an equally virulent and deadly affliction.

The successes, or more often the failures, of nineteenth-century Arctic expeditions are usually viewed as little more than inventories of the foibles of individual commanders—which, if one believes the usual popular historical appraisals, run the gamut from simple incompetency and benign eccentricity to outright, stark-raving lunacy—squared off against a malignant climate and relentless geography. With hindsight, the decisions made and actions taken by some of those commanders do lend credence to the view that the Arctic heaved with an armada of the reality-challenged. But all that arrogance and misapprehension amounts to little beside one simple fact: that many of those who sailed in search of the passage in the nineteenth century did so with their physical and mental health seriously compromised.

These failures cannot simply be assigned to character in the face of history's failure to account for a fundamental truth: That at the very moment when explorers sought to conquer the places of greatest extremity, where success relied on every advantage of technology and human ingenuity and when the consequences of failure were so stark and absolute, a new and unanticipated threat to human health had entered the equation. It was a threat absolutely germane to the debate about character, for it also had the effect of subverting and undermining a commander's mental faculties at the same time as it mugged his body. Yes, the forces of the natural world they encountered were little understood. But even less understood was the "debility" caused by the scorbutic and saturnic diseases that ate away at expedition members, loosening their teeth, blackening their gums, bloating their extremities and clouding their judgment.

The story of how the Royal Navy failed to achieve the Northwest Passage is really that of how the world's greatest navy battled, and was ultimately humbled by, a simple yet gruesome disease—scurvy, allied to a menace of which they could not begin to conceive: lead poisoning. The source of their defeat was not the ice-choked seas, the deep cold, the winters of absolute night, the labyrinthine geography or the soul-destroying isolation. It was found in their food supply, most notably in their heavy reliance on tinned foods.

The landscape of the Canadian Arctic has changed little in the intervening years. The grey tracts of stone, the relentless, grinding course of the sea ice, the violet hues of the late-setting sun, all are today as they were in Franklin's time. Adventurers visiting King

William and Beechey islands this summer or the next, whether burdened by backpacks or man-hauling sledges in a personal struggle
to attain some commonality with a lost world, will find their satisfaction. The romance of the Franklin era of exploration and the
emotional response that it evokes is enduring. What is not is the assumption that great men die only of great causes. For despite the
hostile forces of climate and geography the region represents, it
was something else that had a catastrophic effect on the Franklin
expedition—something human.

Afterword

Discovering Erebus and Terror

AND YET, A great mystery remained: where were the ships? How did two Royal Navy exploration ships simply vanish? And literally, for most of seventeen decades, there was very little evidence of HMS *Erebus* and HMS *Terror* at all. A plank was found, which historians carefully scrutinized and concluded may have come from one of the ships. But there was nothing resembling the sort of debris one might associate with a maritime disaster of such magnitude.

There were Inuit accounts that one ship was prone on her side before being crushed by the ice and sinking quickly, it was understood, off the west coast of King William Island, not far from the point of abandonment. The tradition placed the second of the ships farther to the south, in eastern Queen Maud Gulf. A map based on these accounts published in the *Illustrated London News* had an X marking the spot: "ship here." Inuit reported visiting this ship, and evidence pointed to some crewmen being alive when the ship reached that furthermost point. These reports were provided to searchers, who took what they were told seriously and assiduously recorded it. These accounts have guided many of the investigations over the decades, and, despite the challenges of translation and the vagaries of the transcriptions, they have proved remarkably accurate.

As an example, in 1869 Charles Francis Hall recorded Inuit testimony involving the discovery of evidence of cannibalism at Erebus Bay on the west coast of King William Island. In-nook-poo-zhe-jook told Hall that several years earlier he had seen human bones associated with a cooking site that had been "broken up for the marrow in them." There were also bones that had been boiled. Owen Beattie found human remains on the shoreline of Erebus Bay in 1982, and later surveys by archaeologists recovered bones from an islet in Erebus Bay and another site nearby. Many of these bones showed knife cut marks consistent with early-stage cannibalism, butcher marks made as flesh was removed, as well as possible dismemberment.

However, in 2015, a new study, "Evidence for End-stage Cannibalism on Sir John Franklin's Last Expedition to the Arctic, 1845" appeared in the *International Journal of Osteoarchaeology*. Coauthored by Simon Mays, an expert with the Excavation and Analysis Team of Historic England, and Beattie, the paper went a step further. It investigated the bone collected by Beattie to see if there was any evidence for late-stage cannibalism—the breakage and boiling of bones to extract marrow fat.

The results of that investigation support In-nook-poo-zhe-jook's testimony, as the authors found evidence for "pot polish," the polishing of broken edges of bones during boiling. This is, according the study by Mays and Beattie, "the first osteological evidence of end-stage cannibalism among members of the expedition."

"Breakage of bone ends and pot polish suggest deliberate fracturing and heating of bones to aid marrow or grease extraction," Beattie and Mays argued.

Their study not only corroborates the Inuit testimony, but also underscores a degree of desperation that is hard to conceive. It is possible that these particular remains of Franklin sailors were targeted not once, in the efforts of survivors to stave off starvation, but again, and possibly again, perhaps over a prolonged period. Not only days, but even maybe over weeks or months, if cold conditions favoured nutrient preservation. It is a terrible thing to contemplate.

SINCE REMNANTS OF the horror could still be found on beach ridges after so many decades, including bone found at Erebus Bay as recently as 2013, it raised the question: then why not the ships? Surely they had come to represent the greatest possible source for knowledge about the Franklin expedition.

Sooner or later, *Erebus* or *Terror* (or both) would be found, and it would be very exciting to glimpse these submerged artifacts that no doubt would eventually become the basis of a virtual diorama of Victorian Arctic exploration. And who knows, they might also offer some valuable insight into the disaster itself, or answers to some of the enduring Franklin questions.

For example: if a ship reached Queen Maud Gulf, as per the Inuit accounts, then did that ship drift there, perhaps with the ice? Were all hands long dead? The Inuit reportedly found a skeleton on the ship. But Inuit reports raise another intriguing possibility: the witnesses also saw signs of life on the ship, including a recently swept deck and lowered gangplank and fresh footprints from three or four individuals. If Franklin's men were alive, if they had taken the ship there—or even simply if they were alive when the ship drifted or was carried there by ice—then they had connected the dots, joining the final few kilometers of unexplored water and land, and arguably deserve credit for the symbolic completion of the Northwest Passage before they were consumed by it (and in some cases by each other).

DESPITE THE INUIT evidence, the two ships and whatever was aboard those ships remained the two most significant undiscovered Franklin artifacts, short of finding a grave belonging to Franklin himself. That is, until the 2014 Victoria Strait Expedition found one of them.

Interest in the ships had been stoked by important research carried out during the 1990s by David Woodman, a sea captain and scholar of Inuit testimony about Franklin. Woodman, supported in some instances by the Royal Canadian Geographical Society, undertook several expeditions to eastern Queen Maud Gulf, convinced of the accuracy of the Inuit accounts. In 2008 Parks Canada's underwater archaeology team began a systematic multi-year search of the area, painstakingly surveying hundreds of square kilometres of the Arctic seabed.

In 2013, the Canadian government used the Speech from the Throne to announce its "renewed determination" to find Franklin. Britain's Westminster had once been the parliament at which Franklin's fate had been debated. Now, it had become the subject of Canadian political interest, a response to questions of sovereignty and the growing economic importance of Canada's Arctic—and the effect of changing climate that is opening the Northwest Passage to commercial shipping.

In 2014, the government launched the largest Franklin search since the 1850s. In all, four ships and three smaller boats were involved in the multi-partner project, which was led by Parks Canada and involved a half-dozen other Government of Canada departments and agencies, the Government of Nunavut, as well as non-government partners, including the Royal Canadian Geographical Society. The objective was to locate either or both of *Erebus* and *Terror*. According to *Titanic* discoverer Dr. Robert Ballard, they were the two most important undiscovered shipwrecks in the world.

The goal was to bring the greatest possible capability and the very best available technology to the area of the disaster, and search the two locations identified by the Inuit testimony—a northern search area off the west coast of King William Island and a southern search area in eastern Queen Maud Gulf.

Inuit traditional knowledge about the fate of Franklin and his men has persisted. To build on the recorded accounts, Parks Canada consulted Louie Kamookak of Gjoa Haven, the only community on King William Island, Nunavut. An historian who has made the collection of Inuit testimony and oral histories his life's work, for years Kamookak has travelled all over his ancestral lands in pursuit of clues. Franklin and his men were outsiders, but despite that they have become part of the Inuit story too.

If even one of the missing vessels could be located, the potential to answer enduring questions about the expedition disaster would be vastly enhanced. The ships represented storehouses of information about the expedition and its final months.

Conditions in the field contributed to a sequence of events that resulted in the find. Ironically, unexpectedly heavy ice was a critical factor. The original forecast called for the ice in Victoria Strait to melt out completely by the end of August, leading to open water conditions in September. In the past such a forecast would never have been made since prior to 2006 the pack in Victoria Strait was composed of heavy multi-year ice brought by the current from the Arctic Ocean via M'Clintock Channel. Victoria Strait has been described as an "ice sink" because of the congregations of ice. The fact that it took three days for Franklin's crew, even with a burden of heavily laden sledges, to travel the 28 kilometers from the ships to Crozier's Landing indicates serious ice—the kind that beset *Erebus* and *Terror* in the first place. Since 2006, however, that heavy ice was replaced by first-year ice and Victoria Strait cleared every year except 2009 and, it turned out, 2014.

The presence of ice had a profound impact on the 2014 survey plans. Only one vessel, One Ocean *Voyager* (also known as *Akademik Sergey Vavilov*), a Finnish-built, Russian-owned ship operated by partner One Ocean Expeditions of Squamish, B.C., focused on the northern search area in Victoria Strait, and only then in a severely limited area due to the ice. The best technology carried on the expedition, Defence Research Development Canada's Arctic Explorer AUV, which employed an advanced technology called synthetic aperture sonar was deployed off of *Voyager* on six missions in Victoria Strait, in areas in the northern search area identified by Parks Canada as higher probability for a find. In total, these missions, conducted over five days, covered 27.93 km². While small areas in the northern search area were surveyed, the presence of the ice cover forced other vessels in the expedition to concentrate on the southern search area. Two vessels, CCGS *Sir Wilfrid Laurier* and the search workhorse *Martin Bergmann*, operated by Arctic Research Foundation, focused their survey efforts in the open waters of Queen Maud Gulf. (Ice prevented a fourth vessel, HMCS Kingston, from reaching the survey areas).

During the search in the southern area, a helicopter operating off of the *Laurier*, piloted by Andrew Stirling, landed on a small island. Stirling, not just a highly skilled pilot but also an amateur sleuth, wandered along a beach, where he found an iron fitting from a ship, later identified as part of a boat-launching davit. Archaeologist Douglas Stenton later found two broad arrows, signifying its Royal Navy provenance. Stirling also discovered a second object, wooden, possibly a plug for a deck hawse, the iron pipe through which the ship's chain cable would descend into the chain locker below. These were significant finds. They were not the sort of item likely to be carried off a ship by retreating crews, but suggested instead the existence of a wreck in the vicinity.

After concentrating the search in the waters nearby, a towfish sonar pulled by Parks Canada's research vessel *Investigator* captured an image of a wreck. Dive team members Ryan Harris and Jonathan Moore of Parks Canada were the first to see it. Dive team head Marc-André Bernier was summoned from the One Ocean *Voyager*, and subsequent investigation by a remotely operated underwater vehicle (ROV) confirmed it was a Franklin vessel. Even-

262 | FROZEN IN TIME

tually, the Parks Canada experts measured the vessel, confirming the wreck to be HMS *Erebus*, Sir John Franklin's own ship, and presumably the place where he died.

At a news conference held on September 9, 2014, at the Walkley Road, Ottawa, labs of Parks Canada, then-Prime Minister Stephen Harper said, "I am delighted to announce that this year's Victoria Strait Expedition has solved one of Canada's greatest mysteries."

The fate of Franklin has been a global mystery, the greatest in polar exploration history. The discovery of *Erebus*, and then, just two years later, the discovery of *Terror*, promises to fill many of the gaps in understanding, just as the forensic investigation of human remains has done.

A tip from a resident of Gjoa Haven led the crew of the *Martin Bergmann*, who were taking part in the ongoing Parks Canada-led search, to discover *Terror* in September 2016. Its location, in Terror Bay (named for the ship long before the discovery), off the southern coast of King William Island, defied the theories of historians and overturned existing conclusions about the sequence of events at the disastrous end of the expedition. Like that of *Erebus*, in Queen Maud Gulf, the *Terror*'s location suggested Franklin's crews remanned the ship after the initial abandonment and may have steered it to the south, escaping Victoria Strait. With that act, they would have discovered a Northwest Passage. Underwater archaeology is certain to offer valuable insight into the disaster. It remains to be seen whether it will be enough to satisfy our yearning to know more, or whether the Franklin mystery will ever, truly, be solved.

Acknowledgements

THE FIELD and laboratory researches of the Franklin Forensic
Project, and the Franklin Osteology Project, described in this
book, were supported by the Social Sciences and Humanities
Research Council of Canada, the Boreal Institute for Northern
Studies, the Polar Continental Shelf Project and the University of
Alberta. Sincerest thanks go to these organizations and agencies.

Additional support for various phases of the project was
received from the Park Nicollet Medical Foundation, the Science
Advisory Board (NWT), Alberta Workers' Health and Compensation and Taymor Canada.

Without the energy, insight, understanding, co-operation and
dedication of those who participated in the field research, this book
(and the research) would not have been possible. On Beechey Island: Walt Kowal, Eric Damkjar, Arne Carlson, Roger Amy, Joelee
Nungaq, James Savelle, Derek Notman, Larry Anderson, Brian
Spenceley, Geraldine Ruszala and Barb Schweger. And on King

William Island: Arsien Tungilik, Karen Digby, Kovic Hiqiniq and Mike Aleekee. Thanks are also due to Dr. K. Kowalewska-Grochowska, University of Alberta Hospital; Sylvia Chomyc, Tuberculosis Control Unit, Provincial Laboratory of Public Health (Alberta), and the Netsilik Archaeology Project (James Savelle).

The authors would also like to thank the staff of the following institutions for their assistance with historical and archival research: the British Library, the British Archives, the University of Alberta libraries, including the Canadian Circumpolar Library, the University of Toronto libraries and the Toronto Reference Library. In addition, special thanks go to Donald Bray, Sten Nadolney, Patrick Walsh of Conville & Walsh, Matthew Swan of Adventure Canada and Rob Sanders. Margaret Atwood is profoundly thanked.

In memorium: Arne Carlson, who, with his wife Lesley Mitchell, died tragically in December 1998.

IMAGE CREDITS

Photos: All photos are by Dr. Owen Beattie, except: photo on page 144 courtesy of the Department of Culture, Language, Elders and Youth, Government of Nunavut; photo on page 208 (lower) by Brian Spenceley; photo on page 216 "project photograph."

Illustrations: Pictures on pages 20, 37, 39, 40, 42, 49, 59, 63, 80, 82, 89, 90, 164, 215 are reproduced courtesy of the National Maritime Museum, Greenwich, England; pictures on pages 19, 89 (lower) courtesy of the University of Toronto libraries; picture on page 54 courtesy of the British Library; pictures on pages 84, 98 courtesy of the Boreal Institute of Northern Studies, University of Alberta, Canada; pictures on pages i, 94 from the collection of John Geiger; pictures on pages 77, 87 courtesy of Mary Evans Picture Library.

Maps and diagrams: Neil Hyslop and Andrew Barr.

REPRINT CREDITS

Grateful acknowledgement is made to the following for permission to reprint previously published material:

Quotation from *The Rifles* by William T. Vollmann. Penguin Books, New York. ©1995 William T. Vollmann. Reprinted by kind permission of the author.

Quotation from "The Age of Lead" by Margaret Atwood. *Wilderness Tips*. McClelland & Stewart, Toronto. ©1991 O.W. Toad Ltd. Reprinted with kind permission of the author.

Quotation from *Terror and Erebus* by Gwendolyn MacEwen. *The Poetry of Gwendolyn MacEwen: The Early Years* (Volume One), eds. Margaret Atwood and Barry Callaghan. Exile Editions, Toronto. ©1993. Reprinted with kind permission of the publisher.

Chorus from "Northwest Passage" by Stan Rogers. The album *Northwest Passage*. ©1981 Fogarty's Cove Music. Reprinted with kind permission of Fogarty's Cove Music and Ariel Rogers.

Appendix One

List of the officers and crews of HMS *Erebus* and HMS *Terror* taken from their Muster Books, 1845. Source: Admiralty Records, Public Record Office.

HMS *Erebus*

CAPTAIN Sir John Franklin
COMMANDER James Fitzjames
LIEUTENANTS Graham Gore, H.T.D. Le Vesconte, James W. Fairholme
MATES Robert O. Sargent, Charles F. Des Voeux, Edward Couch
SECOND MASTER Henry F. Collins
SURGEON Stephen S. Stanley
ACTING ASSISTANT-SURGEON Harry D.S. Goodsir
PAYMASTER AND PURSER Charles H. Osmer
ACTING MASTER James Reid
WARRANT OFFICERS John Gregory (engineer), Thomas Terry (boatswain), John Weekes (carpenter)

PETTY OFFICERS Philip Reddington (captain of the forecastle), Thomas Watson (carpenter's mate), John Murray (sailmaker), James W. Brown (caulker), William Smith (blacksmith), Samuel Brown (boatswain's mate), Richard Wall (cook), James Rigden (captain's coxswain), John Sullivan (captain of the maintop), Robert Sinclair (captain of the foretop), Joseph Andrews (captain of the hold), Edmund Hoar (captain's steward), Richard Aylmore (gunroom steward), Daniel Arthur (quartermaster), John Downing (quartermaster), William Bell (quartermaster), Francis Dunn (caulker's mate), William Fowler (paymaster and purser's steward), John Bridgens (subordinate officers' steward), James Hart (leading stoker), John Cowie (stoker), Thomas Plater (stoker)

ABLE SEAMEN Henry Lloyd, John Stickland, Thomas Hartnell, **John Hartnell**, George Thompson, William Orren, Charles Coombs, William Closson, William Mark, Thomas Work, Charles Best, George Williams, John Morfin, Thomas Tadman, Abraham Seely, Thomas McConvey, Robert Ferrier, Josephus Geater, Robert Johns, Francis Pocock

ROYAL MARINES David Bryant (sergeant), Alexander Paterson (corporal), Joseph Healey (private), **William Braine** (private), William Reed (private), Robert Hopcraft (private), William Pilkington (private)

BOYS George Chambers, David Young

HMS *Terror*

CAPTAIN Francis Rawdon Moira Crozier
LIEUTENANTS Edward Little, John Irving, George H. Hodgson
MATES Robert Thomas, Frederick John Hornby
SECOND MASTER Gillies A. Macbean
SURGEON John S. Peddie
ASSISTANT SURGEON Alexander MacDonald
CLERK-IN-CHARGE E.J.H. Helpman
ACTING MASTER Thomas Blanky

WARRANT OFFICERS Thomas Honey (carpenter), John Lane (boatswain), James Thompson (engineer)

PETTY OFFICERS Reuben Male (captain of the forecastle), Thomas Johnson (boatswain's mate), **John Torrington** (leading stoker), Alexander Wilson (carpenter's mate), David MacDonald (quartermaster), William Rhodes (quartermaster), John Kenley (quartermaster), Thomas Darlington (caulker), John Diggle (cook), Thomas Farr (captain of the maintop), Henry Peglar (captain of the foretop), John Wilson (captain's coxswain), Samuel Honey (blacksmith), William Goddard (captain of the hold), Thomas Jopson (captain's steward), Thomas Armitage (gunroom steward), Cornelius Hickey (caulker's mate), Edward Genge (paymaster's steward), William Gibson (subordinate officers' steward), Luke Smith (stoker), William Johnson (stoker)

ABLE SEAMEN George Cann, William Shanks, David Sims, William Sinclair, William Jerry, Henry Sait, Alexander Berry, John Bailey, Samuel Crispe, John Bates, William Wentzall, William Strong, John Handford, Charles Johnson, David Leys, George Kinnaird, Magnus Manson, James Walker, Edwin Laurence

ROYAL MARINES Solomon Tozer (sergeant), William Hedges (corporal), Henry Wilks (private), John Hammond (private), James Daly (private), William Heather (private)

BOYS Robert Golding, Thomas Evans

Four crewmen who returned to Britain on the *Barretto Junior* and the *Rattler* before the *Erebus* and *Terror* entered the Arctic: Thomas Burt (armourer), John Brown (able seaman), James Elliot (sailmaker), William Aitken (Royal Marine private)

Appendix Two

Major expeditions involved in the search for HMS *Erebus* and HMS *Terror:*

1846–47	Dr. John Rae (overland)
1847–49	Sir John Richardson and Dr. John Rae (overland)
1848–49	Captain Sir James Clark Ross, Captain E.J. Bird (HMS *Enterprise* & HMS *Investigator*)
1848–50	Captain Henry Kellett (HMS *Herald*)
1848–52	Captain Thomas Moore (HMS *Plover*)
1849–50	Lieutenant James Saunders (HMS *North Star*)
1850–51	U.S. Navy Lieutenant Edwin J. De Haven, U.S. Navy Lieutenant S.P. Griffin (*Advance & Rescue*)
1850–51	Captain Horatio Austin, Captain Erasmus Ommanney, Lieutenant Sherard Osborn, Lieutenant Bertie Cator (HMS *Resolute*, HMS *Assistance*, HMS *Intrepid*, HMS *Pioneer*)*
1850–51	Captain William Penny, Alexander Stewart (*Lady Franklin & Sophia*)*

1850–51   Rear Admiral Sir John Ross (*Felix*)

1850   Captain C.C. Forsyth (*Prince Albert*)

1850–55   Captain Richard Collinson (HMS *Enterprise*)

1850–54   Commander Robert McClure (HMS *Investigator*)

1851   Dr. John Rae (overland)

1851–52   Captain William Kennedy (*Prince Albert*)

1852   Commander Edward Augustus Inglefield (*Isabel*)

1852–54   Captain Sir Edward Belcher, Sherard Osborn, Captain
Henry Kellett, Commander Francis Leopold M'Clin-
tock (HMS *Assistance*, HMS *Pioneer*, HMS *Resolute*, HMS
Intrepid)

1852–54   William John Samuel Pullen (HMS *North Star*)

1853   Captain Edward Augustus Inglefield, William
Fawckner (HMS *Phoenix* & HMS *Breadalbane*)

1853–54   Dr. John Rae (overland)*

1853–55   U.S. Navy Dr. Elisha Kent Kane (*Advance*)

1855   Chief Factor John Anderson (overland)

1857–59   Captain Francis Leopold M'Clintock, Lieut. William
Robert Hobson (*Fox*)*

1869   Charles Francis Hall (overland)*

1878–80   U.S. Lieut. Frederick Schwatka (overland)*

Made significant discoveries of Franklin expedition relics

Bibliography

There are a great many publications relating to the preparation for, and loss of, the 1845–48 Franklin expedition, as well as the subsequent searches and contemporary research. The following bibliography is not definitive, but it does include sources that allow the reader to explore the complexities of historical and scientific research into the disaster. Each of the entries has been used by the authors as information and/or illustration sources.

Anonymous. 1883. Dangers of canned food. *Medical News*. xliii:270.

Amundsen, Roald. 1908. *The North West Passage*. Vol. II. London: Archibald Constable and Co.

Amy, R., Bahatnagar, R., Damkjar, E., and Beattie, O. 1986. The last Franklin expedition: report of a postmortem examination of a crew member. *Canadian Medical Association Journal*. 135:115–117.

Anderson, J.E., and Merbs, C.F. 1962. A contribution to the human osteology of the Canadian Arctic. Occasional Paper 4. Toronto: Art and Archaeology Division, Royal Ontario Museum, University of Toronto.

Back, George. 1838. *Narrative of an Expedition in HMS Terror Undertaken with a View to Geographical Discovery on the Arctic Shores in the Years 1836–7*. London: John Murray.

Banting, F.G. 1930. With the Arctic Patrol. *Canadian Geographical Journal*. Vol. 1.

Beattie, O.B. 1983. A report on newly discovered human skeletal remains from the last Sir John Franklin expedition. *The Muskox.* 33:68–77.

Beattie, O.B., and Savelle, J.M. 1983. Discovery of human remains from Sir John Franklin's last expedition. *Historical Archaeology.* 17:100–105.

Beattie, O.B., Damkjar, E., Kowal, W., Amy, R. 1985. Anatomy of an arctic autopsy. *Medical Post.* 20(23):1–2.

Belcher, E. 1855. *The Last of the Arctic Voyages.* London: Lovell Reeve.

Bernier, Joseph E. 1909. Report on the Dominion Government Expedition to Arctic Islands and Hudson Strait, on Board the D.G.S. 'Arctic.' Ottawa: Government Printing Bureau.

Burwash, L.T. 1930. The Franklin Search. *Canadian Geographical Journal.* Vol. 1, No. 7.

Busch, Jane. 1981. An introduction to the tin can. *Historical Archaeology.* 15:95–104.

Cooke, Alan, and Holland, Clive. 1978. *The Exploration of Northern Canada.* Toronto: Arctic History Press.

Cooper, P.F. 1955. A trip to King William Island in 1954. *The Arctic Circular.* Vol. 3, No. 1.

Cruickshank, Alistair. n.d. *Franklin's Naturalist Mss: Harry Goodsir.*

Cyriax, Richard J. 1939. *Sir John Franklin's Last Arctic Expedition.* London: Methuen.

Cyriax, Richard J. 1942. Sir James Clark Ross and the Franklin Expedition. *The Polar Record.* Vol. 3, No. 24.

Cyriax, Richard J. 1951. Recently discovered traces of the Franklin expedition. *Geographical Journal.* June. 211–14.

Cyriax, Richard J. 1952. The position of Victory Point, King William Island. *Polar Record.* 6:496–507.

Cyriax, Richard J. 1958. The two Franklin Expedition records found on King William Island. *The Mariner's Mirror.* 44:178–189.

Cyriax, Richard J. 1962. Adam Beck and the Franklin search. *The Mariner's Mirror.* 48:35–51.

Cyriax, R.J., and Jones, A.G.E. 1954. The papers in the possession of Harry Peglar, Captain of the Foretop, HMS *Terror,* 1845. *The Mariner's Mirror.* 40:186–195.

De Bray, Emile-Frederic. 1992. *A Frenchman in Search of Franklin: De Bray's Arctic Journal, 1852–1854.* Toronto: University of Toronto Press.

Drummond, J.C., et al. 1939. *Historic Tinned Foods.* Greenford, UK: International Tin Research and Development Council.

Fleming, Fergus. 1999. *Barrow's Boys.* London: Granta Books.

Fleming, Fergus. 2001. *Ninety Degrees North: The Quest for the North Pole.* New York: Grove Press.

Franklin, John. 1823. *Narrative of a Journey to the Shores of the Polar Sea, in the years 1819, 20, 21, and 22, with an Appendix on Various Subjects Relating to Science and Natural History.* London: John Murray.

Franklin, John. 1828. *Narrative of a Second Expedition to the Shores of the Polar Sea, in the Years 1825, 1826, and 1827, including an account of the Progress of a Detachment to the Eastward by John Richardson.* London: John Murray.

Geiger, John. 2001. Exploring Leadership. *National Post.* October 26, 2001.

Gibson, William. 1932. Some further traces of the Franklin retreat. *Geographical Journal.* 79:402–08.

Gibson, William. 1933. The Dease and Simpson cairn. *The Beaver.* 264:44–45.

Gibson, William. 1937. Sir John Franklin's last voyage. *The Beaver.* 268:44–75.

Gilder, W.H. 1881. *Schwatka's Search.* New York: Scribner's Sons.

Gilpin, J.D. 1850. Outline of the voyage of HMS *Enterprise* and *Investigator* to Barrow Strait in search of Sir John Franklin. *Nautical Magazine.*

Glob, P.V. 1969. *The Bog People.* London: Faber and Faber.

Gzowski, P. 1981. *The Sacrament.* Toronto: McClelland and Stewart.

Holland, Clive. 1980. Franklin expedition and search. *The Discoverers; an Encyclopedia of Explorers and Exploration.* H. Delpar, ed. New York: McGraw-Hill.

Huntford, Roland. 1979. *The Last Place on Earth.* London: Pan Books.

Inglefield, E.A. 1852. Unpublished letter to Sir Francis Beaufort, dated 14 September 1852.

Inglefield, E.A. 1853. *A Summer Search for Sir John Franklin with a Peep into a Polar Basin.* London: Thomas Harrison and Son.

International Tin Research and Development Council. 1939. *Historic Tinned Foods.*

International Tin Research and Development Council Publication Number 85 (Second Edition). Middlesex: Greenford.

Johnson, R.E., Johnson, M.H., Jeanes, H.S., and Deaver, S.M. 1984. *Schwatka: The Life of Frederick Schwatka (1849–1892), M.D., Arctic Explorer, Cavalry Officer.* Montpelier: Horn of the Moon.

Jones, A.G.E. 1971. Sir James Clark Ross and the Voyage of the *Enterprise* and *Investigator.* 1848–49. *Royal Geographical Society Journal.* Vol. 137.

Kane, Elisha Kent. 1854. *The U.S. Grinnell Expedition in Search of Sir John Franklin. Personal Narrative.* New York: Harper and Brothers.

Kane, Elisha Kent. 1856. *Arctic Explorations: The Second Grinnell Expedition in Search of Sir John Franklin, 1853, '54, '55.* Philadelphia: Childs and Peterson.

Kane, Elisha Kent. 1898. *Arctic Explorations in Search of Sir John Franklin.* London: T. Nelson and Sons.

Keenleyside, A., X. Song, D.R. Chettle and C.E. Webber. 1996. The Lead
    Content of Human Bones from the 1845 Franklin Expedition. *Journal of
    Archaeological Science.* 23.

Keenleyside, Anne, Margaret Bertulli and Henry C. Fricke. 1997. The Final Days
    of the Franklin Expedition: New Skeletal Evidence. *Arctic.* Vol. 50, No. 1.

Kowal, W., Beattie, O.B., Baadsgaard, H., and Krahn, P. 1990. Did Solder kill
    Franklin's men? *Nature.* 343:319–320.

Kowal, W.A., Krahn, P.M., and Beattie, O.B. Lead levels in human tissues from
    the Franklin Forensic Project. *International Journal of Analytical Chemistry.*
    35:119–26.

Kowal, Walter, Beattie, Owen, Baadsgaard, Halfdan, and Krahn, Peter M. 1991.
    Source Identification of Lead Found in Tissues of Sailors from the Franklin
    Arctic Expedition of 1845. *Journal of Archaeological Science.* 19:193–203.

Kowalewska-Grochowska, K., Amy, R., Lui, B., McWhirter, R., and Merrill, H.
    1988. Isolation and sensitivities of century-old bacteria from the Franklin ex-
    pedition. Poster presented at the Interscience Conference Antimicrobial
    Agents and Chemotherapy. California: Los Angeles.

Lamb, Jonathan. 2002. Captain Cook and the Scourge of Scurvy. www.bbc.co.uk/
    history/discovery/exploration/captaincook_scurvy_01.shtml.

Lieb, Clarence W. 1929. The effect on human beings of a twelve months' exclusive
    meat diet. *Journal of the American Medical Association.* Vol. 93, No. 1.

Lind, James. 1753. *A Treatise on Scurvy.* Facsimile edition (1953), C.P. Stewart
    and D. Guthrie, ed. Edinburgh: University Press.

Loomis, C.C. 1971. *Weird & Tragic Shores.* London: MacMillan.

MacInnis, Joe. 1985. *The Land That Devours Ships.* Toronto: CBC Enterprises.

M'Clintock, F.L. 1908. *The Voyage of the "Fox" In Arctic Seas.* London: John
    Murray.

M'Clintock, Francis Leopold. 1984. Reminiscences of Arctic ice-travel in search
    of Sir John Franklin and his Companions. Ottawa: Canadian Institute for
    Historical MicroreProductions.

McCord, Carey P. 1954. Lead and Lead Poisoning in Early America. *Industrial
    Medicine and Surgery.*

M'Dougall, George Frederick. 1857. *The Eventful Voyage of H.M. Discovery Ship
    "Resolute" to the Arctic Regions, in Search of Sir John Franklin and the Missing
    Crew of H.M. Discovery ships 'Erebus' and 'Terror,' 1852, 1853, 1854.* London:
    Longman, Brown, Green, Longmans and Roberts.

Magruder, W.E. 1883. Lead-poisoning from canned food. *Medical News.*
    xliii:261–263.

Markham, A.H. 1891. *Life of Sir John Franklin and the North-West Passage.*
    London: G. Philip.

Martin, Constance. 1983. *James Hamilton: Arctic Watercolours*. Calgary: Glenbow Museum.

Murchison, R. 1853. Commander E.A. Inglefield—Royal Awards. *Journal of the Royal Geographical Society*. 23:ix–ixi.

Nanton, Paul. 1970. *Arctic Breakthrough*. Toronto: Clarke, Irwin & Co.

Neatby, L.H. 1958. *In Quest of the Northwest Passage*. Toronto: Longmans, Green and Company.

Neatby, L.H. 1970. *Search for Franklin*. Edmonton: Hurtig.

Newman, Peter C. 1985. *Company of Adventurers*. Markham: Penguin Books.

Notman, D., Anderson, L., Beattie, O., and Amy, R. n.d. Arctic paleoradiology: portable x-ray examination of two frozen sailors from the Franklin expedition (1845–48). *American Journal of Roentgenology:* accepted in April, 1987.

Notman, D. and O. Beattie. 1996. The Palaeoimaging and Forensic Anthropology of Frozen Sailors from the Franklin Arctic Expedition Mass Disaster (1845–8): A Detailed Presentation of Two Radiological Surveys. *Der Mann im Eis*. Vol. III. K. Spindler, ed. Vienna: Springer-Verlag.

Nourse, J.E., ed. 1879. *Narrative of the Second Arctic Expedition of C.F. Hall*. Washington: United States Naval Observatory.

Osborn, Sherard. 1856. Notes on the late Arctic Expeditions. *Proceedings of the Royal Geographical Society*. London: Royal Geographical Society.

Osborn, Sherard. 1859. The Last Voyage of Sir John Franklin. *Once A Week*.

Osborn, Sherard. 1865. *Stray Leaves from an Arctic Journal; or, Eighteen Months in the Polar Regions, in Search of Sir John Franklin's Expedition, in the Years 1850–51*. London: Longman, Brown, Green, and Longmans.

Osborn, Sherard, ed. 1857. *The Discovery of the North-West Passage by HMS 'Investigator,' Capt. R. M'Clure. 1850, 1851, 1852, 1853, 1854, Second Edition*. London: Longman, Brown, Green, Longmans and Roberts.

Owen, Roderic. 1978. *The Fate of Franklin*. London: Hutchinson.

Parliamentary Papers. 1850. Arctic Expedition. 58–64. London.

Parry, William Edward. 1821. *Journal of a Voyage for the Discovery of a North-West Passage from the Atlantic to the Pacific; Performed in the Years 1819–20, in His Majesty's Ships "Hecla" and "Griper."* London: John Murray.

Parry, William Edward. 1858. *Three Voyages for the Discovery of a Northwest Passage from the Atlantic to the Pacific and Narrative of an Attempt to Reach the North Pole, Vol. I*. New York: Harper & Bros.

Rae, John. 1855. Arctic exploration, with information respecting Sir John Franklin's missing party. *Journal of the Royal Geographical Society*. 25:246–56.

Rasmussen, K. 1927. *Across Arctic America: Narrative of the Fifth Thule Expedition*. New York: G.P. Putnam's Sons.

Read, P.P. 1974. *Alive: the Story of the Andes Survivors*. New York: Avon Books.

Roland, Charles G. 1984. Saturnism at Hudson's Bay: The York Factory Complaint of 1833–1836. *Canadian Bulletin of Medical History*. 1:59–78.

Ross, John. 1835. *Narrative of a Second Voyage in Search of Northwest Passage, and of a Residence in the Arctic Regions*. London: A.W. Webster.

Savours, Ann. 1999. *The Search for the North West Passage*. London: Chatham Publishing.

Simpson, Thomas. 1843. *Narrative of the Discoveries on the North Coast of America: Effected by the Officers of the Hudson's Bay Company During the Years 1836–39*. London: Richard Bentley.

Spindler, Konrad. 1999. The Tyrolean Iceman and the Seamen from Beechey Island. *OeCulture*. No. 2.

Stackpole, E.A., ed. 1965. *The Long Arctic Search: The Narrative of Lieutenant Frederick Schwatka, U.S.A., 1878–1880*. Mystic: Marine Historical Association.

Stefansson, Vilhjalmur. 1918. Observations on three cases of scurvy. *Journal of the American Medical Association*. Vol. 71, No. 21.

Stefansson, Vilhjalmur. 1970. *Unsolved Mysteries of the Arctic*. New York: Collier Books.

Stone, Ian R. 1996. The Franklin search in Parliament. *Polar Record*. 32:182.

Sutherland, Patricia D., ed. 1985. *The Franklin Era in Canadian Arctic History, 1845–1859*. Mercury Series Archaeological Survey of Canada Paper. No. 131. Ottawa: National Museums of Canada.

Sutherland, Peter. 1852. *Journal of a Voyage in Baffin's Bay and Barrow Straits, in the Years 1850–1851, performed by H.M. Ships 'Lady Franklin' and 'Sophia,' under the Command of Mr William Penny, in Search of the Missing Crews of H.M. Ships 'Erebus' and 'Terror'*. London: Longman, Brown, Green, and Longmans.

Wallis, Helen. 1984. England's Search for the Northern Passages in the Sixteenth and Early Seventeenth Centuries. *Arctic*. Vol. 37, No. 4.

Watt, J., Freeman, E.J., and Bynum, W.F. 1981. *Starving Sailors: the Influence of Nutrition Upon Naval and Maritime History*. Bristol: National Maritime Museum.

Wightwick, T. 1988. Canned vegetables and lead poisoning. *Lancet*. 2:1121.

Wonders, W.C. 1968. Search for Franklin. *Canadian Geographical Journal*. 76:116–27.

Woodward, F.J. 1951. *Portrait of Jane: A Life of Lady Franklin*. London: Hodder and Stoughton.

Wright, Noel. 1959. *Quest for Franklin*. London.

Young, Allen. 1879. *The Two Voyages of the Pandora in 1875 and 1876*. London: Edward Stanford.

Newspapers and magazines used include:

The Anthenaeum, 17 February 1849, 17 November 1849
Blackwood's Edinburgh Magazine, November 1855
Edmonton Journal, 9 September 1930
Edmonton Sun, 24 September 1984, 26 September 1984, 21 October 1984
Illustrated London News, 24 May 1845, 12 October 1850, 18 February 1854,
    28 October 1854, 15 October 1859, 1 January 1881
The Times, 26 April 1845, 12 May 1845, 23 December 1851, 3 January 1852, 5
    January 1852, 20 January 1852
Toronto Globe 4 April 1850, 30 April 1850, 23 October 1854, 25 October 1854,
    11 October 1859

Other material was derived from primary sources, including various Parliamentary Papers of Great Britain (post-1847), the Arctic Blue Books, the Muster Books of the *Erebus* and *Terror,* National Archives (UK); Admiralty medical journal, *HMS Enterprize,* 1848–49, ADM 101/99/4, National Archives (UK); the collection of the Hydrographic Department, Ministry of Defence (UK) for the letter from E.A. Inglefield to Sir Francis Beaufort, 14 September 1852; the Royal Scottish Geographical Society, for the letter from Harry D.S. Goodsir, to his uncle, 2 July 1845; the British Library (Barrow Bequest, Add. Ms. 35306, section 4) for the letter from E.A. Inglefield to John Barrow, 14 September 1852; Donald Bray for the letter from Sarah Hartnell and Charles Hartnell to John and Thomas Hartnell, 23 December 1847.

Index

Page numbers in italic indicate figures.

Admiralty, 18–19, 37, 47–48, 57–59, 65, 73, 146–47

Advance, 69–72, 231

Air support, Beattie expeditions, 107, 119, 130–31, 152–53, 189–90, 204–5, 212

Aleekee, Mike, 107–12

Ambler, James, 250–51

Amundsen, Roald, first transit of Northwest Passage, 19, 100, 189

Amy, Roger: bacteriological analysis, 238–39; Braine autopsy, 230–33; field team 1984, 152; field team 1986, 201, 204; Hartnell autopsy and X-rays, 214–20; polar bear encounter, 159–60; Torrington autopsy, 175–77, 193

Anderson, James, 75–76

Anderson, Larry, 202, 204, 210–14, 217, 230–32

Animals: bears, 63, 159–60, 204, 217–18; dogs, 45, 204, 217–18, 250; foxes, 28, 50, 121; as game, 23, 28, 63; hares, 23, 28, 131; pet monkey, 45; rats, 72, 231

Antiscorbutics: in Arctic exploration, 22–24, 32, 41, 52, 57, 68, 70, 71; fresh meat, eating off the land, 22–24, 28–30, 44, 68, 70–72, 102–3; tinned food (putative), 15–16, 68, 104. *See also* Scurvy

Artefacts and debris: Beechey Island, 63–64, 160; "boat place," 86–87, 97, 134–39; Booth Point, 13; Capes Riley and Spencer, 60–61; Crozier's Landing, 123–26; given to M'Clintock, 79–80; Montreal Island, 75–76; Northumberland House, 163; Peffer River, 80–81; rope, 125; from search expeditions,

161; tin can cairn, 64, 179–81, 203–4; used by Inuit, 75, 95, 131; Victoria Island, 59; Victory Point cairn, 85
Austin, Horatio Thomas, 58–60, 161
Autopsies, 51, 174–77, 193–94, 214–20, 230–33

Back, George, 20, 30–33, 85, 103, 249
Bacteriological analysis, 238–39, 248
Banting, Sir Frederick, 161, 163
Barretto Junior, 44–45
Barrow, Sir John, 18, 20–21, 25–26, 33–35
Beattie, Owen B.: exhumation permits, 146–47, 158–65; in field, 1981, 11–17, 107–12; in field, 1982, 118–39; in field, 1984, 153–77, 178–90; in field, 1986, 201–34; forensic anthropologist, 105–7; lead poisoning hypothesis, 140–47. *See also* Braine, William; Exhumations; Expeditions in 20th century; Hartnell, John; Lead poisoning and Franklin expedition; Torrington, John
Beechey Island: burial of Thomas Morgan, 68; description, 152–53, 155–57; Franklin's winter camp, 82, 92, 151–52; graves discovered, 61–66; map, *viii*; Parks Canada excavations, 160. *See also* Braine, William; Hartnell, John; Torrington, John
Belcher, Sir Edward, 67, 161–63, 185–86
Bellot, Joseph René, 161
Bennett, Gordon, 249
"Boat place," *ix*, 86–88, 97, 134–39
Boats, 27–29, 72, 86–88, 99, 132–33
Bones. *See* Human remains

Bonnett, James, 52
Booth Point, *ix*, 11–17, 109, 111–12
Braine, William, 3, 61, 73, 145, 222–34, 239
Bray, Donald, 199–200
Breadalbane, HMS, 163–64
Burials: Franklin, 90, 101–2; preparation of body, 172, 173, 207, 229; reburials, 96–99, 118, 129, 146–47, 177, 188–89, 220–21, 233–34; Thomas Morgan, 68; Torrington, 196–98
Burnett, Sir William, 57
Burwash, L.T., 101–2

Cairns: Beechey Island, *viii*, 60, 163; Crozier's Landing, 125; found by Schwatka, 98; James Ross sledging party (1849), 52, 53; of tin cans, 64, 179–81, 203–4; Victory Point, 81–85, 122–23. *See also* Notes
Campsites (Beattie and searchers), 119, 125, 129, 153, 202
Campsites (Franklin), *ix*, 59–66, 81, 97, 99, 108, 111–13, 125, 152, 160–64. *See also* Overwintering
Canada, 7, 100, 109–10, 160
Cannibalism: Beattie's evidence, Booth Point, 16–17, 111–13; behaviour patterns of cannibals, 116–17; contemporary reaction, 5, 7, 75–76, 113–15; end-stage, 257–58; Hall's reports (from Inuit), 95, 114; in modern disasters, 115; Rae's reports (from Inuit), 5, 7, 75, 113–14; Schwatka's reports (from Inuit), 114–15
Carlson, Arne: Braine's grave, excavation, 223–30; field team 1982, 118–39; field team 1984, 154, 170, 173;

field team 1986, 201; Hartnell's grave, excavation, 202–3, 205; Torrington autopsy, 175–77

Clothing: boots, 114, 132, 138–39, 250; with Franklin party remains, 80, 86, 97, 130, 171, 184–85, 206–8, 210, 214, 226, 228–29, 230; at Victory Point cairn, 85. *See also* Fabric

Coffins, 165–69, 181–83, 196–97, 202–3, 205–6, 224–26, 230. *See also* Plaques, on exhumed coffins

Collinson, Richard, 58–59, 68

Coombes, William, death of, 49–50

Crozier, Francis, 38–39, 83, 95

Cundy, William, illness and death, 51

Damkjar, Eric, 154, 160–64, 166–67, 201, 203–4, 230–33

Danehower, John, 251–52

Day and night, polar, 23, 50, 165–66

Debility, illness and death on expeditions: De Long expedition, 249–53; early expeditions, 23–24, 28, 31–33, 38; Franklin expedition, 45, 61–65, 83, 86, 241–42; and Polar Failure, 19–20; psychological symptoms, 50, 68–71, 142, 195; and redefined "Franklin mystery," 126; reported by Inuit, 95–96; in Royal Navy, 14–15; search expeditions, 49–57, 67–72, 89–90; tuberculosis, 186, 193–94, 219, 238–39, 241. *See also* Lead poisoning and Franklin expedition; Scurvy

De Haven, Edwin J., 59, 61, 69–70

De Long, George Washington, 249–53

Des Voeux, Charles F., 82, 129

Dickens, Charles, 41, 64, 113–14

Digby, Karen, 12–13, 107–12

Donaldson, Seaman, death of, 32

Enterprise (whaling ship), 45–46

Enterprise, HMS, 48–51, 58, 68

Epitaphs, 61–62, 100, 153–54. *See also* Plaques, on exhumed coffins

Equipment and supplies: Beattie expeditions, 120–21, *211*, 212; 19th-century expeditions, 23, 35, 40–42, 44, 55, 85–88. *See also* Food and diet; Goldner, Stephan; Tinned food

Erebus, HMS and *Terror*, HMS: artefacts from, 75–76; discovery, xvii, 259–62; Inuit reports, 101; logs lost, 99; and Northwest Passage, 95–96; officers and crew, 259–61; outfitting of, 40–42; previous history, 31–35; reports of fate, 79–83

Excavations: Braine's grave, 223–30; and daylength, 165–66; Hartnell's grave, 179–84, 205; by Parks Canada, Beechey Island, 160; techniques, 155, 157–58, 202–4, 222–24; Torrington's grave, 157–58, 165

Exhumations: of Braine, 222–34; ethical and legal requirements, 146–47; of Hartnell, 178–90, 201–21; by Inuit, 95; Sutherland's proposal, 65–66; of Torrington, 151–77. *See also* Trace element analysis; X-ray studies

Expeditions, North Pole: De Long (1879–81), 249–53; Kane (1853–55), 70–72, 231; Peary (1909), 19

Expeditions before Franklin: Back (1836–37), 20, 30–33, 103, 249; Dease and Simpson (1839), 93; James Clark Ross (1839–43), 33–34; John Ross (1818), 21; John Ross (1829–33), 25–30; Parry (1819–20), 21–25

Expeditions in search of Franklin, 262–
63; Admiralty efforts, 47–57, 58–59;
Beechey Island discoveries, 61–66;
Belcher (1852–54), 161;
De Haven (1850–51), 69–70; Hall
(1869), 94–96; international and
private, 58–66, 69–72; interpretations and commentary, 91,
100–102; James Ross (1848–49),
47–57; Kane (1853–55), 70–72, 231;
Kennedy (1851–52), 161; Lady
Franklin's efforts, 77–78;
M'Clintock (1857–59), 78–90;
Penny (1850–51), 59, 61, 161; Rae
(1853–54), 74–76; Richardson and
Rae (1847–49), 47–48; Schwatka
(1878–80), 96–99
Expeditions in 20th century: Beattie
(1981), 107–12; Beattie (1982),
118–39; Beattie (1984), 146–47,
152–90; Beattie (1986), 201–34;
Burwash (1930), 101–2; Rasmussen
(1923), 101

Fabric, 97–98, 130, 158, 165, 170.
See also Clothing
Fitzjames, James, 38–41, 44–45, 65, 83
Food and diet: Beattie expedition
(1982), 120–21, 133–35; early expe-
ditions, 23–25, 28, 32–33; James
Ross rescue expedition, 48; of
Royal Navy, 14–16; spoilage, 64–
65, 236, 237. *See also* Antiscorbu-
tics; Lead poisoning and Franklin
expedition; Scurvy;
Starvation; Tinned food
Forensic anthropology, 13, 16–17, 105–
17, 138, 153–54. *See also*
Beattie, Owen B.
Fox, 20, 78–80, *80*
Franklin, Eleanor, 43

Franklin, Lady Jane (née Griffin),
5–6, 43–44, 59, 67, 77–78, 90, 186
Franklin, Sir John: biography and
character, 36–38, 44–45; death of,
83; historical reinterpretations of,
4–7; influence on Amundsen, 100;
portrait of, *37;* premonitions, 43;
remains and burial, *90,* 99, 101–2;
reputation, 4–7, 77–78, 90, 102
Franklin expedition, known events:
deaths declared, 73; instructions
from Admiralty, 42–43; loss of
ships and overland escape attempt,
81–88, 99; and Northwest Passage,
91–93; officers and crew, 36–40,
259–61; origins, preparations and
launch, 33–46; reasons for failure,
241–42; route, *viii,* 92–93
Franklin expedition, reconstructed
events, 88–91, 95, 99, 116–17, 137–
39, 143, 151–52, 195–98
Franklin mystery, 1–8, 11–12, 41, 64,
76–79, 100, 113–14, 126

Geographic locations and features:
Adelaide Peninsula, *ix,* 95, 98, 101;
Back River, *viii,* 74, 83; Bellot
Strait, 26, 79; Boothia Peninsula,
viii, 26, 74–75; Cape Crozier, *ix,* 86;
Cape Jane Franklin, *ix,* 123; Cape
Riley, 60–61, 156; Cape Spencer, 61;
Crozier's Landing, *ix,* 102, 124–26;
Devon Island, *viii,* 59–61, 156;
Erebus Bay, *ix,* 119, 134–35; Frank-
lin Point, 123; Gladman Point, *ix,*
109–10; Gore Point, 127; Melville
Island, 21–25; North Magnetic
Pole, 26–27; O'Reilly Island, 95–
96, 98; Peffer River, 80–81,
99; Point Le Vesconte, *ix,* 129–30;
Port Leopold, *viii,* 48–51, 53;

Rivière de la Rocquette, *ix*, 131–33;
Simpson Strait, *ix*, 91–93, 99; Somerset Island, *viii*, 48, 51–53, *54;*
Starvation Cove, *ix*, 99, 108; Tulloch Point, *ix*, 109–10; Victory
Point, 26, 81–85, 93, 122–23; Wellington Channel, 82, 92, 151, 161.
See also Beechey Island; Booth
Point; King William Island; Northwest Passage
Gibson, William (1931 survey), 109
Gilbert, W.E., on Crozier's Landing,
    102
Gjoa, 100, 189
Goldner, Stephan, 65, 180–81, 238, 249
Goodsir, Harry D. S., 39–40, 44,
    214, *215*
Gore, Graham, 81–85, 129
Graves: Beechey Island gravesite
    and headboards, 61–63, 153–54;
    Braine's, 222–24, 233–34; Franklin's, 101–2; Hartnell's, 179–82, 188,
    202–3; Inuit and
    explorer graves confused, 109–11;
    Inuit reports of, 12; Irving's, 97, *98*,
    125; reburial by Schwatka, 129–30;
    smell from, 157, 165; Thomas
    Morgan's, 160–61; Torrington's,
    154–55, 157–58; water in, 158–59,
    202. *See also* Exhumations;
    Permafrost
Gray, James, illness and death, 50–51
Grinnell, Henry, 59, 69–72
Griper, HMS, 21–25

Haddington, Lord, 36
Hair, lead levels in, 194, 239–40
Hall, Charles Francis, 12, 94–99, 101–
    2, 114, 145–46
Hartnell, John: descendants of, 199–
    201; discharged dead, 73;

exhumations, studies and reburial,
    178–90, 201–21; gravesite, 3, 62,
    180; scientific importance, 145, 239
Hartnell, Sarah, 200
Hartnell, Thomas, 200
Hecla, HMS, 21–25
Hiqiniq, Kovic, 107–12
Hobson, William Robert, 78, 81–82,
    86–88, 89–90, 129
Hudson's Bay Company, 38, 43, 59,
    75–76, 85, 141–42
Human remains: at "boat place," 86–
    88, 134–38; Booth Point skeleton,
    ix, 11–17, 109, 111–12, *113;* evidence of cannibalism, 111–12, *113*,
    115–17; found by search expeditions, 80–81, 96–99, 118, 129, 130;
    found in 20th century, 100–101; at
    Gladman Point, 110; of Inuit, in
    modern surveys, 109–10; in Inuit
    reports, 95–96, 98–99, 101; skulls,
    14, 111–12, 176; trace element analysis, 111, 140–41, 144–47, 194–95,
    235–36, 239–40, 245–47. *See also*
    Braine, William; Hartnell, John;
    Preservation, of archaeological
    materials; Torrington, John

Ice (sea ice): early expeditions, 21,
    26–28, 31; *Erebus* and *Terror* beset
    and abandoned, 83; hazards of,
    128–29; and James Ross rescue
    expedition, 55; *Jeannette* beset and
    crushed, 250; near King William
    Island, 93
Inglefield, Edward Augustus, 185–87,
    206
Inuit: adaptive lifestyle of, 29–30, 72,
    102–3; brought to England, 73–74;
    Dickens's characterization, 113–14;
    disturbance of Franklin campsites

and graves, 97; and European artefacts, 75, 79–80, 95, 131; Franklin
party, reports of, 74–76, 95–96,
98–99, 101–2, 114–15; gravesite,
report of, 12; lead levels in remains,
141, 145, *246;* mummified remains,
192; skeletons, 109–10; and tinned
foods, 24, 86
Inuit informants: Enukshakak, 101;
Ikinnelikpatolok, 98–99; Nowya,
101; Ogzeuckjeuwock, 115; Qaqortingneq, 101
Investigator, HMS, 48–51, 58, 68, 161
Irving, John, 83, 97, 125

Jeannette, 249–53
Jenkins, David, death of, 51

Kane, Elisha Kent, 61–64, 69,
70–72, 231
Keenleyside, Anne, 247
King William Island: Beattie expeditions, 107–11, 118–39; description
and geography, 11; explored by
search expeditions, 79–80, 93, 95–
99; map and naming of, *ix,* 26–27;
in Northwest Passage, 92; overland
travel, Franklin party, 75–76; visited by Rasmussen, Burwash, 101–
2. *See also* "Boat place"; Booth
Point
Kowal, Walt: field team 1982, 118–39;
field team 1984, 152, 157–58, 165,
179–84; field team 1986, 201, 202–
3, 205, 211–12, 223–33; hair sample
testing, 239

Lead: in bones, 111, 140–41, 194–95; in
exhumed hair and soft tissues, 144–
47, 194–95, 235–36, 239–40, 244–

47; exposure, Victorian and
current, 142–44, 181, 236–38, 244–
55; isotope ratios, 245–46
Lead poisoning and Franklin expedition: Beattie's hypothesis and tests,
140–47, 235–36; contemporary
warnings, 247–48; evidence from
De Long's expedition, 249–53;
evidence from human remains,
194–95, 239–41, 246–47; isotope
analysis, 245–46
Le Vesconte, Henry T.D., 96
Logs and books, 41, 75, 81, 86–87,
99, 198
Lung diseases, in exhumed Franklin
crew, 186, 193–94, 219, 238–39, 241

Martin, Robert, 45–46
Mathias, Henry, death of, 54–55
McClure, Robert, 58–59, 68–69
M'Clintock, Francis Leopold, 20, 51–
53, 56, 78–90, 94
Monuments and memorials, 79, 96,
100, 130, 161, *162,* 163
Morgan, Thomas, death of, 68,
160–61

News and commentary, on Arctic
exploration: *Athenaeum,* 56, 78;
Blackwood's Edinburgh Magazine,
76, 242–43; *Edmonton Journal,* 102;
Household Words, 113–14; *Illustrated London News,* 40–41, 55–56,
60, 74, 91, 94, 99; *Last Voyage
of Capt. John Ross,* 29; *London Gazette,* 73; *North Georgia
Gazette and Winter Chronicle,* 22;
Times (London), 35, 41, 43, 65,
147; *Toronto Globe,* 58, 74–75, 91
Northumberland House, *viii, 162,* 163

Northwest Passage, 18–35, 67, 68, 90–94, 100, 251

Notes: describing Franklin expedition fate, 81–85, 129; left by James Ross sledging party, 52; none at Beechey Island cairn, 64; none at the "boat place," 87; pointing finger, 98; in Torrington's grave, 177; Victory Point, 122–23

Notman, Derek, 202, 204, 210–14, 217, 230–32, 241

Nungaq, Joelee, 152, 154, 201–5, 214, 217–18, 223–30

Officers, of ships, 27–28, 36–40, 83, 241, 259–61. *See also* Shipboard life

Ommanney, Erasmus, 58–60, 64–65

Osborn, Sherard, 60, 62, 63, 65, 66, 90

Overland travel and sledging: Beattie (1982), 120–24, 127–30, 131–35; early expeditions, 21–22, 26–28, 37–38; Franklin party, 74–76, 85, 86–88; river crossings, 131–33; search expeditions, 51–55, 70–71, 72, 89–90, 97; sledges, 63, 86, 107–8, 126–27; and snowmobiles, 107–8

Overwintering, 21–29, 48–51, 53, 61–63, 69–71. *See also* Shipboard life

Parry, William Edward, 21–26, 36, 156

Peglar, Harry, notebook of, 81

Penny, William, 59, 61, 161

Permafrost: excavation in, 157–58, 202–3, 222–24; and ice in graves, 168–69, 181, 205–6; in mud flats, 133; preservation of human remains, 145–46, 158–59, 193

Photography, 41, 154, 190, 201, 205, 222. *See also* X-ray studies

Plaques, on exhumed coffins, 166–67, 182–83, 187, 188, 224–26

"Polar Failure," 18–20

Preservation, of archaeological materials, 125, 145–46, 158–59, 176, 191–93, 232–33. *See also* Artefacts and debris; Human remains

Prince of Wales, 45

Radios, in fieldwork, 120, 130–31

Rae, John, 5, 7, 47–48, 59, 74–76, 85, 113–14

Rasmussen, Knud, 101–2, 103

Reburial. *See* Burials

Richards, George Henry, 20, 67

Robertson, John, 50–51, 55, 56

Ross, James Clark: and debility, 20, 249; early expeditions, 26–27, 33–35, 85; rescue expedition for Franklin, 47–57; Victory Point cairn, 83, 122–23

Ross, Sir John, 21, 25–30, 59, 103

Royal Canadian Mounted Police, 100, 110, 146–47

Royal Navy: broadarrow mark, 124; diet, scurvy and debility, 14–15, 22, 24–25, 33, 254; discipline vs. cannibalism, 113–14; exploration of the Northwest Passage, 18–35; Franklin's career in, 36–37; "Polar Failure," 18–20

Ruszula, Geraldine, 152, 159–60, 165, 169, 177

Savelle, James, 12, 107–12, 201–3, 217–18, 223–33

Schwatka, Frederick, 96–99, 114–15, 118, 129, 130, 132

Schweger, Barbara, 202, 204, 210, 214

Scurvy: in Arctic exploration, 18–35, 253; evidence of, in Franklin party bones, 14, 16–17, 136; and Franklin expedition failure, 86, 103–4; in Franklin search expeditions, 50–51, 55, 57, 67–72, 88–90; Inuit reports of, 98; in maritime history, 14–17; symptoms, 15, 142. *See also* Antiscorbutics; Debility, illness and death on expeditions; Lead poisoning and Franklin expedition

Shipboard life, 22–23, 41–42, 48–49, 69–71. *See also* Overwintering

Shrouds, 97, 170, 184, 206–7, 226, 228

Skeletons. *See* Human remains

Sledging. *See* Overland travel and sledging

Somerset House, 27–28, 53

Spenceley, Brian, 200, 201, 206

Starvation, 38, 74–76, 103, 114–17, 250

Stefansson, Vilhjalmur, 102–4

St. Roch, 100

Sutherland, Peter, 65–66, 72, 181, 186–87, 206

Technology, Victorian, 16, 35, 236–38, 242–43, 253–55

Tennyson, Alfred Lord, 76, 100

Terror, HMS. *See Erebus*, HMS and *Terror*, HMS

Thoreau, Henry David, 64

Tin cans: in Beechey Island cairn, 64, 179–81, 203–4; in Inuit cache, 98; Inuit reports of, 101; lead solder, 142–43, 181; on Montreal Island, 76; opening of, 22, 24; recycling of, *144;* Victorian canning technology, 16, 236–38

Tinned food: advantages and use by Royal Navy, 15, 24–25, 33; on Arctic expeditions, 22–25, 28, 32, 41, 44, 48, 52–53, 70, 86, 240, 251–54; Inuit reports of, 96, 98–99; as lead source, 142–43, 236–38; as putative antiscorbutic, 15–16, 68, 104; spoilage and quality, 56–57, 64–65, 180–81

Torrington, John, 3, 62, 73, 145, *155,* 157–77, 192–98

Trace element analysis, 111, 140–41, 144–47, 194–95, 235–36, 239–40, 245–47

Tungilik, Arsien, 119, 126–27

University of Alberta, 12, 16, 105

Victorian society: Crimean War, 76; equipment hauled by Franklin party, 86–88; "exhibit" of "Esquimaux," 73–74; image of polar regions, *20;* Romanticism, 4, 77–78, 79; sources of lead poisoning, 141–44, 236–38, 244–55. *See also* Technology, Victorian

Victory, 25–27

Water: drinking, on Beechey Island, 157; in graves, 158–59, 202; for melting permafrost, in excavations, 168–69, 184, 205, 206, 229, 230; meltwater and overland travel, 108, 121; shortage, in Kane expedition, 70; for X-ray development, 211–12

Weather and climate: field season, 1982, 121, 134, 165; field season, 1984, 178; field season, 1986, 202; and 19th-century Arctic exploration, 23, 70, 128–29; at Torrington's burial, 198

X-ray studies, 210–14, 217, 230–32, 241

York Factory Complaint, 141–42

Young, Alexander, death of, 32